THE WORLD'S GREATEST
ARCHITECTURE
PAST AND PRESENT

THE WORLD'S GREATEST
ARCHITECTURE
PAST AND PRESENT

D.M. FIELD

CHARTWELL
BOOKS, INC.

This edition published in 2007 by
CHARTWELL BOOKS,INC.
A division of BOOK SALES, INC.
114 Northfield Avenue
Edison, New Jersey 08837
USA

Copyright © 2007
Regency House Publishing Ltd.

For all editorial enquiries please contact
Regency House Publishing Ltd at

www.regencyhousepublishing.com

ISBN 13: 978-0-7858-2239-4
ISBN 10: 0-7858-2239-9

Printed in China
by Sino Publishing House Ltd.

PAGE 2: *Fontainebleau.*

TITLE PAGE: *Taj Mahal.*

OPPOSITE: *Doge's Palace,*
  Venice.

PAGE 6: *Reichstag, Berlin.*

CONTENTS PAGE: *Saint*
  Peter's, Rome.

Contents

*A*rchitecture is the one art that we cannot avoid. It is constantly before our eyes, indeed we live in its works, in the sense that all buildings are designed or planned, if not by Brunelleschi or Sir Norman Foster. At the same time architecture is probably the least highly regarded of the visual arts. This is partly due to the fact that it is functional, it serves a practical purpose, which in the West, though not in other cultures, is regarded as somehow downgrading. It becomes a 'mere' craft, and subject to compromises imposed by economic, political or social constraints, though the greatest artists also worked for patrons, and aimed to earn a living. But to some extent, the inferior status of architecture is due to popular disillusionment with the works of Modernism – all those sub-Miesian glass towers and mock-Corbusier concrete blocks that disfigured many a European cityscape in the years after the Second World War. Architecture of earlier periods is, for most people, more easily categorized as art, largely because age is considered to confer virtue. But, at the beginning of a new millennium, there are signs that the popular prejudice is changing. It is not, we are discovering, necessary to revert to a pastiche of the past to avoid the ugliness of the present. The 20th century may not have produced many indisputably 'great' buildings but it did produce an unparalleled number of, if not all 'good' ones, creative, innovatory, and visually spectacular buildings.

The aim of this book is to offer a panoramic view of the marvels of world architecture by looking at nearly 300 individual buildings. Inevitably, Western examples far outnumber those of the East, because of their greater variety, number, influence and, not least, durability; in eastern Asia, the traditional building material was wood, with the result that very few buildings in China have survived from earlier than the Ming dynasty, 1368–1644. If the subjects highlighted in this book had been chosen on aesthetic criteria alone, probably the European majority would have been smaller and the Islamic section larger. In general, the buildings have been chosen because they are, for one or several reasons, outstanding in themselves or typical of an important type; but no strict qualifications have been demanded and some are present (or absent) largely as a result of personal preference. Although one or two family houses are here, in general large, spectacular or monumental buildings – cathedrals rather than churches, skyscrapers rather than bungalows – are preferred.

The buildings are arranged first by geographical region, second by chronology, but with exceptions in both cases. For instance, Islamic buildings in India, something of a special case, will be found under South Asia, but Islamic buildings in Europe will be found under Islam. Most modern buildings in Asia, even if designed by Western architects, are placed in the appropriate region unless, for example, they are closer to international Modernism than indigenous tradition. But there are some borderline cases. A few small liberties have been taken with chronology too, when it is desirable to place two buildings together for purpose of comparison although, if strict dating were adhered to, one would appear earlier or later. However, it is in any case difficult to put a precise date on many buildings, as they were often built over many years, even centuries.

This book is designed for the general reader. Abstruse theories and technical terms have been excluded as far as possible. Sometimes they cannot be avoided, in which case the term may be found in the glossary at the end.

The Ancient World

Chapter One

Stonehenge

Great Pyramid, Giza

Ziggurat, Ur

Abu Simbel

Temple of Amun, Karnak

Ishtar Gate, Babylon

Knossos

Persepolis

Pyramid of the Sun, Teotihuacán

Machu Piccu

Mesa Verde

Architecture is usually considered an activity exclusive to the human species, but building is not, since many animals practise it with remarkable aptitude. The bowerbird, indeed, decorates his alluring arbour with flowers and shells in a display, were the bowerbird human, of what might be called taste. Still, we would not describe the bowerbird as an architect.

Building is an ancient human activity. Even Palaeolithic hunter-gatherers, constantly on the move, must have made shelters of leaves and branches. But serious building, meant to last, only became possible when people settled down in one place, something they could not generally do until they had learned how to grow crops and keep animals. When buildings were no longer merely temporary expedients, they ceased to be merely functional and acquired other characteristics. They became architecture. As Vitruvius defined it in the 1st century AD, architecture is building that fulfils three criteria: it is useful, soundly built, and venustas, *meaning delightful, attractive or – a work of art.*

Until quite recent times, the buildings that have survived are almost exclusively temples, palaces, castles, and the like. Ordinary houses were built of less durable materials such as adobe or wood and naturally received far less care and expenditure than was lavished on the homes of gods and rulers. It is no surprise that the earliest works of architecture were predominantly religious buildings, such as the great temples of ancient Egypt or Greece. Increasingly, other kinds of building became prominent as time passed, but spiritual motives have generally been responsible for the peaks of architectural achievement: think of the cathedrals of medieval Europe, the Baroque churches of the Counter-Reformation, the mosques and madrasas of Islam, the Hindu and Buddhist temples of south and south-east Asia. The decline of religion in the contemporary West may explain why today, although we have an unprecedented number of fine architects, we have no indisputably great buildings.

Stonehenge

Stonehenge, which stands amid the bleak expanse of Salisbury Plain in southern England, is the most famous megalithic monument in Europe. The earliest construction began before 3000 BC, and the building remained in use, sporadically at least, for nearly two millennia. It consists basically of an incomplete circle of roughly worked standing stones up to 22ft (7m) above the ground and arranged in a ring.

Archaeologists distinguish three main periods of construction. In Period I, Neolithic workmen using picks made from antlers dug a circular ditch nearly 327ft (100m) in diameter, backed by a circular wall. Two large stones, one still surviving, marked the entrance. In Period II,

about 2100 BC, two concentric circles of 80 bluestone pillars weighing up to four tonnes each were erected in the centre. Period III, 100 years later, saw the erection of the circle of sarsen uprights capped by sarsen lintels, fashioned with stone hammers, which largely form the monument as it is today, after centuries of climatic erosion and pillage by builders. There is no natural stone nearby. The sarsen stones came from the Marlborough Downs, about 20 miles (32km) away, but the only known source for the huge bluestones is South Wales. Numerous theories, many patently absurd, have been put forward to explain how the monument was constructed and what its purpose was. It certainly had nothing to do with

the Druids, who did not appear on the scene until centuries later, and this puzzle is unlikely to be solved, though it is generally accepted that Stonehenge was a place of worship. The construction of Period II is aligned with the rising sun at the summer solstice, which is clearly not a coincidence, but its significance remains a mystery. It has been widely supposed that the bluestones were brought overland to the site by rollers and by water on a raft. An attempt to reproduce this operation in 2000, however, ran into serious difficulties. Another theory holds that the bluestones were a relic of the Ice Age, deposited on Salisbury Plain thousands of years earlier by glaciation.

Stonehenge: the slightly controversial reconstruction has made it appear less of a ruin than it once was.

The Great Pyramid, Giza

Although Egyptian architecture remained remarkably constant for nearly 3,000 years, there were changes. Pyramids, built chiefly to contain the bodies of pharaohs, were restricted to the Old Kingdom (c. 2575–2134 BC). They developed from the earlier, low, flat-topped *mastaba* but, due partly to the menace of thieves, were replaced in about the 18th century BC by tombs cut deep in the rocks, which were unfortunately not thief-proof either.

About 100 pyramids are known today, but the great majority are no more than piles of rubble. The earliest is the Step Pyramid, or Ziggurat, of Zoser, a king of the 3rd Dynasty of about 2800 BC, which was originally about 200-ft (60-m) high. The true pyramid, with four smooth sides on the plan of a square sloping inwards to a point, developed in the 4th Dynasty. There is reason to think, however, that the most notable survivals, the three pyramids at Giza on the outskirts of modern Cairo, are the finest. They are regarded as one of the Seven Wonders of the Ancient World, and are the only survivor of the seven.

The largest and oldest of the three is the Great Pyramid of Khufu (Cheops). Measuring 756ft (230m) along each side at the base, it rose originally to a height of 482ft (147m). It covers an area of about 13 acres (5 hectares), more than the five largest European cathedrals put together, and is said to contain about 2,300,000 blocks of stone with an average weight of 2.5 tonnes. Buried deep within were three separate chambers, reached by intimidating, angled passages and heavily buttressed against the oppressive weight of stone.

Though still an awe-inspiring sight, it is not untouched by time, and the encroachment of the city is a growing threat to its integrity. Today, it has lost about 39ft (12m) of its original height, and it lacks its outer layer of smooth and dazzling limestone, appropriated by the builders of Cairo. Though about 4,500 years old, the Great Pyramid remains one of the largest and most splendid of human works.

OPPOSITE
The three pyramids at Giza.

BELOW
The outer facing of the pyramids has largely disappeared except for a section towards the top of the Great Pyramid.

generally dry climate such material, which would be practically useless in more temperate regions such as northern Europe, lasts a remarkably long time, although, of course, it does not last as well as stone. The reason why the ziggurat at Ur is comparatively well preserved is that its sloping walls were carefully faced with sun-dried bricks set in mortar made from mud. An interesting feature is that the facing of the wall is interrupted at intervals by shallow vertical channels which, experts suggest, were made to allow the mud-brick core to 'breathe', preventing cracking during the wet season. The remaining lower stages have recently been restored to their original appearance.

The ziggurat was originally built by Ur-Nammu, a king of the 3rd Dynasty, during the last two centuries of the 3rd millennium BC, when Ur was the leading Mesopotamian power. It is roughly 1,000 years later than the earliest giant temples of the Sumerians such as those at Eridu and Uruk. The form of the earlier buildings – basically a monumental temple with buttressed sides raised on a huge platform – led to the ziggurat, or temple tower, which was the essential form at Ur. Ziggurats were often built on the same sites as archaic temples and have many features recalling them in form.

The great ziggurat at Ur is essentially a truncated pyramid, built in a series of platforms of diminishing area, and accessed by stairways. On the topmost platform would have been the temple of the Moon god Nanna, the chief god of Ur, although there is no trace of it now. The large temple enclosure includes royal residences and the royal tombs, which have yielded treasures of extraordinary sophistication.

The restored lower section of the Ziggurat of Ur.

Ziggurat, Ur

The Sumerians in southern Mesopotamia (roughly modern Iraq) are generally credited with being the earliest of ancient civilizations, followed closely by those of Egypt, China and the Indus valley. The focus of Sumerian life was the temple, the house of the god who ruled the city, the king at that time being merely his agent. In southern Mesopotamia, little stone or wood was available for building, but what did exist in huge quantity was alluvial mud, from the frequent flooding of the river. In the

Abu Simbel

Abu Simbel lies about 174 miles (280km) south of Aswan, in ancient Nubia. The region was first conquered by the Egyptians during the Middle Kingdom (2134–1786 BC), and was ruled by them, with intervals, until the late 8th century, when the position was reversed and the Nubians briefly ruled Egypt, until driven out by the Assyrians.

The great temple of Abu Simbel was built during the long reign of Ramses II (1304–1237 BC) and proclaims the formidable power of that mighty pharaoh. On the rock-cut façade are four colossi of Ramses, each about 65-ft (20-m) high, accompanied by comparatively tiny figures of his family, who cluster at his feet like satellites around a planet. The plan of the temple is in the customary form, with two large, hypostyle (pillared) halls, surrounded by other chambers and apartments. The temple was built so that at the most important festivals of the year, 20

February and 20 October, the rays of the sun would shine directly along the main axis to illuminate the sanctuary. The inner walls were

decorated with painted low-reliefs celebrating the activities of the divine king, including his famous battles against the Hittites in Syria, the first military campaign in history that can be reconstructed from surviving records. There is also a rather more attractive, smaller temple, dedicated to Ramses' chief wife, Nefertari.

The proposal to build the Aswan High Dam in the 1960s threatened Abu Simbel with inundation, and a remarkable rescue effort was mounted under the auspices of UNESCO. The entire complex was dismantled in pieces and raised to a position 200-ft (60-m) higher, where it was reassembled and protected from the vast piles of rock introduced to emulate its original setting by a gigantic concrete dome. The whole operation took four years and cost over $40 million, a modern technological achievement to match the skill and effort of the original temple builders.

Ramses II built seven major temples at Abu Simbel, including the Great Temple. The so-called Small Temple (left) was associated with his Great Royal Wife, Nefertari, who appears inside being crowned as a goddess. Below are details of the exterior and interior decorations at Abu Simbel.

Temple of Amun, Karnak

Little remains to be seen of the ancient city of Thebes, capital of Egypt during the New Kingdom (c.1550–1070 BC), but the two great temples of Luxor and especially Karnak, which stand close by on the east bank of the River Nile, are notable exceptions.

The temples of ancient Egypt were not places of worship but dwelling places for the gods. Few temples earlier than this have survived, and it can often be assumed that the surviving building, as at Karnak, replaced an earlier one, perhaps dating back to the Old Kingdom, and for about 1,500 years the style hardly changed. These temples are huge, Karnak in fact being the biggest, and are built along an axis. The main entrance takes the form of a pylon gateway, leading to a colonnaded court and a hypostyle hall. Walls bear rich decorations, typically in low-relief, representing rites of the cult, deeds of the pharaoh, and sometimes more domestic scenes. They form an integral part of the building.

The Egyptians were not interested in experimenting with interior space, and the vast hall is somewhat cramped by the profusion of columns. But it was merely a 'hall', in the sense of an anteroom. Beyond lay the holiest chamber, the sanctuary, comparatively dark and narrow, where the cult statue in which the god resided was housed within a shrine. Ordinary people were not admitted, but at festivals, which were extremely elaborate, the images of the gods were carried outside the temple to make contact with them. The annual ceremony at Karnak, when the image of the god was

carried by water to Thebes, lasted for a month. It was conveniently celebrated during the Flood season, when no work could be done in the fields.

The great temples, something like medieval monasteries, were substantial, largely self-contained units, containing craftsmen's workshops and schools. In the 12th century BC, the Temple of Amun at Karnak employed about 10,000 people.

Ishtar Gate, Babylon

Although the city of Babylon existed in the 3rd millennium BC, it only became important in the first half of the 18th century BC, when Hammurabi made it the capital of an empire comprising most of Mesopotamia, from the Persian Gulf to the borders of Anatolia. It was raided and sacked by the Hittites and others in succeeding centuries and was dominated by Assyria from the 9th century until the fall of Assyria in 612 BC. Under a dynasty of Chaldean kings, notably Nebuchadnezzar II (602–562 BC), it again became a major political power in the Near East.

The new Babylon, whose ruins, first seriously excavated at the beginning of the 20th century, can still be seen on the River Euphrates about 55 miles (90km) south of Baghdad, was essentially the creation of Nebuchadnezzar. Straddling the river and guarded by a three-part wall, it covered an area of up to 12 miles (19km) in circumference, and contained such fabulous structures as a seven-staged ziggurat that has been popularly identified with the Tower of Babel and Nebuchadnezzar's palace with its alleged Hanging Gardens, one of the Seven Wonders of the Ancient World. In fact, excavations have shown that the palace was much smaller than might have been expected.

The main entrance to the city was through the Ishtar Gate, which led to the Processional Way, the main central avenue that bisected the city. The glazed brickwork, decorated with heraldic animals, sometimes in relief, adorned the Processional Way and Nebuchadnezzar's palace, as well as the Ishtar Gate which, carefully restored, is now in the National Museum in Berlin. The animals, not only real ones such as lions and bulls but also obscure mythical ones, were originally modelled on a large panel of soft clay. The panel was then cut into bricks, fired, and reassembled on the wall. Colours, on a deep blue background, are bright and varied. The technique was not new, but it had never been employed on such a large scale before. It so impressed the Persians, who under Cyrus the Great captured Babylon in 539 BC, that they took Babylonian craftsmen back to decorate their capital at Susa.

The Ishtar Gate, preserved and restored, is now in Berlin.

Knossos

The Bronze Age Minoan civilization of the Aegean was one of the most remarkable discoveries of the 20th century. Excavations in Crete began under Sir Arthur Evans in 1900, and although the palace of the legendary King Minos had practically disappeared, some parts, especially the alleged royal apartments on the eastern side, were restored in a bold attempt to recreate their original appearance, some say rather insensitively, the characteristically short, heavy, red-painted columns, which were originally of wood, being made of concrete.

The first palace was built soon after 2000 BC, and apparently consisted of a series of individual buildings grouped around a courtyard. In about 1720 BC it was destroyed by an earthquake and was rebuilt in a more elaborate form, while retaining the large central courtyard. This is the building whose remains are visible today. The palace occupies a hilly site and the buildings, which vary in height between two and five storeys, were connected by shady colonnades and flights of stairs. They were surmounted by an emblem representing the horns of a bull, a sacred animal in Crete as the famous painting of the intriguing rite of 'bull-dancing' confirms. Carved in stone and gilded, these images, mounted on the outward edge of the flat roofs, must have produced a brilliant effect in the Mediterranean sunlight.

The palace was virtually a city in itself: it contained thousands of rooms, and the site would have comfortably accommodated two full-sized football pitches. It must have been almost as confusing a place for the newcomer in the 2nd millennium as it is today for the tourists, as they wander through endless rooms and corridors, surrounded by the evidence of a sophisticated society which remains largely unknown, despite the evidence, unfortunately fragmentary, of the surviving wall paintings. The effort to recapture the decorative scheme was taken farthest in the Throne Room. The great frieze of mythical beasts around the walls is modern, but based on fragments discovered during excavation. The high-backed throne of alabaster is original.

Knossos survived the Mycenaean takeover in the 15th century BC, but was destroyed early in the next century by fire, probably the result of a natural disaster.

ABOVE
One of the pillared halls at the Palace of Knossos, thought to have been private apartments.

LEFT
A restored section in the eastern part of the palace; the red columns are concrete replicas of the wooden originals.

FAR LEFT
Some of the storage jars or pithos, *many with sophisticated decoration, found at Knossos.*

Persepolis

In the 6th century BC the Persians, under Cyrus the Great, rapidly swallowed up all the territories of the various earlier empires of the Near East. The ceremonial capital at Parsa, better known by its Greek name of Persepolis ('City of the Persians'), was founded by Darius I in the late 6th century BC, and completed by Xerxes and his successors. It was an unsuitable administrative capital, being remote and inaccessible, but for nearly two centuries it was the chief royal residence.

Although the Greeks had never heard of Persepolis until Alexander the Great conquered it in 331 BC, it bears traces of Greek influence, although it is thoroughly unGreek in spirit. Figures from the processional frieze in the palace of Darius I show Greek influence in the drapery, but are more closely related to Assyria than to Athens.

The Achaemenids, the founders of the Persian royal family, were not great originators, but expertly exploited and refined the achievements of their predecessors. As in Assyria, the whole complex is raised on a huge limestone platform, creating a level surface on sloping ground. In the east, it is backed by the Kuh-e Rahmat (Mount of Mercy), which also provided the greyish stone from which the complex was built. The other three sides were guarded by a wall that ranged up to 41ft (12.5m) where the ground level is lowest. A magnificent stairway on the west led to the top. The colossal royal palaces were built according to the trabeated technique of post and lintel, like the Greek temples. The lofty stone columns that survive from the Audience Hall of Darius rise from a curved base to a complex decorative capital, to support wooden beams. Besides the palaces of Darius I, Xerxes and Artaxerxes III, the buildings included a treasury, a harem, and the Hall of One Hundred Columns, Xerxes' Throne Room. Extremely large stone blocks were used, meticulously masoned, and parts still stand without the aid of mortar.

Persepolis was largely destroyed by a vengeful Alexander, when it remained as capital of a Macedonian province, but gradually declined. The south wall still bears Darius' inscription, 'God protect this country from foe, famine and falsehood'. He didn't, but enough of Persepolis remains to make it one of the world's most impressive monuments.

OPPOSITE
This overall view reveals the vast scale of the monumental Persian citadel.

BELOW
Part of the ceremonial staircase of the Tripylon.

23

Pyramid of the Sun, Teotihuacán

About 2,000 years ago, a little-known people (whose language is still not understood), who had settled in what was then a fertile offshoot of the Valley of Mexico about 400 years earlier, began to build a massive ceremonial complex north-east of modern Mexico City, which grew into the greatest city of Mesoamerica. At its height in the 6th century AD, it covered about 8sq miles (20sq km), housed over 100,000 people, and outposts of Teotihuacán's empire eventually stretched to the Gulf Coast and Guatemala. The city was planned on a formal grid pattern, with even the streams channelled to conform to the rectilinear layout. The manner in which streets and buildings are aligned suggests some astronomical significance. The main north-south thoroughfare is called the Avenue of the Dead because the buildings that lined it, probably residences of the great, were once thought to have been tombs. It runs south from the Pyramid of the Moon, with the somewhat larger Pyramid of the Sun standing to the east. Both date from the earliest period of construction.

Like all the temples of Teotihuacán, the Temple of the Sun has disappeared; but the gigantic ziggurat that supported it remains, along with its ceremonial plaza. It measures roughly 735ft (225m) on each side and is 240-ft (73-m) high, consisting of five great 'steps' with sloping sides, the fourth stage being much smaller than the others. On the west, facing the Avenue of the Dead, a grand staircase rises from three stepped terraces. The core of the pyramid is earth – nearly 1 million cubic metres of it. It is faced with a red volcanic stone found locally and lime-plastered.

Teotihuacán began to decline after about 600 and it was sacked by the Toltecs, probably soon after 650. Later settlers, impressed by its grandeur, respected the place, though it never recovered its former power or population. The Aztecs, who would have recognized many of the gods portrayed in murals and sculpture, believed that the city had been built by the gods and made occasional pilgrimages there.

ABOVE
Head of the god Quetzalcoatl, in high relief.

RIGHT
A general view of the Pyramid of the Sun with the Avenue of the Dead in the foreground.

Machu Piccu

The dominance of Andean civilization by the Incas, whose empire at the time of the Spanish conquest extended over most of South America west of the Andes, from Ecuador to central Chile, was a recent achievement. Inca legends go back no further than AD 1200, and it was not until the mid-15th century that the power of the Incas, the 'Children of the Sun', was established in Peru. The greater empire was won in the last quarter of the century, only to be extinguished by the arrival of the Spaniards under Pizarro in 1532.

The Inca empire was a notable triumph over its topography, most of its cities, including Cuzco, the capital, being situated far up in isolated mountain valleys. Good roads, though never travelled by wheeled vehicles, connected the towns and outposts, although

quite how the Incas managed to overcome the communications problem, there being no conventional written language, remains something of a mystery.

Another mystery surrounds the exact function of Machu Piccu, today the most-visited of the Inca sites, which is set in a spectacular position on a high precipice surrounded by almost sheer mountain peaks. In fact the Spaniards never knew it was there: abandoned for centuries, it was first rediscovered by the American archaeologist, Hiram Bingham, in 1911. There may have been some religious association responsible for its location, and its architecture supports this supposition, as it seems too substantial to be merely a frontier strongpoint. A notable feature of the site, the carved, natural stone Intihatana, enclosed by

curving walls, must have had some ritual significance, no doubt connected with the Sun god. The careful planning and orderly layout suggests that this was probably a state enterprise, perhaps organized from Cuzco, which is about 50 miles (80km) away to the south-east.

As well as fine stone buildings the city also combines extensive agricultural terraces. The extraordinary skill of the stonemasons and engineers is famous, for they worked with primitive tools and without mortar, yet managed to fit the stone blocks together with extraordinary precision, building on simple lines, generally based on squares and rectangles. They did not employ the arch, and the buildings of Machu Piccu are quite devoid of sculpture.

Two views of Machu Pichu. The site is in serious danger from erosion: in 2001, a survey reported that a large section was in imminent danger of destruction.

The Cliff Palace at Mesa Verde. The circular structure in the foreground is a kiva, *revealed by excavation.*

Mesa Verde

The Mesa Verde National Park in Colorado, south-west USA, was established in 1906 to protect the ancient dwellings of the Pueblo people, which had been cut into the sheer cliffs. Long deserted, they were rediscovered in about 1890 by cowboys. Nearly 2,000 years ago, the site was occupied by Basket Makers who were able to raise crops such as maize, beans and squash on the green (*verde*) table tops (*mesa*) of the cliffs. They made circular pits for storage which, lined with stone and roofed, they later adapted as dwellings. Later they built stone houses, sometimes of two or more storeys, above ground.

The famous cliff dwellings were constructed by their descendants between the 12th and 14th centuries, probably as a defence against marauding Navajo and Apache. The ground floor had no doors or windows, and access to the higher floors could only be reached by ladders, easily removed when danger threatened. Access to the ground floor was through a hole in the ceiling, and upper storeys were reached by the same means. There were also sacred chambers, called *kivas*, below ground level.

The main construction material was hand-cut stone, fashioned with great skill, and adobe (mud) mortar. Ceilings were built by laying cross-beams which supported laths made from smaller branches, plastered over with adobe. Ascending storeys were recessed, creating a terraced effect, like a ziggurat. Living rooms average about 194sq ft (18sq m). A large number of different groups combined to build these massive communal residences, the most spectacular of the ruined buildings being the so-called Cliff Palace, which was inhabited between about 1100 and 1300. It contains about 200 rooms, plus 23 *kivas*.

The buildings were abandoned early in the 14th century, when the people moved farther south to construct smaller *pueblos* with better access to water. The move may have been prompted by the raids of nomadic tribes or dissension among the different tribal groups, but archaeologists have identified a severe drought between 1272 and 1299 which may also have contributed to the abandonment of Mesa Verde.

A general view of the site, tucked into the cliff. The population must have been well in excess of 400.

THE CLASSICAL WORLD

CHAPTER TWO

Temples of Paestum

Temple of Apollo, Bassae

Parthenon, Athens

Erechtheion, Athens

Theatre, Epidaurus

Stadium, Olympia

Pont du Gard, Nîmes

Maison Carrée, Nîmes

Colosseum, Rome

Pantheon, Rome

Baths of Caracalla, Rome

Diocletian's Palace, Split

The driving force of ancient Greek architecture was religious: the search for the perfect temple, the home of a god, which they believed was a matter of proportions, in fact a mathematical enterprise. Although not immune to foreign influence (the Ionic Order was ultimately of Eastern origin), the Greeks had a profound respect for tradition, and were in general conservative. Decorative details such as metopes and triglyphs derived from functional aspects of a wooden structure, the ends of the cross-beams and the spaces between them, and their stone or marble buildings followed the same form as their wooden predecessors, being based on the post and lintel. This is an architecture of straight lines, though, in fact, owing to the Greek grasp of entasis, perfectly straight lines are rare in, for instance, the Parthenon. This Athenian temple is often called the nearest thing to a perfect building and represents the culmination of about 150 years of evolution of the Classical Doric Order. Other beautiful buildings, such as theatres, were built in Classical Greece, and in the Hellenistic era, from the late 4th century BC, different types proliferated. Gifted artists were even engaged for private houses, and decoration became more elaborate, with the Corinthian Order displacing the pure simplicity of the Doric.

The Greeks were not ignorant of the arch, it was simply irrelevant to them. The arch makes possible the vault and the dome, and where Greek architecture is based on straight lines, Roman architecture is rounded. The Roman answer to the Parthenon is the Pantheon: although strongly influenced by Greece, Roman architecture is remote from Greek in both spirit and technique, although, ironically, the actual architects of Roman buildings were often Greeks. The chief structural element in Greece, the column, in Rome became merely decorative. In a basilica, the most characteristic Roman building, the columns are inside, their structural function taken over, as in the Maison Carrée in Nîmes (p. 39), by walls. Types of Roman building are more varied, including palaces, baths, amphitheatres, etc., often of colossal size, ingenious design and in later times elaborately decorative, as at Split in Croatia (p. 44–45). The Romans were excellent technicians who were willing to experiment. What made their domes and vaults, and hence their vast interiors, as in the Baths of Caracalla, (p. 43), possible, was their development of concrete, often used together with brick. Their technical ability produced many utilitarian structures, some, like the apartment blocks of Rome, to poor standards; others, like the Pont du Gard (p. 38), ageless monuments to their style and efficiency.

Temples of Paestum

Paestum, the Roman name for the Greek colony of Poseidonia in southern Italy, on the shores of the Tyrrhenian Sea, about 60 miles (100km) south of modern Naples, flourished during the 6th–4th centuries BC. It sometimes happens that Classical Greek remains in Italy and Sicily are better preserved than counterparts in Greece; at Paestum there are two large, early Doric temples of about 460 BC, almost contemporary with the Temple of Zeus at Olympia, plus a smaller, slightly later one. Although there have been losses since Piranesi engraved the remains of the Temple of Hera (formerly called 'the Basilica' because its patron was unknown) in the 18th century, both this and the so-called Temple of Neptune (the Roman Poseidon) are still remarkably well preserved. The exterior columns are standing and, inside, there are survivals of both tiers of the two storeys.

Work in the colonies was generally less refined than in Greece, and the Paestum temples are built of travertine stone, common in Italy, though they would have been covered with marble stucco. The Temple of Neptune has 14 columns, while the Temple of Hera has 18, and nine on the ends, an unexpected number in relation to the dimensions, but no doubt planned to create an effect no longer evident. The columns in the *cella* have a considerable convex curve (*entasis*), greater than in any other known temples. That makes them seem taller and stronger but, compared with the Parthenon, these temples have a rather heavy look.

Another characteristic of buildings outside Greece was that the builders felt less strictly bound by convention, for instance in introducing Ionic features in the Doric Order. The flutes of the columns of the Paestum temples end in a semicircle, usually an Ionic characteristic, and they have an almost unique feature in the rounded band of the capitals, known as the *echinus*. Normally plain, they are carved with a decorative pattern, each one different from its neighbours. The only other known example of this occurs in the small temple, usually called the Temple of Ceres, built a generation or two later.

The former Greek colony was taken over by Latins (Romans) in 273, whereupon the Temple of Poseidon (below) became the Temple of Neptune.

The site at Bassae with archaeological excavations in progress.

Temple of Apollo, Bassae

The Temple of Apollo at Bassae is remarkable in representing all three of the Classical Greek Orders. A hexastyle temple, with six columns across the front of the porch, and 13 columns along the sides, it was built in about 430 BC, in grey limestone with a marble frieze and *metopes*, by the little state of Phigalia as thanksgiving for deliverance from plague. The architect was Ictinus, architect of the Parthenon. Although there is a family relationship to the Parthenon, in some respects the temple at Bassae, though probably built later, harks back to earlier traditions. A possible explanation is that it was influenced by the earlier Temple of Apollo at Delphi, the god's chief shrine, a theory supported by the unusual orientation of the temple, which faces north, towards Delphi. It is Doric outside and Ionic inside, but it also had at least one Corinthian capital (the earliest known) on a solitary free-standing column, which supported the frieze between *cella* and *adytum* (the inner sanctuary), where there is usually a wall, and probably others on adjacent half-columns. (It may be significant that the Corinthian Order is better suited to angles than the Ionic.)

High in the mountains of Arcadia, the temple was unknown except to locals until it was discovered by a French architect in 1765. His investigation was cut short by murderous bandits, but his report aroused widespread interest and resulted in the first major international archaeological expedition (British, Germans, Scandinavians and others) in 1811–12. Given the early date, it was carried out in a responsible, scientific manner and was a great success; the archaeologists seem to have enjoyed themselves eating roast kid, drinking rough wine from goatskin flasks, and watching rustic dances. Some of the marbles eventually found their way to the British Museum, but the Corinthian capital was unfortunately not among them. Though there are more colourful explanations of its disappearance, it was probably inadvertently left behind on the site.

32

Parthenon, Athens

The Parthenon, the shrine built by the Athenians for their patron goddess Athena is possibly the world's most famous building, and is as near as possible to perfection. It represents the climax of the Doric style, the first of the three Orders, and the one that engaged the Greeks longest and most intensely. Aesthetically, the main criticism of the Doric Order is that it is inclined to be heavy, but the Parthenon, though much the largest temple in Greece, demonstrates by the beauty of its design that this effect is not inevitable. Unusually, it has eight (not six) columns across the porch, and 17 along each side. The temple stands on the highest point of the Acropolis, and would have been visible from any spot in Periclean Athens. Built in Pentelic marble (the whitest) between 447 and 436 BC, its architects were Ictinus and Callicrates. The sculpture was by Pericles' friend, the genius Phidias, though naturally many hands were employed. Originally it contained an image of the goddess 40-ft (12-m) high, by Phidias, in gold and ivory.

At close quarters, the sheer size of the temple is a surprise, being disguised by the perfection of the proportions and subtle devices such as the slight convex curve of the columns (*entasis*) to correct the optical illusion that makes straight columns look concave. Such devices required extraordinary mathematical calculation as well as building skill. The columns are over 34-ft (10-m) high and measure 74in (188cm) in diameter at the base. A well-built man leaning against one fits into the curve of a single flute.

Renaissance drawings show that the Parthenon survived two millennia in good condition, but in 1687 it was partly destroyed by an explosion during war between Venice and the Ottoman Turks, who had turned it into a mosque and were currently using it as an arsenal. Thereafter it deteriorated steadily, a process currently accelerating due to atmospheric pollution. In 1801–05 Lord Elgin rescued, though the Greeks say stole, the famous Elgin marbles (now in the British Museum), including substantial fragments of Phidias' masterpiece, the frieze, which was 524-ft (160-m) long. The frieze was 40ft (12m) above the floor and therefore quite hard to see so, in order to compensate, Phidias designed it with the background to the figures tilted slightly forward.

The Parthenon is a larger, subtler and more refined version of the Paestum temples and represents the climax of the Classical Doric Order.

BELOW
Detail of the frieze.

Athenian heroes Erectheus, for whom the temple is named, and his brother Butes. It was sited, according to legend, where Poseidon, brother of Zeus and god of the sea, who first claimed possession of the city, thrust his trident into the ground. The result was that a salt-water well sprang up within the precincts of the Erechtheion. (Zeus later granted precedence to Athena on the grounds that the olive tree she had planted predated Poseidon's well.)

The decorative sculpture of the Erectheion is of the same superlative quality as that of the Parthenon. The best-known feature of the building is the south porch, associated with the cult of Athena, in which the columns are replaced by *caryatids*, sculpted female figures, which are slightly more than life-size and combine the Classical attributes of strength and beauty. As the temple appears today, the second *caryatid* from the left is a copy, cast in Portland cement, the original having been removed by Lord Elgin. (One of Elgin's associates planned to deconstruct the whole temple and take it back to England but was frustrated by lack of available shipping.)

The Erechtheion, with the caryatid porch to the right. This remarkable little Ionic temple flaunts the rules with perfect assurance.

Erechtheion, Athens

The Erechtheion belongs to the great reconstruction of the Acropolis of Athens, set in motion by Pericles after the Persian Wars, and stands to the north of the Parthenon. The finest building in the Ionic Order, which, having originated in the cities of Ionia, was just becoming fashionable in mainland Greece, it is sometimes attributed to Mnesicles, who designed the Propylaea, the monumental gateway to the Acropolis. It was built in marble between 421 and 406 BC, and its plan is peculiar and unique, since it has three façades or porches, east, north and south. All of these are at different levels, the result of a sloping site and a profusion of divinities, for the temple was dedicated to not one but three – Athena, Poseidon, and Hephaestos – as well as to the

Theatre, Epidaurus

Most Greek theatres were radically changed in later times: the large theatre at Epidaurus is the best surviving example that retains its original form, though it has been considerably restored in recent times. It was probably built around 300 BC and is ascribed to Polykleitos the Younger, who also designed the Tholos, a rare circular building with a cone-shaped roof, in the same area.

Greek theatres were built in the open on a hillside, exploiting the natural slope to provide clear sight lines for a large audience. The audience sat on benches, first wooden, later of stone, in a semicircle. A central block of seats at the front, originally occupied by the priests of Dionysus, whose rites were the starting point for the development of Greek drama, was reserved for important persons, but otherwise seating arrangements seem to have been democratic. Entrance was at one time free, and even after admission charges were introduced the poor did not have to pay. 'Tickets' in the form of bronze tags have been found. The performance took place in a large circular, later semicircular, space called the *orchestra*. The altar to Dionysus, once placed in the centre, had been removed by the 4th century BC, though its position can still be seen in the theatre at Athens. Behind the *orchestra* was a permanent structure, the *skene*, somewhat resembling a temple façade. It contained the actors' dressing rooms, the few props and stage machinery, the main item of which was a kind of crane enabling an actor impersonating a god to descend from the sky – the original *deus ex machina*. The theatre at Epidaurus had a raised stage with a ramp connecting with ground level. The *orchestra* and the seating have been restored, but not the buildings.

The theatre measured about 390ft (119m) across: though large, it was not unique, having a similar audience capacity to the theatre at Syracusa of about 14,000, a figure to make contemporary impresarios blink. Its acoustics are famous, and it is still in use for the annual summer festival of the Greek National Theatre.

The theatre at Epidaurus was one of the last to preserve the circular orchestra *(not visible here).*

The stadium was originally situated next to the Temple of Zeus, but was later moved farther east, out of the sanctuary precincts.

Stadium, Olympia

Olympia was the centre of the biggest religious festival of ancient Greece, and of the associated Olympic Games which, according to tradition, were first held in 776 BC. The Olympia complex is something of a jumble as town planning did not interest the Greeks; but at its heart was the Temple of Zeus, built between 470 and 456 BC and at that time the largest building in Greece. The stadium was originally next to it, but was later moved farther east, out of the sanctuary precincts. Events, in which only men took part, though women's races were probably held in the Archaic period, included wrestling, boxing and chariot-racing, as well as track and field events, especially foot races.

What was then just a slight depression in the ground became the centre of intensive German archaeological exploration in 1936, inspired by the Olympic Games in Berlin that year, and continued, after a gap imposed by war, until the 1960s. The end result was the virtual restoration of the stadium to the form it had taken in the 4th century BC. Races were not run, as now, on an oval track, but in a straight line, so that the main area of the stadium was a narrow rectangle, measuring about 208 x 33yd (190 x 30m). The athletes began from a starting gate and ran from end to end. The shortest race was the *stade* (the origin of the word stadium), which was one length. There was also a medium-distance (two lengths) and a long-distance (20 lengths) race, the athletes rounding a post at each end. Athletes competed naked, but there was also a race for armed men. The excavations revealed the foundations of other details, including bathhouses with hot-air furnaces to heat the water and provide underfloor heating, the umpires' box about halfway down one side, hand weights held by long-jumpers to gain momentum, and a 4th-century BC building that appears to have been something like a luxury hotel for the richer competitors. Access to the arena was through a tunnel passing under the sloping bank where spectators sat, latterly on tiers of stone benches.

Pont du Gard, Nîmes

The Romans regarded nature as a challenge to be overcome in much the same way as they regarded their enemies. The straightness of their roads is often remarked upon, and although the Romans were not so foolish as to build a road up and over a hill if there was an easier way around it, they did take satisfaction in overcoming natural obstacles. Armies would ford rivers, or build a temporary 'bridge' of boats, but it was preferable to demonstrate mastery over water by building bridges. Permanent bridges and aqueducts were usually built of stone, and many still stand.

A good water supply was essential in any Roman town, where the liking for frequent bathing raised consumption, and sometimes water had to be brought from a very long distance – ideally by tapping a mountain spring from which it would run for miles downhill. Aqueducts best demonstrate the skill of the Romans as construction engineers. The aqueduct at Segovia is over 900-yd (820-m) long with two tiers of arches made of granite blocks without mortar. The Pont du Gard, in the south of France, is one of the most impressive sights imaginable. It is a relatively short section of an aqueduct that was nearly 15-miles (24-km) long, built by Agrippa (also responsible for the original Pantheon in Rome) around 14 BC to supply the thriving settlement of Nemausus (Nîmes).

The bridge that carries the aqueduct across the gorge of the River Gard for about 300yd (275m) consists of two tiers of arches each about 65-ft (20-m) high, with a third tier of much smaller arches. The channel on the top of that, about 180-ft (55-m) above the river, is about a 3-ft (1-m) wide and has cemented sides covered with stone slabs. The first tier carries what until recently was the main road, and it is also possible to walk along the water channel, providing you are not affected by vertigo.

The Pont du Gard is a testament to the Romans' determination to ensure a constant supply of clean water.

Maison Carrée, Nîmes

Roman temples, up to about the 1st century BC, generally followed Greek design, at least in principle, and were indeed sometimes built by Greek architects. However, there were also differences: the Romans were less inclined to respect the Greeks' strict purity of style or order, and they were given to elaborate on ornamentation, sometimes to a fault. It is not surprising that the Corinthian Order was their favourite because it offered greater decorative opportunities than Doric, which the Romans disdained, or Ionic. Many of the differences, however, were more fundamental, and can be traced to native Italian, especially Etruscan, sources.

Some of these are demonstrated in the little temple known as the Maison Carrée, in Nîmes (Roman Nemausus), in Provence, a place that in the 1st century AD, when the temple was built, has been described as 'more Roman than Rome'. The large raised platform or podium is over 11-ft (3-m) high, with a flight of steps providing access to the façade, features found in Etruscan temples. The *cella* is set well back, the porch being three columns deep in the common Greek manner, and is broad enough to cover the entire width, so that the lateral columns are engaged with the *cella* wall and the peristyle, or colonnade, disappears. This too is characteristic of Etruscan temples.

It is a particularly beautiful building: its harmonious proportions and the fine sculptural decoration of the entablature and Corinthian capitals have been ascribed to the fact that a Greek colony existed here before the town, founded by well-subsidized Roman army veterans. However, the temple has imperial

associations. It bears an inscription to the sons of the Emperor Augustus, and it is likely that the architect was an imperial appointee.

The Maison Carrée, which would have stood originally in the forum, is a gem, a perfect example of its type; but it owes its fame to some degree to the fact that it is so miraculously and uniquely well preserved, the exterior remaining virtually unchanged since it was built.

The Maison Carrée from the side, showing the high base and the engagement of the flanking columns with the cella *wall.*

39

*The Colosseum was used
as a handy quarry by
local house builders until
the pope declared it a
Christian shrine in the
18th century.*

OPPOSITE
*The floor has disappeared
to reveal the maze of
subterranean rooms.*

Colosseum, Rome

It is difficult to imagine the people of Periclean Athens enjoying the kind of entertainment that occurred in the Colosseum in Rome, at any rate in later imperial times, and the amphitheatre, though with obvious similarities to a theatre, is a type of building not found in ancient Greece. At least three Roman amphitheatres have survived in a fair state of preservation, good enough still to be used, though not for gladiatorial combats or mass slaughter, in Arles, Nîmes and Rome itself.

They are all similar, but the Roman Colosseum is the largest and finest. Besides its aesthetic merit, it is of great structural interest because of the special problems facing the builders, such as security and access, and the ways in which they solved them. It is sometimes said that an architect who could build an amphitheatre could build anything.

The Colosseum, built in AD 70–80, is about 160-ft (49-m) high and 615-ft (187-m) across at the widest point, and held nearly 50,000 people. Much of the four-tiered exterior arcades is still standing, and demonstrates the Roman method of building a massive structure with a combination of order and arch – Greek decoration and Roman construction. The three main tiers illustrate the three Greek Orders, Doric, Ionic and Corinthian in ascending rank. The fourth, walled tier was added later and was originally of wood, and statues once stood in the open arches of the first three tiers. The walls are brick or stone, but the carved decoration and seating is marble. Staircases within the walls give access to passages separating blocks of seats, and each tier has two adjacent circulating corridors. The vaulting problem alone was

enormous, as changing levels, tapering diameters and varying angles, caused by the oval plan, had to be catered for. There was a retractable canvas roof to keep the sun off, which was maintained by professional sailors. The arena itself, 278ft (85m) by 180ft (55m), was supported on joists. Underneath was space for gladiators and wild animals.

*ABOVE and BELOW
Details of the rotunda.*

*BELOW RIGHT
Façade of the portico.*

Pantheon, Rome

The Pantheon is probably the most admired of all Roman buildings for its combination of aesthetic quality and structural brilliance. A circular temple with a rectangular porch, it was built from AD 118–c.128, probably supervised by that most cultured of Roman emperors, Hadrian, and was a replacement for another older building built in 25 BC by Agrippa, the son-in-law of Augustus. The original inscription to Agrippa was retained, which caused much confusion over the dating of the Pantheon for many years.

Considering what it has suffered, the Pantheon's very existence is something of a miracle. It survived the Barbarian invasions and the vandalism of early Christians. It was plundered by rulers such as the Byzantine Emperor Constans II, who stole the gilded bronze plates from the dome and re-covered it in lead, and Pope Urban VII, who removed the bronze beams of the porch in 1625 because he had another use for them.

Unusually for a Classical temple, the interior is far more spectacular than the exterior, and the one obvious design fault is the clumsy junction of porch and *cella*. The porch has 16 columns, each cut from a single block of grey granite, with the rear ones red. Capitals and bases, in the Corinthian Order, are in Pentelic marble and, before the temple was converted into a Christian church, a bronze relief of Zeus crushing recalcitrant Greeks filled the tympanum. The bronze doors, almost unparalleled for their workmanship, were originally gilded.

The *cella* is a brilliantly planned masterpiece of lighting and proportions. The diameter is 142ft (43m), and the total height is the same, divided equally between wall and dome. The dome, which is slightly larger than that of St Peter's, was made possible by the Romans' command of building in concrete. Above the coffered panels, it consists of alternate layers of concrete and brick, about 21-ft (6-m) thick at the base, diminishing to less than 5ft (1.5m) at the crown. Weight, which is further diminished by reducing the specific gravity of the mortar towards the top, is concentrated on four massive but unobtrusive piers. The only natural light comes from the circular opening, or *oculus*, at the centre of the dome.

Baths of Caracalla, Rome

In Roman society, the public baths fulfilled a variety of social functions that it would be difficult to find nowadays all in one place, if within one city, and could certainly not be obtained so cheaply, sometimes, indeed, for nothing. There were over 800 such establishments in imperial Rome, though they varied greatly in size and quality. Roman citizens went to the baths for many purposes, besides bathing: they were a place of leisure, for general social gossip or perhaps for conducting important business affairs. After bathing, the client could have a massage, perhaps medical treatment, and he (rarely she)

could eat and drink, play games and sports, and enjoy live entertainment. The larger establishments included restaurants and theatrical performances, gardens and fountains, perhaps a sports stadium, and large public halls for lectures and debates.

The bathing itself, in a society which placed bodily and spiritual health on a roughly equal footing, was quite a complex process. One might start in the hot room (*caldarium*), have a rub-down with a strigil (scraper), then into the cold swimming bath, followed by a massage and a rub-down with scented oils.

Many emperors built public baths, but the finest surviving are the Baths of Caracalla (AD 212–216), ruined of course, but less than others, and with a graphic record going back to the Renaissance, when more was intact. They

covered an area of over 270,000sq ft (25,000sq m), including the huge central hall of 183 x 79ft (56 x 24m), which was covered by intersecting barrel vaults and supported on massive piers. Being higher than the surrounding buildings, it was lit by a clerestory. The moderately heated *tepidarium* and the hot *caldarium*, heated by hot air from furnaces blown though openwork bricks, were covered by a dome, while the *frigidarium*, which had plenty of room for spectators, was open to the sky. While the exterior was rather plain, constructed of brick and stucco, the interior was lavishly decorated, with marble floors and walls and a great deal of sculpture, some of it from Greece, which was to be thoroughly plundered during the Renaissance.

The sheer scale of the ruins of the Baths of Caracalla, which were not the largest in Rome, Trajan's baths being larger, strikes the visitor with awe.

Diocletian's Palace, Split

The Palace of Diocletian at Spljet (Split, or Spalato), on the Dalmatian coast of Croatia, was more than a residence, being more like a small, fortified town. Nevertheless, besides being a statement of imperial power and prestige, one of Diocletian's purposes for building it was as a retirement home, and he moved there on abdicating his imperial office in 305.

Like a Roman fort, the palace (and, today, the medieval town) is contained within a rectangle measuring about 700 x 580ft (213 x 177m), and is guarded by walls and projecting square towers on the three landward sides. At the centre of each wall was a gateway flanked by octagonal towers, the main gateway being the Porta Aurea (Golden Gate), still in reasonable condition on the north side. The south side, fronting the Adriatic, was occupied by the Grand Gallery, where the imperial apartments were located beyond a colonnade. A seaward gate in the centre gave access to the interior via an underground passage. Intersecting cross-streets met at the centre of the rectangle, and the most sacred buildings, including the barrel-vaulted Temple of Jupiter and the Emperor's domed, octagonal Mausoleum, were in the southern half.

Over the centuries, Split has been subjected to the usual ravages of time and unsympathetic inhabitants, and much has been lost or obscured. Some has gone since the great English Neoclassical architect Robert Adam visited it and made the careful drawings engraved for his book on the palace in 1764. More recently, painstaking archaeologists have disinterred and restored other parts. The Mausoleum, the most important building,

probably benefited from being turned into a church around the 9th century, the Romanesque bell tower that now looms over it being raised in the 13th century. Much of the Temple of Jupiter, built of finely cut limestone blocks, also survives, in particular the coffered vault and some marvellously rich sculptural decoration in the Corinthian capitals and entablature. Otherwise, little of the imperial apartments of the palace – baths, halls, temples, libraries, gardens – can now be seen, having succumbed to medieval building when Split was a prosperous commercial entrepôt for Balkan-Venetian trade: but the extensive basements remain, preserved by centuries of rubbish-dumping.

OPPOSITE
The peristyle of
Diocletian's palace.

RIGHT
The 13th-century
Romanesque bell tower.

45

THE MEDIEVAL WORLD

CHAPTER THREE

Santa Maria Maggiore, Rome	Windsor Castle	Cloth Hall, Ypres	Cathedral of St Vitus, Prague
Hagia Sophia, Constantinople (Istanbul)	Wartburg	Palazzo Pubblico, Siena	Ulm Cathedral
San Vitale, Ravenna	Edinburgh Castle	Burgos Cathedral	Rambouillet
Charlemagne's Cathedral, Aachen	Krak des Chevaliers	Castel del Monte, Apulia	Guarda Cathedral
Mont-Saint-Michel, Normandy	Laon Cathedral	Château d'Angers	Vienna Cathedral
Gravensteen, Ghent	Chartres Cathedral	Marienburg Castle	Milan Cathedral
Strasbourg Cathedral	Notre Dame, Paris	Rochester Castle	Kremlin, Moscow
Château de Chillon	Bourges Cathedral	Doge's Palace, Venice	Old Hospital, Beaune
Saint Sophia, Kiev	Royal Chapel, Palermo	Caernarvon Castle	Seville Cathedral
Durham Cathedral	Salamanca Cathedrals	Cologne Cathedral	Frauenkirche, Munich
Ely Cathedral	Amiens Cathedral	Rouen Cathedral	Palaces of Sintra
Canterbury Cathedral	Leaning Tower of Pisa	Münster Cathedral	Christiansborg
Tower of London	Reims Cathedral	Regensburg Cathedral	
Abbey of Cluny	Beauvais Cathedral	Salisbury Cathedral	
Mainz Cathedral	Santiago de Compostela	Toledo Cathedral	
Worms Cathedral	Borgund Church, Norway	Florence Cathedral	
	Château de Blois	Palace of the Popes, Avignon	
	Brussels Cathedral		

When Christianity became the religion of the Roman Empire in the 4th century, church-building began on a large scale. Two main types emerged: the West favoured the Roman basilica, a rectangular building that in time produced transepts and became cruciform. The East preferred the round church, dramatically, in the miraculous Hagia Sophia in Constantinople (p. 50–51), an early example of Byzantine architecture which was not equalled in the next millennium. It was also an early example of the principle of the pendentive, which solved the problem of erecting a dome on a square base. Byzantine architecture had interesting offshoots in Armenia and in Russia, while in the West there was little of note until the Carolingian period (8th–10th centuries), of which the most notable survivor is Charlemagne's church at Aachen (p. 53).

The Romanesque style was established by the 10th century (some would include Carolingian) and is especially associated with the Abbey of Cluny (p. 64) and its offshoots. The Christian religion was the main unifying factor as, like its successor, Gothic, the Romanesque style was subject to marked regional variations. The English variety is known as Norman, being associated with the Norman Conquest of 1066. Another complication is that builders were becoming more willing to experiment, and constant rebuilding meant that comparatively few purely Romanesque buildings have survived.

Romanesque is the architecture of the round arch and the barrel vault. Churches are clearly planned, sometimes with a series of apses in the east, or with chapels off an ambulatory. Shafts or piers, often with geometric patterns, are heavy, and interiors tend to be dark. Gothic, which first appeared in the mid-12th century abbey of St-Denis, near Paris, is by contrast an architecture of light, with huge windows of stained glass, made possible by the pointed arch in accompaniment with weight-reducing features, such as the rib vault and the flying buttress. None of these features was entirely unknown in the Romanesque period and to a large extent the changes were motivated by aesthetic as much as structural considerations. There is no functional reason for the immensely high vaults to which Gothic builders aspired.

Gothic architecture covered a wider area than Romanesque and, while the great Gothic cathedrals stand supreme as the finest achievement of European art in any period, with the growth of towns and a wealthy merchant class, the ever-changing Gothic style was adapted for secular buildings. The Cloth Hall at Ypres (p. 86) and the Doge's Palace in Venice (p. 94–95) are examples, not only of different types of building, but also of the great stylistic differences contained under the umbrella of 'Gothic'.

Santa Maria Maggiore, Rome

Christian churches began to appear in the Roman Empire after the Emperor Constantine adopted Christianity in 313. Two types developed, the basilica, a rectangular hall with lower side aisles to allow for a clerestory, and the round or octagonal church. S. Maria Maggiore (c. 432–440) is an example of the first type, which came to be almost universal in the West, while S. Vitale in Ravenna is an example of the second type, which was preferred in the Byzantine Empire and produced the astonishing Hagia Sophia in the 6th century.

One of the advantages of the basilica church was that it offered the opportunity for a splendid colonnade dividing the aisles from the nave. In S. Maria Maggiore, lines of Ionic columns form stately margins to the broad nave. They carry a Classical entablature and, above, the upper walls of the clerestory have muted Corinthian pilasters between the windows, below which are mosaic panels illustrating incidents from the Bible. Mosaics also cover the arch that extends into the apse.

The church is an example of a recurring phenomenon in the history of Western architecture, the revival of Classicism. At one time scholars thought that the building must date from the 2nd century because in style it resembles the architecture of the reign of Trajan (AD c. 53–117). (Methods of dating have since improved; for instance, it has been possible to date early brick churches in Rome by the width of the mortar between the bricks.) S. Maria Maggiore is associated with a revival of an earlier, Classical style of about the time of Pope Sixtus II, and was one of several

large religious foundations in what was a time of prolific church-building.

Although it is not hard to visualize the original appearance, the church has been considerably altered since the 5th century. The apse was rebuilt and a transept added in the 13th century. The coffered ceiling and aisle vaults belong to the Renaissance, the *baldachino* over the altar to the 18th century. Much of the rest of the fabric has been restored, but in the original style.

Santa Maria Maggiore has been much altered, but behind the Baroque façade the early Christian church is still recognizable.

Hagia Sophia, Constantinople (Istanbul)

Early in the reign of Justinian (527–565), riots broke out in Constantinople, in the course of which several important buildings were destroyed. They included the Church of Divine Wisdom (Hagia Sophia), which was both the cathedral church of Constantinople and the palace church of the emperor. Imperial prestige demanded rapid reconstruction; moreover, the new church was expected to be far more magnificent than the one it replaced, a building to astound the eye of the beholder. Justinian entrusted the job to Anthemius of Tralles in Lydia, a scholar not known to have ever produced another building, and his nephew, Isidorus of Miletus. In just five years, between 532 and 537, they had built what is universally regarded as the supreme masterpiece of Byzantine architecture.

The crowning glory of Hagia Sophia is the dome. Here Anthemius' background in geometry was undoubtedly useful. Built in brick and measuring 106ft (32m) in diameter, it was an extraordinary feat of engineering, though it collapsed after an earthquake in 568 and was rebuilt by another Isidorus. Of course, the Romans had built domes and they had also used brick, though not for domes. But to build a dome on circular walls, as in the Pantheon, is comparatively simple compared with raising a dome over a square. Anthemius overcame the problem by the device of the pendentive, a concave, triangular section with the point at the right-angle of two walls or arches, rising to form a quarter-circle at the height of the arches. Such a structure transmits the weight of the dome evenly to the main supports at the

Views of the interior and exterior of Santa Sophia. The Church of Divine Wisdom is an example of a work of genius that, springing almost from nowhere, was imitated but never equalled. The church became a mosque in the 15th century.

corners. Screened aisles and galleries were employed to conceal the supports, so that the dome appears to float miraculously heavenward, a mysterious effect enhanced by the contrast between the well-lit central space and the dark surrounding aisles. The glittering mosaics, carved capitals and coloured marble

helped to justify Justinian's boast, when he first entered the finished building, that he had 'triumphed over Solomon'.

When the Ottoman Turks took Constantinople in 1453, Hagia Sophia became a mosque, and a model for other mosques. Today it is a museum.

San Vitale in Ravenna, the first great monument to the Byzantine style.

San Vitale, Ravenna

The city of Ravenna, about 60-miles (100-km) north-east of Florence, first flourished when its port became the main base for the Roman fleet in the Adriatic under Augustus. In the early 5th century, it was the imperial capital, and Theodoric the Goth made it his seat as ruler of Italy. When the generals of the Byzantine Emperor Justinian reconquered the West, Ravenna became Byzantium's western capital. The architecture of 6th-century Ravenna reflects a mixture of Italian and Eastern influences, notably in the characteristically Byzantine art of mosaics, which remained in fashion for 1,000 years. They are the most famous element of S. Vitale (built c. 540–48).

Sometimes called the first truly Byzantine Church, S. Vitale is Justinian's greatest monument after Hagia Sophia in Constantinople. In the 4th century, the earliest Christian churches had followed the general plan of the Roman basilica, but S. Vitale is centrally planned. The general form is octagonal, with a second, smaller octagon rising above the first, topped by a dome. The outline is broken by an apse in the east, a porch in the west, and several attendant chapels. Built in brick and plaster, its exterior appearance is plain, with understated buttressing pilasters at intervals along the walls and otherwise little decoration. Inside, it is a different story. The overall impression is of space and light, an effect enhanced by the pale marble columns and lofty arches. The Byzantine love of ornament is given full reign, with richly carved capitals and, especially in the presbytery, mosaics occupying every suitable space. Some of them depict the Byzantine court, including hierarchical portraits of the Emperor and his equally famous wife, Theodora, whose jewellery is represented in mother-of-pearl. The advantage of wall-mounted mosaics over their traditional use for floors, was that the artists could make more use of coloured glass cubes, too fragile to be satisfactory under foot. The effect of the stately procession, with figures ranged from left to right and the pale, large-eyed, solemn faces framed in a marvellous arrangement of brilliant colours, represents the apogee of Byzantine art.

Charlemagne's Cathedral, Aachen

The imperial chapel of Charlemagne is the finest surviving example of Carolingian architecture. When, in the late 8th century, Charlemagne chose Aachen (Aix-la-Chapelle) as his capital, he planned to create something that would rival the great imperial centres of Rome or Ravenna, both places he had visited. He attracted to Aachen such men as the Frankish scholar Einhard and the learned Englishman Alcuin, together with the finest available artists, craftsmen and scholars, which included Italians, Greeks, Provençals, Jews and even Arabs.

The basic form of the building is an octagon with a projecting apse. It is usually said to have been modelled on the Church of S. Vitale in Ravenna (opposite), although its simple strength is more Roman in spirit than Byzantine. The interior of the octagon, with its three tiers of arches and marble-columned arcades, appears much as it did in Charlemagne's time, and the simple, marble throne on which Charlemagne sat and later Holy Roman emperors were crowned, is still in place.

Otherwise the building has been greatly altered. The Carolingian apse was replaced in the 14th century with a lofty Gothic choir, the tall outer roof of the octagon was added in the 17th century, and the western steeple dates from 1884.

Its founder endowed the church with many relics and sacred objects, now housed in the treasury with other, later precious objects. In the 13th century, Charlemagne's remains were transferred to a shrine of gilded silver and copper, decorated with coloured enamels and gems. The figure of the emperor is shown holding the church in his hand, his crown informally tilted, and is in contrast to the solemn saints flanking him. In the 14th century, a silver and gilt bust was made to contain Charlemagne's brain case. An interesting addition to this piece, of unknown origin, reminds us that Charlemagne is claimed to be a founder of both the German and French nations; the shoulders of the bust bear a jewelled costume with German eagles, while a plinth on the base of it is studded with the French *fleur-de-lis*.

Gothic additions to the Carolingian chapel.

53

Mont-Saint-Michel from the landward side.

Mont-Saint-Michel, Normandy

The steep, rocky island of Mont-Saint-Michel, less than 3,280ft (1000m) in circumference and accessible overland at low tide, though the sands are treacherous, is crowned by the ancient abbey. It is one of the most famous sights in France, familiar to those who have never been there from tourist posters and advertising. Seen across a calm sea in the evening sunlight, it is a breathtaking sight.

According to legend, the Archangel Michael instructed Bishop Aubert in a dream to build the original chapel on the mount in the 8th century, when it attracted pilgrims then, as it still does today. It became a Benedictine abbey in the 10th century, and the oldest structure found is a Carolingian church of that time. Construction of the present buildings, originally in the Norman Romanesque style, dates from the early 11th century, but part of the abbey and the village below were burned by the Bretons in 1203, the monks later successfully defending themselves against English attacks during the Hundred Years War. Later buildings are Gothic. Part of the 13th-century reconstruction was La Merveille, which became the main monastic building. Because of the limited space, it was necessary to build upwards rather than out, and La Merveille is on three storeys. The vaulted Knights' Hall (Salle des Chevaliers), a beautiful specimen of Norman Gothic that was originally the Scriptorum, is on the second storey, with the refectory and cloister above it. The choir of the church was rebuilt in the Flamboyant style in the 15th century, and the tower and spire, topped by a gilded St Michael and the Dragon, 570-ft (174-m) above the sea, were erected in the 19th century.

The abbey gained a reputation for learning in the 12th century and held a famous library, which may explain why it was not damaged by the vandals of the French Revolution. However, monastic life had declined disastrously, and when the monastery was dissolved in 1790 there were only seven monks at Mont-Saint-Michel. It became a state prison under Napoleon, until it was rescued in 1863 and subsequently restored.

Gravensteen, Ghent

The people of Ghent have always manifested a sturdy desire for independence or, in the words of a medieval chronicler, an 'overbearing arrogance'. Their revolt of 1539, for example, brought upon them the vengeance of the Emperor Charles V who, in spite of having been born in the city, executed the leaders and quartered his underpaid troops all over town, with no instructions to be kind to their hosts.

The Gravensteen was the medieval stronghold of the counts of Flanders, and though now near the city centre, it would have been outside the town in the 9th century when it was first built. The site offered no natural topographical advantages, and the castle was protected by a wide moat which, however, failed to prevent two successful sieges in the 14th century. By 1539, however, the counts had moved out and the castle had passed into the hands of the dukes of Burgundy. Thereafter the history of the Gravensteen was less important and less violent. Various parts were converted into government offices and, for a time in the 19th century, even a factory.

The castle has an unusual appearance, chiefly due to the hanging turrets along the curtain wall, providing covering fire for the walls, which may have derived from experience of the Crusades. There are other indications of familiarity with Byzantine practice and the chapel has an unusual window in the form of a cross; but there is no known architectural prototype. Another striking feature is the gatehouse, defended by machicolated towers, which is large enough to suggest a kind of subsidiary castle in itself. The keep, with large halls on two floors, is massive, and still dominates the city. The castle contains the usual horrors, a torture chamber and an *oubliette*, which was entered only by a trapdoor in the ceiling (and rarely left again).

There are some remains of the original building in the base of the keep: otherwise, the Gravensteen today looks like an unusually well-preserved 13th-century castle, though this is chiefly due to a careful restoration in the late 19th century.

A restorative spruce up in recent times cannot conceal the turbulent heritage of the Gravensteen.

Strasbourg Cathedral

When the cathedral, of which only the crypt and parts of the east end remain, was first built in the early 11th century, Strasbourg was a powerful German city, and German architecture was approaching its zenith. The original building was destroyed by fire in 1176 and the cathedral was subsequently entirely rebuilt, changing in the course of the 13th century from heavy Romanesque into an harmonious example of High Gothic, whose aspiration to height, perhaps augmented by the comparatively tall houses of medieval Strasbourg that crowded around it, gives it a particular dynamism. In 1439 the spire eventually rose to 480ft (146m), the highest in Europe, and was a structure as bold, it was said, as the Tower of Babel. The impression of soaring growth is heightened by the tense upward momentum of towers, buttresses and gables, although the nave is less high than in most French contemporaries. Much of the design is credited to Erwin von Steinbach, who probably planned the sculpture of the west front, though it was not completed until the late 14th century. Building still continued thereafter, but in spite of the great span of years, Strasbourg maintains a remarkable artistic integrity.

During the Reformation, Strasbourg became Protestant, and many of the figures of saints were removed from the interior along with tombstones and a number of altars, making it today seem comparatively austere. The greyish sandstone, quarried locally, has also darkened with time. Strasbourg returned to Roman Catholicism when Alsace was ceded to France in 1681 but suffered more damage during the French Revolution, when many sculptures on the exterior were torn down and a law, fortunately disobeyed, was passed calling for the demolition of all church steeples. Of the surviving sculpture, perhaps most notable are the tympanum of the Death of the Virgin and the figures of the Church and the Synagogue. They flank the south transept, which inside contains the unusual, sculptural Judgement Pillar, marking the place where the bishop dispensed justice and mystery plays were performed. Like the Church and Synagogue figures, it was apparently the work of a group of itinerant craftsmen who were in Strasbourg in 1225, having previously worked at Chartres. Surprisingly, a good deal of medieval glass has survived, including two rose windows from the 12th century.

Château de Chillon

From a distance, the Castle of Chillon, with its cluster of turrets and pitched roofs, has a picturesque appearance that belies its strength as a fortress. Once the stronghold of the dukes of Savoy, whose territory straddled the French-Italian border, it stands on a rocky island not far from the shore of Lake Geneva, near Montreux, with the mighty slopes of the Alps providing a suitable backdrop. It was first built in the 10th century, and the lower portion of the donjon, or keep, dates from that time. It was expanded in the 11th century, and the Tower of the Dukes was built at the northern end. There was further, extensive rebuilding in the 13th century and, bar a few later accretions, it is the building which we see today.

Besides the surrounding water, the castle is guarded on the landward side by a double wall, with the outer walls interrupted by round, machicolated towers. The drawbridge has been replaced by a permanent bridge, leading through a gatehouse into the outer courtyard. A second gate gives access to the inner courtyard, which is virtually divided in two by the bulky keep. On the far side are two great halls, with magnificent 13th-century vaults and, to the north, the ducal apartments and Tower of the Dukes, including the red-ceilinged *camera domini*, or lord's chamber, the most interesting room in the castle.

Although the dukes moved their chief residence to Chambéry in the 13th century, and the castle was taken over by the city of Berne in the 16th century, it remained in occasional use. Lord Byron visited Chillon in 1816 and subsequently wrote his poem, *The Prisoner of Chillon*, which commemorates François

Bonnivard (1496–1570). A political enemy of the Duke, Bonnivard was held for six years in the impressive vaulted cellar, partly carved from the rock under the Great Hall, chained to a pillar. Byron scratched his name on what he believed to be the pillar in question.

The Castle of Chillon, exceedingly well preserved, is enhanced by its site, with the lake on one side, the mountains on the other.

The 13 domes of the cathedral, some of which are just visible above the trees, set a style which spread throughout Russia.

Saint Sophia, Kiev

In 988 Prince Vladimir, ruler of the old Russian state of Kiev, under the influence of Byzantium, adopted Greek Orthodox Christianity. When he returned to Kiev, bringing Byzantine icons, crosses and other sacred objects, he ordered the pagan idols of Kiev to be thrown into the river, where a few days later his people came to be baptized. These events mark the beginning of the Christian Middle Ages in Russia, in which Byzantine art and the Orthodox Church together formed the major theme of Russian culture.

The earliest churches of Kiev have not survived, though we know they were Byzantine in character and based on the form of a Greek cross. The Cathedral of St Sophia, founded in 1037, is probably the oldest survivor, but there is not much evidence of its original appearance, which is now that of a fine example of Ukrainian Baroque. A reconstruction of the original building shows a basilica with a brick dome and five aisles terminating in round apses, with cloister-like arcades on the other three sides. The exterior was banded with alternating horizontal courses of brick and pinkish mortar, producing a novel effect. Another striking feature, not derived from Byzantium, was the total of domes which, including the large central one, numbered 13, representing Christ and the Twelve Apostles. But the addition of new aisles and domes in the Baroque period obscures the 11th-century church.

It was designed to rival Hagia Sophia in Constantinople, whose dedication it shares, and inside, the immediate impression is of the skill with which the Byzantine architects handled the admission of daylight, a notable feature of the earlier Hagia Sophia. The chief decorative

features are frescoes and mosaics, the Orthodox alternative to the stained glass and sculpture of the Latin Church. Most famous is the powerful, almost intimidating mosaic of Christ Pantocrator ('Ruler of the Universe') in the central dome, which is lit by windows below. The largely glass mosaics illustrate the painstaking detail employed in their creation: in the huge mosaic of the Virgin Orans ('praying Virgin'), more complex parts such as a human face contain about 26 cubes per square inch.

Durham Cathedral

Durham Cathedral, built from 1093–1133, together with the bishop's palace and castle – a powerful combination of lay and ecclesiastical power in Norman England – share a spectacular site, high on a wooded, cliff-like peninsular all but circled by the River Wear far below. Seen from the west, the three great towers of the cathedral convey an impression of massive invulnerability and which nearly 1,000 years of history confirms.

Durham is the finest example of the Anglo-Norman version of the Romanesque style. Not only does it contain more Norman work unaltered by later generations, it is also the one Romanesque cathedral in England of truly remarkable design. It contains all the main Gothic features – pointed arches, ribbed vaults (probably the earliest in Europe) and flying buttresses (concealed above the vaults of the aisles), but remains essentially Norman in character and possesses a stylistic unity rare among English cathedrals. The massive central tower, for example, was built in the late 15th century but, lacking the usual pinnacles, it confirms the Anglo-Norman character of the whole structure.

Durham contains a famous relic, the body of St Cuthbert (died 687), once believed to work miracles, which was brought here by the monks of Lindisfarne in 995 to save it from the depredations of the Vikings. An elaborate shrine was built to house it, and the Chapel of the Nine Altars built around it. The unusual Galilee porch was built in about 1170 at the west end, after a previous attempt to build it at the eastern end was thwarted by cracking, interpreted as a sign of St Cuthbert's disapproval.

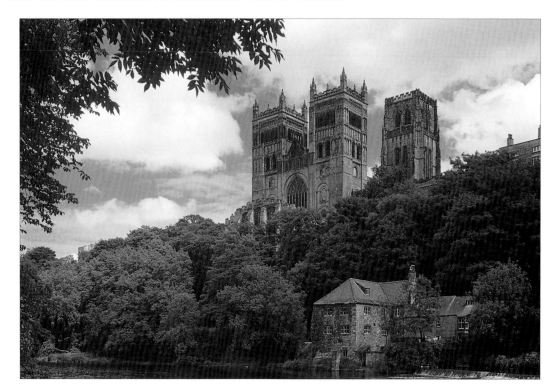

The interior, perhaps unexpectedly, is scarcely less impressive than the exterior. Great round columns decorated with geometric patterns, combining power and vigour, march down the nave alternating with composite piers, each about 10ft (3m) in diameter. Among the most interesting furnishings are the Neville Screen, carved in Caen stone with alabaster images.

Durham, untypical and in advance of its time, is one of the outstanding buildings of medieval Europe. Today, it is sited in what may seem a rather remote region, but in St Cuthbert's time and later, the early Anglo-Saxon kingdom of Northumbria was one of the most civilized places in Europe. The cathedral is a reminder of that heritage.

Durham Cathedral, high on a bluff above the River Wear, has some very advanced features which influenced architectural developments elsewhere.

Ely Cathedral

Driving north from Cambridge through the dead-flat fens of eastern England, the Cathedral Church of the Holy and Undivided Trinity appears above the ground-clinging mist like a heavenly apparition. This magnificent building is situated within a market town of little more than 10,000 people which has changed comparatively little in essence since the cathedral was built.

Of the Saxon original, developing from a 7th-century religious foundation endowed by a daughter of an East Anglian king, there is no trace, except for the 7th-century Cross of St Ovin, unearthed in archaeological excavations, and a window in the *triforium* (below the clerestory). The house was later destroyed by

the Vikings, but a new Benedictine monastery was founded on the site in the late 10th century, and the present cathedral was begun under the first Norman abbot in the 1080s. The nave, characteristically lengthy, at 208ft (63m), the lower part of the grand western tower that replaces the common arrangement of twin towers, the southern transept, and the superb Prior's Door with its tympanum of Christ in Glory, are Norman, all in place before the end of the 12th century, though the tower fell in the early 14th century and was rebuilt by Alan de Walsingham, who appears to have been responsible for the innovation that makes Ely Cathedral unique. The cruciform plan of most English cathedrals had the disadvantage that the central crossing, with four massive columns and arches at the corners to support a tower or steeple, was rather cramped. The solution at Ely, credited to Walshingham, was an octagon, in the Decorated style, with the arches of the nave and choir set obliquely, to open up the central space. The late 14th-century lantern at the top of the western tower repeats the octagonal form, with four long sides and, at the angles, four shorter ones.

After the octagon, the most famous feature of Ely is the beautiful, airy Lady Chapel, by a pupil of Alan de Walsingham from among the monks of Ely, and built in the second quarter of the 14th century. From 1566 to 1938 it served as a parish church.

Canterbury Cathedral

Canterbury Cathedral incorporates the entire history of the Christian Church in England since Pope Gregory I sent St Augustine to convert the English in Kent in 597. There are no visible traces of the original building, although the world of demons and monsters encapsulated in the capitals of the crypt embodies pre-Christian superstitions, and there are some fragments of the early Norman Benedictine abbey.

The double transepts of Canterbury were to influence other English cathedrals, such as Salisbury; but the most remarkable feature of the building is the length, especially of the eastern end, begun by William of Sens in 1175 and completed ten years later by William 'the Englishman', which was nearly twice as long as the 197-ft (60-m) nave of the 1390s. The latter is the work of a great 14th-century architect, Henry Yevele, and its slender piers and high arches make it one of the most spacious and distinguished interiors in the whole of medieval architecture. Despite this and other examples of the 14th-century Perpendicular style, Canterbury belongs predominantly to the Norman and Early English Gothic styles. It was constructed mainly in the warm stone imported from Caen in Normandy, but Purbeck marble was extensively employed inside, particularly in the choir, transepts and the Trinity Chapel, where the shrine of Thomas à Becket once stood.

Due to Canterbury's position as the seat of the English primate and importance as a place of pilgrimage, more of the stained glass, some of it from the same workshop as that of Chartres, has survived here than anywhere else in England. The windows of the Trinity Chapel, having escaped iconoclasts, 'improvers' and

German bombs, depict the miracles associated with the cult of Becket, the former chancellor and friend of King Henry II, who appointed him archbishop in the hope of securing his co-operation in subordinating the Church to the royal will. Becket's unexpected and bitter defiance led to his martyrdom at the hands of four of the King's toadying vassals in 1170, and the king himself, who understood public relations as well as any modern politician,

inaugurated the tradition of pilgrimage by walking barefoot to Canterbury to seek absolution. After him came thousands of pilgrims, guided by the long-vanished gilded angel on the top of the central spire, which was replaced by the lovely Bell Harry Tower, the crowning feature of this emotive building, built in the 1490s by John Wastell, architect of King's College Chapel, Cambridge.

BELOW LEFT
The Bell Harry Tower, which replaced the famous angel steeple that guided pilgrims from afar.

BELOW
One of the figures of English kings that give Canterbury a marked association with royalty.

The White Tower is little changed since Norman times, though Wren altered the windows. The curved projection contains the Chapel of St John.

OPPOSITE
Traitor's Gate, the view of the tower from Tower Bridge.

Tower of London

The strategically placed castles of the early Norman period in England were built as a defence not so much against enemies as against the Anglo-Saxon population. The Tower of London is the most famous of these, erected on the Thames at the south-eastern corner of the old walled city. William the Conqueror was responsible for the White Tower, whitewashed in the late 12th century, hence its name, which has changed very little since, except for the somewhat dubious onion domes and the windows, which were enlarged in more peaceful times by Sir Christopher Wren. The remainder of what is probably the greatest medieval fortress in Europe, dates mainly from the 13th century, although no intervening century has passed without additions and alterations.

The Tower has served many purposes. It was a royal palace until the 17th-century Civil War, an arsenal and, for over 400 years, home of the Royal Mint. In the 13th century it was also a zoo, begun when the Emperor Frederick II gave Henry III three leopards, and the animals were only moved when London Zoo was opened in 1834. The English Crown Jewels were lodged there in a secure vault below the 19th-century Wellington Barracks, and the unparalleled collection of weapons and armour includes the codpiece of Henry VIII, which childless women once stuck pins into in the hope of conceiving.

But the Tower is popularly remembered as a prison, especially for traitors, of whom about 50 were executed on Tower Hill. The most recent internees were spies captured during the Second World War. The princes who were confined there in the 15th century by their uncle, Richard III, were probably held in what was later named the Bloody Tower. The Bell Tower was the final residence of several of Henry VIII's victims during the Reformation, and Elizabeth I was briefly held there by her Catholic half-sister, Mary I. A few prisoners endeavoured to escape. A rebellious Welsh prince made a bid for safety in 1244 but fell to his death; more fortunate was Lord Nithsdale, a supporter of the exiled Stewart dynasty, who slipped away the night before his appointed execution in 1716, disguised as a girl.

Old traditions are zealously maintained, including the nightly Ceremony of the Keys, over 700-years-old, the Yeomen Warders, or 'Beefeaters', in their pantomime Tudor uniforms, and the daily feeding of the ravens, whose departure from the Tower will foretell its fall.

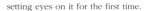

A single tower is practically all that remains of the greatest abbey in Europe.

Abbey of Cluny

As the centre of the great reforming movement in monasticism in the 11th century, the Abbey of Cluny in Burgundy was one of the most influential places in Europe, with some 2,000 religious houses affiliated to it. It was virtually independent of any secular authority, and its church, the largest in Christendom, with its huge basilica and vast cluster of towers and chapels, must have had a dizzying effect on pilgrims setting eyes on it for the first time.

The abbey was originally founded in 910 and built (the second or third rebuilding) in its final form between 1088, when the foundation stone was laid by the Pope's emissary, and 1130. The finely ordered Burgundian Romanesque style that it typified was to be echoed, even imitated, in later Cluniac houses and can be seen today, especially on the pilgrims' route to Santiago de Compostella, in Spain, which Cluny supported.

According to Abbot Hugh, the abbey was built at the direction of St Peter and St Paul, who outlined its dimensions on the ground with a long rope. The speed with which the buildings were completed confirms that Cluny was extremely well endowed, as the costs must have been enormous. The church, whose nave was about 200-ft (60-m) long, could hold thousands of worshippers, and its size provoked some criticism, possibly the cause of Abbot Hugh's insistence that he was only following the saints' instructions. There was also controversy over the results of the Cluniac belief that the House of God (the 'lobby of the angels', as Hugh described it) should testify to his glory and be sumptuously adorned with the finest works that artists could provide. Such ostentation was fiercely attacked by St Bernard of Clairvaux, who joined the new Cistercian Order (1112).

Today it is possible to trace the outline of the abbey on the ground; but of the actual structure, all that remains besides traces of the basilica is one solitary tower and the south transept. The abbey was badly damaged in the French Wars of Religion and closed during the Revolution. The building was then demolished.

Mainz Cathedral

The three great Romanesque cathedrals of the Rhineland, Mainz, Speyer and Worms, form a close-knit group, perhaps because it would be possible to see them all in one day, though a less hectic schedule is preferable. They have obvious affinities: all are constructed of the same reddish sandstone from local quarries and, though Worms is later, all were built in roughly the same period. They make it easy to see why the Romanesque was less easily displaced by Gothic in this region than elsewhere.

The Romans noticed the strategic significance of the site where the Rivers Rhine and Main come together; Mainz is one of the oldest cities in Germany. Though frequently damaged by restless 'barbarian' tribes, it was an early centre of Christianity, and St Boniface, the first archbishop and primate of Germany, set out from there to convert the pagans in the 8th century. During the High Middle Ages, it was a rich imperial city, known as 'Golden Mainz', with a population not much smaller than it is today.

The cathedral is a memorial to the ecclesiastical patronage of the emperor Henry IV (1056–1105), though his cathedral building arose largely from his dispute with the pope. Of the three Rhineland cathedrals, Mainz is perhaps the grandest and certainly the most spacious, partly through the effect of later restorations and partly through certain Gothic features. Among these are the dominant western twin towers, usually considered a characteristically Gothic arrangement. In fact, the west end of the cathedral was built in the 13th century, but in the same style as the east end of over 100 years earlier. Gothic additions, such as the upper stages of the polygonal towers, appear sympathetic to the character of the building.

The cathedral has a turbulent history. The original basilica burned down on the day it was dedicated in 1009, and it was destroyed again in 1081. Fires, earthquake, a hurricane, shortage of finance, local riots and political quarrels, all interrupted construction of the present building. By the Renaissance it was set on a long decline, not arrested until Napoleon, shocked at its disrepair, ordered a major restoration in 1814

Mainz Cathedral, one of the great kaiserdome *(imperial cathedrals), has been much restored. The two crossing towers are 19th century.*

65

Worms Cathedral

Worms was the seat of a bishop in the 7th century, and perhaps earlier. There was also a palace where Charlemagne stayed and his daughter Emma was allegedly courted by the great Carolingian scholar, Einhard. The present cathedral was founded in the 11th century by Bishop Burchard, a powerful figure in the region, but the citizens of Worms (the name probably comes from the German *wurm*, a worm or maggot) later gained a degree of independence as a free imperial city. Worms was a frequent meeting place of the imperial diet, or legislative assembly, where in 1521 Martin Luther took his famous stand before the emperor Charles V. The citizens subsequently embraced Lutheranism, the cause of much damage during the Thirty Years' War, though the cathedral is now Roman Catholic.

Lacking limestone, most German cathedrals were built of materials such as sandstone that are much less durable, with the result that frequent restoration was necessary. There is very little that remains from the 12th century, but despite many later alterations, additions and restorations, the cathedral of St Peter and St Paul remains a noble example of German Romanesque architecture.

The plan is simple. The doubling up of major elements conveys a pleasing sense of order. A distinguishing feature, derived from the Carolingian style, is an apse at each end, though the eastern apse is concealed by a straight wall. This plan rules out a grand western façade, as in French Gothic cathedrals, and also a western entrance, the doors instead opening into the aisles of the nave, north and south. Another common feature is the twin round towers at each end. A shorter, octagonal tower over the central crossing is again echoed by a similar tower in the west, flanked by the slimmer round towers. Certain Italian features, such as the open galleries in the two octagons and the western twin towers, can be explained by the inclusion of Italy in the emperor's domain.

The interior is cool and stately, with scarcely any ornamentation, the tall, cliff-like walls and solid piers ascending austerely into Romanesque shadows.

The round towers of Worms Cathedral, with the octagonal tower between them, and Gothic additions in the foreground.

Windsor Castle

Windsor Castle has been a residence of the English monarchy for nearly 1,000 years, which makes it unique. There was a royal residence nearby in Saxon times, but William the Conqueror selected a site 2-miles (3-km) away, on a loop of the River Thames, when he came to build a *motte* castle here, one of several similar strongholds guarding, or threatening, London.

In plan, the figure-of-eight outline, stretching half-a-mile (1km) from east to west, reflects the 12th-century castle. A central *motte*, or mound, later surmounted by the Round Tower, or keep, divides the Lower Ward, in the west, from the Upper Ward, in the east. The modern entrance leads into the Lower Ward via Henry VIII's Gate.

Norman castles, which had to be put up fast, were originally wooden, though some believe that Windsor was stone from the start. Little, it seems, had been built by William's death in 1087, and little more was done until the reign of Henry II (1154–89), who built spacious royal apartments and started the enclosure wall and towers. Under John, the castle was twice besieged by rebellious barons, but not taken. It has never suffered another siege, although it was occupied by Parliamentary forces, who indulged in minor acts of anti-royalist vandalism during the Civil War of the 17th century. Later monarchs restored and expanded the castle over the centuries. Edward III founded St George's Chapel for his order of the Garter, though the present chapel dates from 1528.

The biggest reconstruction took place during the reign of George IV (1820–30). The architect was Sir Jeffrey Wyatville, who raised the Round Tower by nearly 32ft (10m), rebuilt the royal apartments and created many of Windsor's present splendours, including the Waterloo Chamber, scene of state banquets. Comparing the present castle with pre-Wyatville prints reveals enormous differences. What one sees now is predominantly his work.

Wyatville was less interested in domestic comforts, and Queen Victoria complained about the smell from the ancient cesspools. Bathrooms were also extremely scarce. The castle contains a variety of attractions for the hordes of tourists, besides its architecture. Here are housed the Queen's collection of Leonardo drawings and a remarkable doll's house belonging to Edward VII's queen. A disastrous fire, by no means the first, destroyed the north-east corner in 1992, but the contents were saved and restoration was completed within five years and, remarkably, under budget.

LEFT
The so-called Norman gateway, actually dating from the 14th century.

BELOW
The Round Tower, the upper part of which is a 19th-century addition.

Wartburg

The Wartburg is the name of a rocky peak south of the town of Eisenach in Thuringia, and of its crowning castle, once the residence of the landgraves of Thuringia. At first appearance, little about the castle suggests a defensive function. With its half-timbered, red-roofed buildings, it looks more like a prosperous late-medieval village or manor; but the site gives the game away.

It was probably founded by an obscure ancestor of the future landgraves in the mid-11th century, but was considerably enlarged in the late 12th century, when the landgrave, a cousin of the emperor, Frederick Barbarossa, was at the height of his power, ruling Hesse and the Palatinate as well as Thuringia. During the 13th century the Wartburg was the centre of the *minnesingers*, predecessors of the *meistersingers*, who celebrated chivalry and courtly love. A contemporary poem describes a poetry competition supposedly held at the Wartburg in 1207. It was the home of Elizabeth of Hungary who, after the death on crusade of the landgrave, her husband, devoted her life to the care of the poor and was later canonized, and briefly, of Martin Luther, in flight from pope and emperor after the Diet of Worms (1521), who stayed at the Wartburg under the transparent disguise of 'Junker Jörg'.

Such events contributed to the almost mythic awe the Wartburg inspired in Romantic German nationalists in the 19th century. By then the castle was in decay, and a huge programme of reconstruction took place, much of it directed at satisfying Romantic conceptions rather than historical accuracy. Some of this was corrected when a second major restoration took place under the auspices of the East German government in the 1950s.

The most impressive building is the landgrave's residence, now restored to its medieval state and one of the finest secular Romanesque buildings in Europe. It stands east of the main courtyard on an awkward, sloping site, with arcades running the full length of the main storeys, providing light. Rooms include the deeply vaulted Rittersaal (knights' hall), where the capitals of the abbreviated columns are carved with bizarre eagles and, on the next floor, the Sängersaal (singers' hall), its massive timber ceiling supported by a pair of stone pillars, where, presumably, the *minnesinger* contests took place.

A half-timbered penthouse structure covers the wall-walk of romantic Wartburg. In the background is the reconstructed belfry; the landgrave's house is just visible on the extreme left.

Edinburgh Castle

Edinburgh Castle looks as though it has grown out of the vast rock of volcanic basalt that raises it over 300ft (90m) above the city streets. The site, dominating the entrance to the River Forth, was fortified in the 6th century, probably by Edwin, king of Northumbria, who is sometimes credited with giving his name to Edinburgh but, having been continually occupied throughout the past 13 centuries, there is no archaeological evidence until much later times. The oldest surviving building is the little chapel of St Margaret, English queen of Malcolm III Canmore (Ceann Mor), who died a few days after her husband in 1093. The chapel, still occasionally used, dates only from the early 12th century, though it may contain elements from an earlier chapel contemporary with Margaret, a great ecclesiastical patron.

It must be admitted that Edinburgh Castle is notable more for its historical heritage than its architecture. Always a working castle, frequently in English hands, destroyed by Robert Bruce when he finally captured it in the year of his victory at Bannockburn (1314), it has been constantly reconstructed according to the needs of the moment, and the bulk of it dates from the 16th century or later. King David II added what appears to have been a characteristic Scottish tower house in the south-east in 1367. The base of it was incorporated into the Half Moon Battery, originally built in 1574 but subsequently reconstructed. The palace buildings date from the time of James IV (1488–1513), who was also responsible for the Great Hall with its fine hammer-beam ceiling; but the building of Holyroodhouse and the susceptibilities of

Mary, Queen of Scots, whose son, the future James I of England, was nevertheless born in the castle, ended its long career as a royal residence two generations later. The esplanade was levelled in the mid-18th century as a parade ground, 'a bow-shot wide'. It is now the scene of the floodlit Military Tattoo held annually at the time of the Edinburgh Festival.

Among interesting artifacts are 'Mons Meg', a five-ton 'bombard' or cannon, with a 20-inch (500-mm) calibre, made for James II in the 15th century, and the 'Honours of Scotland', the crown jewels, more venerable though less costly than those of England.

LEFT
Edinburgh Castle floodlit for the popular Military Tattoo.

BELOW
The buildings of the castle seem to have grown directly out of the rock.

Krak des Chevaliers, Gebel Alawi

Krak des Chevaliers is the most famous of the castles of the Christian Crusaders in the Near East. It stands at the edge of the Syrian desert, commanding a pass between the desert and the coast and guarding the road to Tripoli. On a low rocky hill between converging *wadis*, the site is well defended by nature. It was already fortified when the Crusaders arrived in 1096.

In 1142 the Christian Count of Tripoli sold the castle to the Knights Hospitallers of St John, the military order which, with the Knights Templar, provided the most effective Christian forces during the Crusades. Over the next 140 years, and interrupted by various setbacks, including an earthquake, the Hospitallers created the castle as it appears today.

Krak is an outstanding example of the concentric plan, a double ring of fortifications, in castle architecture. The original 12th-century castle was contained within what became the inner wall when the outer one was built after 1202. The main gate, in the east, was approached up a steep and rocky slope, and in the second construction a vaulted ramp, with 'murder holes' in the vault, was built between inner and outer walls, presenting attackers who broke through the outer gate with a virtually impossible passage to the inner gate. The most vulnerable side was the south where another formidable defensive structure was created, a massive, outward-sloping stone bulwark, ending with a 32-ft (10-m) sheer drop to a ditch. On the south, the ditch was enlarged and lined with stone, creating a combined moat and reservoir. Within, other elements, such as the Great Hall, its adjoining cloister and the large chapel, were more elegant.

Krak was virtually impregnable to mining or siege. Capable of holding 2,000 men, it was latterly seriously undermanned. After the failure of the Eighth Crusade (1270), no reinforcements could be expected and the castle was besieged by the determined Sultan Baybars in 1271. A letter from the Grand Master of the Hospitallers, whether or not it was recognized as a forgery, persuaded the Knights to abandon a hopeless cause, and Krak became a mosque.

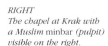

RIGHT
The chapel at Krak with a Muslim minbar *(pulpit) visible on the right.*

FAR RIGHT
Overall view of the greatest of the Crusaders' castles.

Laon Cathedral

Driving along the autoroute towards the Channel ports, through the blessedly deserted countryside of northern France, the distant view to the south of the early Gothic Laon Cathedral, perched on a steep hill, rises like a welcome beacon.

Its history is, of course, less tranquil. Its predecessor was partly destroyed by fire in 1112 during a violent revolt against a notorious bishop, who had revoked the citizens' charter. A new bishop sent out the canons far and wide to collect funds for reconstruction, one group venturing as far as England. The building was soon functioning again, but 50 years later the canons were out again, collecting for a complete rebuilding, which began in 1160 and was largely completed by 1230.

In some ways the result was an innovatory structure, as is immediately evident from contemplation of the vigorous west façade, a prototype much imitated throughout the 13th century, with its deeply recessed arches and gabled porches, and the extraordinary openwork pattern of the towers. The interior, with comparatively slim columns, is unusually light, lively, and uncommonly long, especially by French standards, and the choir, is also unusual in being square-ended, though its predecessor was polygonal, which became the typical form. Although the orderly arrangement of ascending stages derives from the Norman Romanesque style, the contrast with a building such as Durham, only a couple of generations older, with its massive piers, is striking. The design of the transept apses is, in the light of the development of the Gothic style, the most advanced feature of Laon. Polygonal in form, the boldly projecting buttresses that separate the windows virtually eliminate the wall. An advantage of the polygonal over a semicircular form is that the glass of the windows is flat and more manageable for stained glass. At one time Laon dazzled with 2,000 stained-glass windows, though few remain.

The most charming, and probably most famous features of Laon are the carved stone oxen, commemorating those that hauled the stone up the hill, which look out placidly from high in the western towers over the quiet countryside.

BELOW LEFT
Detail of figures in one of the portals.

BELOW
The west front conveys a sense of strongly sculptural energy with its deeply recessed porches, bold relief and open towers.

Chartres Cathedral from the south.

Chartres Cathedral

Chartres has become a symbol of the Gothic age, a name that conjures up an image of the Middle Ages which, if more poetically than historically accurate, still makes an impact on the modern mind.

At first glance, Chartres is not particularly spectacular. Approaching from the west, the portals seem rather cramped and the unmatched spires strike a dissonant note. Yet, if one imagines the later Flamboyant spire in the same form as its southern partner, with its assured proportions and brilliant switch from square to octagonal at roof height, the integrity of the building would not be enhanced and something would certainly be lost. After five centuries of close association, even unlikely partnerships seem to work.

Chartres is really the first incontrovertibly Gothic cathedral. The chunkiness of the flying buttresses, characteristic of the general geometry of Chartres, suggests Romanesque influence, but more importantly they form, for the first time, an integral part of the structure. The quadripartite (four-part) vaulting was also new, and set the common pattern for High Gothic churches.

The cathedral was built quickly in a burst of civic enthusiasm and all but the transepts were completed in a single generation by 1220. The master mason based his elevation on the Golden Section of antiquity: the height of the shafts corresponds exactly to the width of the nave between the columns, bestowing a sense of divine equilibrium. Chartres was a centre of pilgrimage (relics included the Virgin's shift) in the Middle Ages and was also the greatest cultural centre in northern France outside Paris. It is a testament to the spirit of northern humanism which is displayed in the beautiful sculpture and, above all, in the stained glass which, then and now, is frequently likened to jewellery. Most of the windows date from the 12th and 13th centuries, and the earliest predate the fire of 1194 that necessitated reconstruction. Not only do they represent the highest achievement of this medieval art, but they are also pleasingly simple to understand. The dominant colour is a deep, mystical blue, which modern technology has failed to reproduce, nor can photographs recapture its effect. Chartres is undoubtedly a building that must be visited to be appreciated.

Notre Dame, Paris

The Cathedral of Notre Dame de Paris is one of the world's most familiar buildings, rivalled only by the Eiffel Tower as a symbol of its favourite capital. For centuries a centre of Parisian life, housing market stalls, minstrels, a hostel for the homeless, even an employment exchange, it has witnessed momentous events, and few churches have suffered such affronts at the hands of men. Execrable alterations were made in the 18th century, which had no sympathy for the Gothic. The stalls were destroyed, the columns overlaid with marble slabs and the stained glass knocked out of the windows to give more light. Worse came with the Revolution, when an actress was crowned Goddess of Reason on the high altar and the cathedral was auctioned to builders for its stone, a disaster prevented by Napoleon's seizure of power. Notre Dame was saved by the great planner of 19th-century Paris, Viollet-le-Duc, who carried out the restoration of the building – even the gargoyles are his. He recalled that he had wandered there as a boy and thought how the great rose windows seemed to break into song when the organ began to play. His work is not universally approved, but on the whole we should be grateful.

The cathedral was begun in 1163, and at the time it surpassed all rivals. It owed much to a remarkable bishop, Maurice de Sully, a forester's son, who appears in the tympanum of St Anne's portal that shows him with a kneeling King Louis VII at the dedication of the cathedral. A double-aisled plan was adopted, necessitating the fabulous array of flying buttresses which do so much to create the impression, remarked on by so many, of a great oared ship sailing up the Seine towards some heavenly harbour. From the west, the cathedral presents a strong, squarish front 164-ft (50-m) wide, growing steadily lighter in texture as it moves upward from portals to towers, and seeming to proclaim the resilience of medieval French culture. It might be difficult, as the saying, attributed to Zola goes, to 'teach the towers of Notre Dame to dance', but that is not their purpose. What they do convey is a calm image of noble strength.

LEFT
Notre Dame viewed from across the Seine.

RIGHT
The powerful towers of Notre Dame de Paris.

Bourges Cathedral

Bourges is almost at the dead centre of modern France, about 125 miles (200 km) south of Paris. It is dominated by the Cathedral of St-Étienne, one of the most remarkable of French Gothic churches. The archbishop and moving spirit in the construction of the present building was a brother of the founder of Notre Dame de Paris and there are obvious affinities, although the end result is quite different. The building was mainly completed in the first half of the 13th century, though significant additions appeared in the centuries following.

Approaching from the west, the visitor is confronted by a façade of battered majesty with two asymmetrical towers, the southern tower of the 13th century and the northern tower in 15th-century Flamboyant style. But the most striking impression is of sheer width. Above the broad steps, five large and splendid portals march across the front. Walking around the building, one is almost shocked by the total absence of transepts (already minimal at Paris), which results in a long, straight, uninterrupted line of flying buttresses that may be regarded as slightly monotonous.

It is the interior that makes Bourges unique. Here there is no jumble of styles but perfect unity and, most remarkably, an almost springlike atmosphere of light and space. The significance of the breadth of the building, which like Paris adopts the double-aisled pattern, contributes, though the exhilarating effect owes even more to the extraordinary height of the arches, and thus of the vault which, at 125ft (38m), is only 10ft (3m) short of the breadth. The inner aisles reach an unprecedented height of 69ft (21m), abundantly admitting the light lacking in Paris, whose obstructing galleries are absent from Bourges.

There is not much decoration, and not much wall to decorate; but the other outstanding feature of Bourges is its stained glass, which is second only to that of Chartres. As was usually the custom, the windows were presented by various guilds, the beautiful window of the Good Samaritan being the gift of the weavers.

FAR RIGHT
The absence of transepts gives Bourges its slightly parade-ground air. In fact the nave broadens imperceptibly towards the choir, while the aisles narrow proportionately, a device to correct the optical illusion of parallel lines converging.

RIGHT
Detail of the outstanding stained glass.

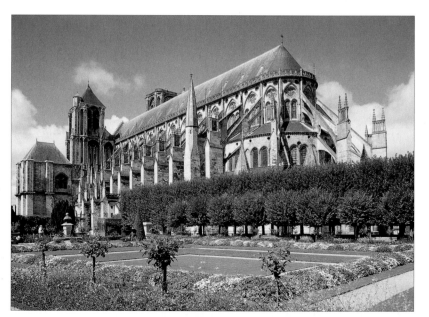

Royal Chapel, Palermo

Medieval Italy was a country which experienced frequent upheavals that left a complex, mixed heritage. In the 11th century, the country contained provinces of the Byzantine empire, Lombard duchies, a claim to overlordship by the Holy Roman emperor, the empire-building Normans in the south and a Muslim state in Sicily. Muslims from North Africa had launched a persistent series of attacks on Sicily in the 9th century, gradually driving out the Byzantine forces. In 1016 a Lombard ruler invited the Normans to Italy as mercenaries, a dangerous move when, playing off their employers against one another, they soon began to conquer the country for themselves. In the late 11th century they drove the Muslims from Sicily, and in 1139 Roger II was recognized as king of Sicily by the pope.

The interchange of cultures in Sicily is almost unique and produced a complex artistic style, broadly a mixture of Western, Byzantine and Muslim influences, which suggests a greater degree of cultural unity in the 12th-century Mediterranean region than might be expected from the general picture of mutual hostility.

The finest example of this style is the Capella Palatina, or royal chapel, the jewel of Roger II's palace in the west of the Old Town of Palermo. Besides the fine marble of the lower walls and floor and the wonderful mosaics, probably the work of Sicilian artists working in the Byzantine tradition, the crowning glory of the chapel is the ceiling, below a dome and small cupolas, which dates from about 1140. This shimmering work of art, its beaded stalactite at first glance suggesting an almost abstract pattern, is of inlaid and painted wood.

The painting, of both decorative and figurative subjects, is probably by Fatimid artists (the Egyptian Fatimids were culturally the leading Islamic dynasty), and gains added importance as it is almost the only major surviving example of Fatimid painting other than on pottery. Since

Roger was apparently well pleased, the decoration of the royal chapel confirms the identification of the hard-headed northern Europeans with the fascinating culture of medieval Sicily.

Detail of the Byzantine mosaics in the Royal Chapel, Palermo.

Salamanca Cathedrals

There are two cathedrals in the fabled, golden city of Salamanca. The old cathedral, built in the 12th century, presses against the southern flank of the new cathedral, dating from the late Gothic era, which, being larger, higher, and more ornate, tends to dominate, perhaps over-dominate: to make space for it, the northern transept of the old cathedral was demolished, and the only entrance to the Romanesque building is via the new cathedral. The celebrated, domed and turreted Romanesque Torre del Gallo is diminished by the Renaissance cathedral looming over it.

The bold, square, western tower has an interesting history. Its core belongs to the old cathedral, as the much-restored frescoes inside confirm; but when the new cathedral was begun in 1512 it was refaced in more contemporary style. The old wooden belfry remained, but in the 18th century it was destroyed by lightning. A new belfry and lantern were built but proved too heavy, and the earthquake of 1755 caused cracks and an ominous twist to the spire. Experts advised demolition, but their advice proved so unpopular that a compromise was reached in which the entire structure was encased in stone. Thus the old tower was preserved, though totally invisible!

The plan of the new cathedral is basically a rectangle, the transepts extending no further that the appendant chapels. Although construction continued over two centuries, the final effect is homogeneous. But passage into the old cathedral may cause slight culture shock. Founded in 1102, this solemn building represents the transition from Romanesque to Gothic. The nave was meant to be barrel-vaulted in the Romanesque manner, but by the time that stage was reached, the builders opted for a quadripartite vault. The large human and animal heads above the capitals are not merely decorative: they support the ribs of the vault.

One of the greatest treasures of Salamanca is the 15th-century curved *reredos* of 55 wooden panels painted with scenes from the Life of Christ by a Florentine artist, who also painted the marvellous Last Judgement in the curve of the apse above.

The old cathedral is dominated by the vast Gothic pile erected in the 16th century,

Amiens Cathedral

The cathedral at Amiens, which could have held the entire medieval population of about 10,000, represents the peak of the High Gothic style of the 13th century. If one were trying to choose a single building to stand for all the great cathedrals of France, Amiens would be a candidate.

The environment of the cathedral has changed a great deal since the Middle Ages and the heart of the city has moved. The best approach is through the narrow streets to the south-east, when the cathedral springs dramatically into view, a perfectly proportioned, though not quite as originally built, vision of slender but steely vertical forms, whose dramatic effect depends on lightness and precision. Contemporary glass-walled buildings sometimes contrive to look heavy: the stone of Amiens appears scarcely heavier than the air. The pigeons fly freely through the flying buttresses, and even the tracery of the windows is minimal. Walls are relatively thin and the vault, the highest in France after neighbouring Beauvais, is supported by slim, uninterrupted shafts. Among its other virtues, the cathedral might be cited as a fine example of economy in the use of materials.

The foundation stone was laid in 1220 by Bishop de Fouilloy, whose bronze tomb is in the nave, and the first master mason, in charge for nearly 30 years, clearly had Reims in mind, though Amiens is altogether more slender. It was the fourth church on the site, and construction began, unusually, at the west end, so that the church to the east could be used until the last moment. Despite a serious fire in 1258, the cathedral was basically complete 11 years later.

For many people, Amiens Cathedral represents the peak of High Gothic art.

The famous figure of the Vierge Dorée was probably already in place on the south transept. The Virgin is frankly portrayed as a fashionable lady – 'the soubrette of Amiens' – Ruskin called her, and though no longer gilded (*dorée*), her charm remains irresistible. In general, the sculpture is hardly excelled anywhere, even at Reims, partly because so much has survived. The serene assurance of the building is finally expressed by the welcoming figure of Le Beau Dieu at the west door.

77

Leaning Tower of Pisa

The Cathedral of Santa Maria Maggiore and its attendant buildings allegedly owe their origin to the gratitude of the citizens of this powerful medieval city for a naval victory in 1063, though work was not begun until about 15 years later. The entire Romanesque complex, favoured by perceptible Byzantine and Lombard, as well as Classical, influences, forms one of the most rewarding architectural vistas in a country not short of them. Despite a period of construction of over 200 years, with the exception of the Baptistery, given Gothic additions in the 14th century, it displays a pleasing conformity.

The campanile (bell tower), better known as the Leaning Tower of Pisa, is probably the best-known architectural phenomen in the world, familiar to schoolchildren everywhere. Because it is so famous for its tilt, it is easy to overlook the fact that it is also the most beautiful Romanesque tower in southern Europe, eight circular storeys of arcaded perfection, with the final stage, the belfry, of lesser diameter than the superb cylinder it surmounts.

It was begun in 1174, and was only half built when, towards the end of the 13th century, the anxious citizens of Pisa observed that it was shifting slightly from the vertical, the result of a soggy site and insufficient foundations. Experts were consulted, without, it seems, much effect, and building optimistically continued. The belfry was not installed until 1350. In a sense, the optimism proved justified, since the tower stood for centuries. Nevertheless, the tilt continued imperceptibly to increase, until it became evident that, eventually, the tower would fall. Numerous schemes were proposed over the years and some of them were ineffectively implemented, at least one actually aggravating the situation. Bold new techniques in the 1990s, which were completed in 2000, appear to have averted the imminent disaster, and are designed to reduce the tilt to a less dangerous angle without restoring the tower to the vertical, which would now be unacceptable. The Leaning Tower must lean.

RIGHT
The campanile at Pisa owes its fame not to its exquisite design but to the fact that it tilts.

OPPOSITE
The tower in context.

Reims Cathedral

Clovis, the ancestor of the Merovingian dynasty, adopted Christianity at Reims nearly 1,500 years ago, and Reims became the coronation church of later French kings. Appropriately, the cathedral, which has benefited from the clearing away of buildings that used to crowd it, is perhaps the grandest in France. It proclaims a proud, if battered, majesty. The addition of blind portals flanking the three main porches, a device copied from an earlier Reims church, gives it a feeling of solid width lacking at, for instance, Amiens, which is actually a slightly larger building.

It was begun in 1211 after the earlier building had been destroyed by fire, and that may account for the uniformity not only of the structure but also of the sculpture, in spite of the fact that construction, slowed by the Hundred Years War, took over 200 years. The upper stages of the towers were completed in 1427, and two years later Charles VII was anointed king at Reims in the presence of Jeanne d'Arc. The battered appearance of the cathedral is chiefly due to damage in the First World War, when, perilously near the Western Front, it received direct hits from German artillery. Looking at photographs of the damage, it seems remarkable that so much was rescued.

The chief glory of Reims is the sculpture of the west façade. The sheer quantity of the sculptural decoration is extraordinary, although it is arranged in perfect symmetry with no sense of clutter. Almost the first thing that strikes the observer on examination of the sculpture is its affinity with Classical models. The frieze of figures rising from their coffins on the Day of Judgement gives the lie to the common supposition that Gothic artists could not convincingly portray the human nude. The larger, draped figures include some of the most famous examples of medieval sculpture anywhere. The impish Smiling Angel (Le Sourire de Reims), the first successful attempt at such an expression, is entirely convincing, and altogether at Reims we see a new spirit of naturalism where Classical balance, pagan identification with Nature (over 30 plants have been identified in the lavish decorative foliage), and Christian charity are wonderfully combined.

The west front of the royal cathedral of Reims.

Beauvais Cathedral

The devout builders of the medieval cathedrals aspired to Heaven, and the hallmark of Gothic ecclesiastical architecture is verticality, upward movement. We may well find the results of this aspiration equally inspiring, if in a different way. But among all the citizens of the still-small French kingdom, except for the poorest classes, more than spiritual aspirations were engaged. They wished to outdo their neighbours. Higher and higher rose the columns and the vaults. Laon set the record, Paris exceeded it, Chartres just topped that, then Amiens leapt ahead by nearly 17ft (5m).

At Beauvais, begun around 1220, 30 miles (50km) south of Amiens, the limit was reached. The choir of the Cathedral of St Peter rose to the fantastic height of 157ft (48m), a jump of nearly another 17ft. A building of 25 floors could have been placed inside without touching the vault. For sheer daring, the builders of Beauvais are unparalleled.

In 1284, the walls of the choir began to bend outwards, and the roof sagged and fell to the ground. But such disasters were not uncommon, and the ambitions of the citizens of Beauvais remained undiminished. Nearly 300 years later a huge spire was erected, in spite of the fact that the nave was still incomplete because the money for construction had been spent restoring the choir, now rebuilt with additional, strengthening piers. A few years later the spire collapsed, and the choir had to be rebuilt again.

The cathedral was never finished. The central tower was not replaced and the nave was never completed. Today, Beauvais remains, a splendid, wounded giant, held together internally by iron rods and externally by massive, three-tier buttresses. The beauty of the stained glass and the heavenly vault (still a record) remain and, in its permanently incomplete state, Beauvais has assumed a unique if unusual appeal of its own.

Beauvais, a wounded giant, and a monument to spiritual endeavour.

Santiago de Compostela

The popularity of the pilgrimage in medieval Europe is easily understandable. The purpose might be a solemn one, but there was no reason why people should not have enjoyed themselves on the journey in a unique opportunity to take a long holiday. All kinds of people, like those in Chaucer's *Canterbury Tales*, became pilgrims.

Although God is present in any church, or, as the priests say, anywhere else, to most worshippers the most vivid presence was the patron saint, a presence powerfully enhanced if the church possessed actual relics of the saint. Some pilgrimages were undertaken for the purpose of securing relics, but less ambitious pilgrims brought back a token of their journey

in the form of a little metal badge. Many of these have survived, and one of the most common is the scallop shell of St James of Compostela, whose shrine is in the north-west corner of Spain.

The Apostle James the Great was said to have brought Christianity to Spain and after his martyrdom his body was returned there, eventually reaching Compostela. By the 10th century his shrine was the greatest centre of pilgrimage in Europe apart from Rome.

The Romanesque pilgrim churches have a certain similarity: long, barrel-vaulted naves, tall arcades with spacious galleries, aisles circling the apse to allow the pilgrims to circulate, with the main artistic emphasis on the shrine in the east. They later acquired various accretions, chapels off apse and transepts, and the Romanesque structure at Compostela, built between 1075 and 1128, is not at first apparent. What meets the eye is a stately, twin-towered Baroque façade, begun in 1667. It overlooks the plaza, built in the Churrigueresque style, like the central section of the façade. Inside, St James's remains are enshrined in a tremendous, gilded Baroque sanctuary. Otherwise, the interior is austerely Romanesque. The 12th-century Portico de la Gloria, with its figures of apostles and others, just west of the nave, has been called 'one of the greatest glories of Christian art'.

FAR LEFT
The sensational Baroque façade of the pilgrimage church of St James.

LEFT
Detail.

Borgund Church, Norway

In regions, such as China, where the chief building material was wood, old buildings are understandably uncommon; thus there are few buildings of great antiquity in China. In Europe, similarly, domestic buildings built more than 200 years ago are rare except when built by those who could afford stone or brick. Not only does timber tend to rot, it is also highly inflammable, and fires in stone churches, which of course also contained much wood, were surprisingly common: Old St Paul's in London was merely one of many casualties.

Timber was used as the structural material for churches only in the forested regions of Scandinavia and Romania. Fortunately, several wooden churches whose foundation dates to within a few generations of the acceptance of Christianity have survived in Scandinavia, chiefly Norway. The Borgund Church in western Norway dates from the mid-12th century, although little, if anything, of the existing material is original. For those accustomed to Romanesque basilicas, the church on first appearance must have been a

shock. It seems to bear little resemblance to contemporary churches in the rest of Europe and the dragon heads (probably 13th-century) that launch themselves from the gables are a disconcerting reminder of the warships of the pagan Vikings.

These buildings are called stave churches, and the structural technique resembles barrel-making. The walls are made up of slightly curved vertical timbers that fit into horizontal beams at top and bottom. This method has the advantage of keeping the wall members clear of the ground and therefore making them less liable to rotting. Although the profusion of steep, shingled roofs is confusing, the basic plan is actually a simple rectangle, based on four tall central posts set in a square. Sometimes, as at Borgund, there is a small square chancel, sometimes aisles were added to the nave, with further elaborations as time advanced; timber churches continued to be built into the 13th century. These churches also contained extensive carved decoration, most famously at Urnes, not far from Borgund, which has given its name to the style.

The Norwegian stave churches are unique, but, being wooden, few have survived, Borgund, exceptionally, being the outstanding exception.

Château de Blois

The counts of Blois were powerful figures in medieval France who became the ancestors of later kings. Sons of Count Estienne (d. 1102) included Henry, a future bishop of Winchester, and Stephen, a future king of England. It was from Blois that Jeanne d'Arc set out in 1429 to dispel the English besiegers of Orléans, and in the 16th century the 'city of kings' was virtually a second capital. The old château has witnessed sensational events, including the escape down a rope of the portly queen mother, Marie de Médicis, when confined by her son Louis XII, and later the assassination of the Duc de Guise on the orders of Henri III (1588).

In the centre of the château country of the Loire valley, Blois is in many ways typical. There are substantial medieval remains, including the 13th-century great hall where the States General twice met during the reign of Louis XIII, although the main elements of the château, seen from the central courtyard today, date from the 16th and 17th centuries. During the 15th century, Charles d'Orléans demolished part of the old castle to build more comfortable accommodation, which included that part of the east wing now turned into a museum. Renovations by Louis XII included the gallery along the front linking the rooms, a comparatively new idea in 1500 when it was normally necessary to move from room to room. The wing added by François I is little more than a decade later, but in the meantime the Italian Renaissance had made itself felt. Perhaps the most striking feature of the whole château is its exterior staircase in an attached, highly decorated, octagonal tower. Originally the centrepiece of the façade, it was displaced by the ambitious plans of François Mansart on behalf of Gaston d'Orléans in the 17th century. Had they been fulfilled, Blois would have been grander than the Luxembourg Palace, but finance called a halt. As it is, Mansart's block is a minor masterpiece and displays probably the first example of the type of double-sloped roof named after him.

ABOVE
An equestrian statue of King Louis XII over the entrance gate of the Château de Blois.

LEFT
François I's striking exterior staircase tower.

Brussels Cathedral

St Gudule was a rather obscure saint of the 7th century, and the 13th-century church dedicated to her is popularly known as Brussels Cathedral. It stands on the slope of what was once called Mont-Saint-Michel, St Michael being the second patron saint; a gilded copper figure of him, twice life-size, is mounted on the spire of the hôtel de ville in the Grand-Place. The church was founded in 1220 after its predecessor had been burned down, and most of the east end appears to have been completed by 1273, although the nave was not finished until the 15th century, closely followed by the towers and west façade, which have a uniformity somewhat lacking elsewhere.

This is practically the first significant Gothic building in the Low Countries, where the style arrived slightly later than in France, and there are remaining traces of the Romanesque, notably in the apse. There are no fundamental distinguishing features of the Brabantine Gothic, at least until the 15th century, as seen at Brussels or in the cathedral of Antwerp, though churches tend to be shorter and wider than in France which, obviously enough, was the dominant influence. However, the southern Netherlands was included in the diocese of Cologne, and considerable German influence, strongest in the Romanesque period, continued to percolate. At St Gudule's, moreover, it is possible to detect slight affinities with the Early English Gothic style, though this could be a matter of chance rather than imitation.

The mixture of influences, the time of construction, and the many restorations make the architecture of St Gudule's rather complicated. The general plan of abbreviated transepts without aisles, and wide chapels flanking the choir on both sides, is typical of the Low Countries, and the style of the carved foliage on the capitals of the circular columns is characteristically Brabantine. Notable features of the interior are the 16th-century oak pulpit, carved with a scene of The Fall, and some very fine medieval stained glass, some of which was restored in the 19th century.

The Cathedral of St Gudule, or Gertrude, is characteristic of the mixed influences at work in the southern Netherlands.

85

Cloth Hall, Ypres

The biggest industry in the Middle Ages was clothmaking and the wool trade. As early as the 12th century the cities of Flanders, such as Ghent and Ypres, were important clothmaking centres, partly because the country raised many sheep and partly because urban enterprise was encouraged by the counts of Flanders. As it grew, the Flemish clothmaking industry soon came to depend largely on high-quality English wool. Merchants of all countries came to the great Flemish fairs, and the wealthy Flemish towns had few rivals. It was a serious blow when, in the 14th century, the English began to make their own, albeit generally inferior cloth, though political factors, not to mention reactionary efforts by the towns to preserve their monopoly, also contributed to the gradual decline.

It is therefore not surprising that Flemish architecture was generally most distinguished in civic buildings, in the weavers' guild halls, town halls and lofty bell towers. Structurally, Gothic was more obviously suitable for churches than secular buildings, but in the Netherlands, the churches were usually outshone by sumptuous secular buildings, even though these sometimes lost sight of constructional needs on which the Gothic style depended. There are several spectacular examples, such as Ghent's guild houses or the 300-ft (90-m) belfry and market hall of Bruges; but perhaps the most distinguished architecturally is the Cloth Hall at Ypres.

Sober, restrained, and perfectly proportioned, the Cloth Hall was built as an exchange for the cloth industry between 1201 and 1304. It has been called 'Europe's outstanding secular medieval building'. Its plan is a relatively narrow rectangle, with small spires at each corner; the façade is 440-ft (134-m) long, broken only at the centre by a large and dignified tower.

What is now the small town of Ypres was the scene of some of the most hideous fighting in the First World War, in which the Cloth Hall was destroyed. It has since been carefully and thoroughly restored.

In medieval Flanders, as in northern Italy, civic and commercial buildings rival the architectural dominance of the Church.

Palazzo Pubblico, Siena

During the 13th century, the city of Siena, already becoming an important centre of banking, was a self-governing commune. It was not altogether a peaceful development, and was marked by a long struggle for ascendancy between the nobles, who at first controlled the government, and the increasingly powerful – and vocal – burghers, who resented the nobles' exemption from taxation.

The city was also prone to plague and wars, notably against its neighbour and rival, Florence. A great victory of the Sienese and their allies over the Florentines in 1260 crushed Florence for many years, which roughly coincided with a long period of good government by the burghers, after they had overcome the power of the nobles.

The influence of French Gothic was more acceptable to Siena than it was, for instance, to Florence. The cathedral, in black-and-white marble, which if ever completed as planned would have been one of the largest in Europe, is a fine example. Another is the Palazzo Pubblico, the seat of government.

It was built between about 1290 and 1310, and its most distinctive feature is the bell tower, called the Torre del Mangia, which at 334ft (102m) is the highest in Italy and a splendid expression of the pride of Siena's merchant class. The palazzo itself, though massive and palatial, with its curved façade and whimsical crenellation, is the reverse of overbearing. It is built of brick except for the ground floor, which is stone and lined with characteristic Sienese arches in which a round arch is set within a pointed one.

There are many treasures of Sienese art within, including a fountain by the sculptor Jacopo della Quercia. The panoramic frescoes in the Sala della Pace on the apposite theme of the effects of just and unjust government were painted by Ambrogio Lorenzetti in the 1330s. One of the two halls on the ground floor has a fine Resurrection by the Renaissance artist known as Il Sodoma, while in the Sala del Mappamondo is the *Maestà* (1315), a Virgin and Child with attendant saints, of Simone Martini, after Duccio the prince of Sienese painters.

The campanile of the Palazzo Pubblico rivalled the spires of church and cathedral.

Burgos Cathedral

Burgos Cathedral stands on a steep slope below the castle of the old city, approached by steep cobbled streets or stone steps. It is closely integrated with its surroundings, with various outbuildings clustering around the massive pile from which emerge intensely ornamented towers and spires.

Burgos, the city of El Cid, and in more recent times the headquarters of General Franco, was the capital of Old Castile, a state that grew from the struggle of the Christians to reconquer Spain from the Muslims. The cathedral, in one sense a gesture of triumph, was founded in about 1221 and, like León and Toledo, was based on French models, with early master masons coming from France or England. Construction continued off and on until well into the 16th century; its original French High Gothic appearance almost disappeared in the wealth of decorative additions of the late 15th and early 16th centuries, which include no less than 22 ornately crocketed spires and pinnacles. This was the work of three generations of the Colonia (Cologne) family. The western steeples were built by Juan de Colonia (Hans of Cologne), the beautiful Constable's Chapel to the east by his son Simon in the 1480s, and the present, almost too exuberantly Flamboyant, central tower with its swarming sculpture, by his grandson Francisco in the 1540s, which replaced an earlier version by Juan himself.

The decoration, inside and out, which of course owes a great deal to Islamic tradition, is what chiefly distinguishes the cathedral; it coincided with the period of the city's greatest prosperity. Visiting in the 19th century, Théophile Gautier was dazzled by Burgos, which he regarded as the finest cathedral in the world. Standing in the crossing, he looked up at 'a giddy abyss of sculptures, arabesques, statues, miniature columns, ribs, lancets and pendentives. One might look at it for two years without seeing everything'. He was puzzled by 'a great staircase of most beautiful design, with magnificent carved chimeras'. In fact, the staircase connects the north transept, which was built on a higher level to accommodate the slope, with the body of the church.

The west front of Burgos Cathedral. The great size and exuberant ornamentation are characteristics of Spanish cathedrals.

Castel del Monte, Apulia

Castel del Monte, dating from around 1240, is probably the most famous and most attractive of the castles of the Emperor Frederick II, king of Sicily (1197–1250), where he grew up and preferred to live, and was emperor from 1220. It has been called the Crown of Apulia, a name suggested by its shape and situation, on a low hill commanding the surrounding plain, near the Adriatic coast. Well-preserved, modest in scale, and the colour of pale honey, it is supposed to have been designed by Frederick as a place of leisure, but it is a much more formidable stronghold than it appears. The elegant Classical doorway was probably protected by a portcullis, and the building itself may have been planned as the keep of a larger structure whose walls were never built. Aspects of the building deriving variously from Classical, Christian and Islamic traditions, and its strict mathematical plan, lend strength to the notion that Frederick himself, a man of wide and eclectic knowledge, had a hand in the design.

The highly symmetrical plan is a double octagon around a central courtyard, with the plan repeated in the octagonal towers at each angle of the outer wall. (There may have been special significance in the fact that an octagon can be seen as midway between a square, representing the Earth, and a circle, representing Heaven.) Towers and wall are now the same height, but originally the towers would have been 6½ft (2m) higher. The mixture of styles is evident at the doorway, where a Gothic window appears above the Classical pediment. Further evidence of Gothic principles exists plentifully within, in ribbed vaulting, column capitals, etc., although at this time the Islamic influence is more evident, and would have been more easily appreciated when the original furnishings – marble floors, tapestries, Eastern carpets, as well as sculpture – were in place. The plumbing was advanced, with running water for baths and latrines supplied from cisterns in the roof.

In fact, the Emperor seems to have seldom used the castle, and may never have stayed there at all. In later times Castel del Monte was used as a prison.

FAR LEFT
Its perfect symmetry largely explains the appeal of Castel del Monte.

LEFT
The Classical entrance.

Château d'Angers

The town of Angers on a tributary of the Loire is still dominated by the remains of the castle, which is a genuine medieval fortress rather than a decorative palace of the type generally associated with châteaux of the Loire.

The original fort was built around 1000, but no trace of it remains. Its successor was built during the reign of that most admirable of medieval monarchs, Louis IX, Saint Louis (1214–70). Its purpose was to defend Anjou, recently regained after long possession by the kings of England. Construction began in 1228 and was largely completed within ten years.

The site is raised above the land around it, and this rocky platform was exploited to raise the effective height of the curtain wall and its towers, the line of plinth that supports them continuing through natural rock. The plan is an irregular heptagon. One side faces the river, the others are guarded by the massive curtain wall and its frequent towers. The towers are round, and made from layers of slate, sandstone and granite, giving a striking banded effect that is the one concession to decoration. The entrance, in the east, was via a drawbridge across the deep moat to a gatehouse. To the north is the Tour de Moulin, which would once have housed a mill, the only one of the towers that stands at its original height, the rest having been reduced to the level of the walls during the French Wars of Religion (1562–98). There is scarcely anything left of the original structures within, though there is a 15th-century chapel with a charming little gatehouse to the gardens.

A major attraction of Angers is the tapestries, now housed within a special gallery. They were commissioned by Count Louis I of Anjou in the late 14th century and fashioned in the workshop of the premier *tapissier*, Nicolas Bataille of Paris. Based on the unusual but visually rewarding theme of the Apocalypse, in the Book of Revelations, they once hung in the Great Hall, and although not all survive, the whole work, which was about 470-ft (143-m) long and 18-ft (5.5-m) deep, can be reconstructed from records.

Marienburg, home of the Teutonic Knights, was largely rebuilt in the 19th century.

Marienburg (Malbork) Castle

The Polish town of Malbork was formerly in East Prussia, and better known historically by its German name, Marienburg. The castle was built for the Teutonic Knights, and was their headquarters for over a century.

The order was founded by merchants from Bremen and Lübeck to provide medical services during the Third Crusade and took its name from the Hospital of St Mary of the Germans, or Teutons, in Jerusalem. It soon developed into a military-religious order like the Templars and Hospitallers, its membership restricted to German nobles who took monastic vows of poverty, chastity and obedience. After the loss of Acre, the order, under the leadership of Hermann von Salza, became involved in German colonization of the east, the *Drang nach Osten*, and embarked upon the conquest of what became Prussia. The headquarters of the order was moved from Acre, via Venice, to Marienburg in 1308. It was independent of all political authorities except the papacy from which, at its own instigation, it held its extensive lands as a fief.

The castle was founded a generation earlier on a hill near the River Nogat. As the headquarters of the Grand Master of the Teutonic Knights, in the 14th century it became one of the largest and most powerful castles in Germany. It was built of brick, with steepish red-tile roofs and turrets in a recognizably 'Baltic' style, seen also in the cities originally responsible for the founding of the Order. The Grand Master ruled his Baltic empire in some style, and great banquets were held under the immensely high vault of the great hall. This is one of the most impressive buildings of the old

castle, along with the chapel. This was, after all, the home of a religious order, and the knights never entirely forgot their religious responsibilities.

The castle's heyday was short. The defeat of the knights by the king of Poland at Tannenberg in 1410 marked the beginning of their decline.

In 1466 Marienburg passed to Poland, and later Polish kings occasionally resided there. It returned to Prussia as a result of the partition of Poland in 1772, and was largely rebuilt in the 19th century by the Prussians. After the destruction of the Second World War, it was restored by the Poles.

Rochester Castle

The English town of Rochester, between London and Canterbury, is full of literary and historical memories. There is a memorial to Charles Dickens, who lived on Gad's Hill, in the cathedral, and the house that was a model for Miss Havisham's in *Great Expectations* can still be seen. The city's eventful history is largely due to its situation at the lowest point at which the River Medway can be forded, on the route followed by the invading Romans. The original cathedral was founded by St Augustine in the 7th century, destroyed by the Vikings and rebuilt in the late 11th century by Bishop Gundulf, who also started the Norman castle.

Though there are earlier remains, including parts of the Roman walls, the core of Rochester castle, which still stands, was the massive great tower, or keep, one of the finest survivals of its type in England. It belongs to the years 1127–42, after the castle passed to the archbishops of Canterbury. Practically square in plan, about 70ft (21m) along each side, it has towers at each corner and a fortified entrance on the north side. The walls are over 10-ft (3-m) thick at ground level and rise 113ft (34m) to the parapet, with the flanking towers another 10ft higher.

During the rebellion of the barons against King John in 1215, the castle was held for the barons and became the object of a famous siege. The south-east tower was successfully mined after a large number of fat pigs had been used as incendiary devices to fire the timbers that supported the sappers' tunnel. However, the attackers were held up by the inner wall, and the garrison held out until it was eventually starved into surrender. The castle was restored and a round tower replaced the casualty on the south-eastern corner. Besieged again in 1254 by Simon de Montfort, it was restored under Edward III, damaged during the Peasants' Revolt (1381) but once again patched up. By the 18th century, years of neglect had rendered it liable to demolition, but it was rescued by the City corporation and restored in the late 19th century.

Rochester Castle was built at the lowest fordable point of the River Medway.

93

Views of the west façade (below and opposite) from the Grand Canal. The walls of the upper storeys have the appearance of a fine silk fabric. The ornamental window (below right) has the Lion of Venice (symbol of St Mark) superimposed above it.

Doge's Palace, Venice

According to tradition, the first doge of Venice was elected in 697. However, his powers were subject to constraints and by the time Venice became a rich empire, due to accessions from the defeated Byzantines, he was little more than a figurehead.

The first palace was built in the early 9th century, though even its form is now uncertain, and the present building, arguably the most spectacular secular building in Europe's most beautiful city, was built in about 1340, largely as a meeting place for the Venetian Assembly, and was completed by the early 15th century. The most familiar image of the palace is its unique façade, which overlooks the lagoon. A masterpiece of Italian Gothic, it is also a brilliant combination of East (Byzantium) and West, as befits a city poised between the two. Above the spacious arcades at ground level are delicately ornamental arches, while the upper half, basically a flat wall, has a colourful geometric pattern of pink and white marble. The most novel element of the design, it is pierced by seven widely spaced windows, the central one ornamented and with a small balcony. Closer examination of the fine, mainly 14th-century sculptural decoration reveals portraits of two Byzantine emperors as well as Venetian contemporaries. Between the palace and the basilica of St Mark a gateway, the Porta della Carta, opens into the courtyard, flanked by rich and various buildings, mostly Renaissance though with some Gothic remnants, with a sight of the domes of St Mark's beyond. The overall effect is slightly disorderly by comparison with the façade. At the top of the monumental Staircase of the Giants, with Jacopo Sansovino's flanking figures of Mars and Neptune (1554), the doge used to stand to receive his cap of office.

Among the impressive state rooms, the Sala delle Quattro Porte contains Tintoretto's frescoes celebrating Venice's maritime supremacy. Veronese's vast painting of the Battle of Lepanto, a famous naval victory over the Turks (1571), and Tintoretto's paintings in tribute to various doges, are in the Sala del Collegio, where the doge met important visitors. A fire in 1577 destroyed many earlier masterpieces, but the Doge's Palace is still a treasure house of Venetian art and history.

Caernarvon Castle

Of the four great castles built by the English King Edward I (reigned 1272–1307) to subdue the Welsh, Beaumaris is aesthetically the most satisfactory, Harlech the most picturesque, and Conwy the most threatening. But the grandest is certainly Caernarvon, as befitted the intended seat of royal government in North Wales. The polygonal towers, which perhaps owe something to Constantinople (a city that Edward had visited when on Crusade), may have been a deliberate attempt to add a touch of distinction to Caernarvon compared with his other castles, which lack them.

Although the remains of a Roman fort can be seen on rising ground beyond the medieval town, the first fortifications in Caernarvon were the work of the Norman Earl of Chester in about 1100. Edward's castle, nearly 200 years later, was built on a flat spit of land projecting into the Menai Strait, dividing mainland Wales from Anglesey. Originally it had water on three sides, but the river that used to flow into the Seiont east of the castle has since been built over. The medieval town on the north was entirely enclosed by the walls extending from the castle, which still stand.

The plan is unusual, like an irregular figure-of-eight, with the residential quarters located in the 13 massive towers along the walls, no two of which are exactly alike. The largest is the Eagle Tower, named for the stone eagles adorning the turrets. This would have been occupied by the justiciar, or royal governor, of North Wales, who as the king's representative lived in some style. The Eagle Tower is large enough so that, after deducting the great width of the walls, there remains an apartment about 40-ft (12-m) across. According to legend it was in the Eagle Tower, in reality not yet built, that Edward I scored a propaganda coup by presenting to the Welsh people his newborn son, a prince 'born in Wales who speaks no English'.

Caernarvon Castle at night, with the Eagle Tower at left.

Cologne Cathedral

Cologne Cathedral is one of the most awe-inspiring buildings in Europe, rising above the city almost as if it belonged to another planet where everything is larger and proportions are different. It is the largest Gothic church in northern Europe, its heritage is ancient, and it

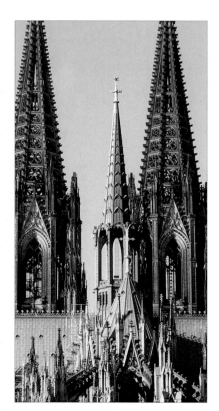

contains many magnificent treasures, including the gold shrine of the Magi, a supreme example of the art of the medieval goldsmiths, and a superb early-15th-century painted panel of the Adoration above the altar. Yet Cologne has never attracted the admiration or affection often lavished on apparently lesser buildings. There may be many reasons for this, but undoubtedly the proportions are slightly jarring. The cathedral is uncommonly broad in comparison to its length (275:466ft/84:142m), and the vault of the nave is almost as high as Beauvais. The two western towers, 512-ft (156-m) high, are so massive that not only do they exclude a central window, they also seem to be preparing to shoulder one another aside.

Medieval Cologne was a wealthy city whose ruling prince, the archbishop, was one of the seven imperial electors. Conflict between

archbishop and citizens was frequent and often violent. Of the cathedral, started in 1284, little more than the choir was built in the following two centuries. A stationary crane sat on the base of the south tower for over 100 years, and during the Napoleonic Wars (1800–15) the cathedral was used as a barn or a military prison.

The surge of nationalism provoked by French occupation provided the impetus the cathedral needed. A special tax was levied to pay for the work, and luminaries like Goethe and the king of Prussia contributed. Remarkably, the original plans were discovered and between 1820 and 1880 the cathedral was finished, more or less in the style originally intended. It was severely damaged by bombing during the Second World War but has since been completely restored.

BELOW
From a distance, the vastness of Cologne Cathedral suggests a structure from another dimension.

BELOW LEFT
An unusual view, from the roof, of the twin spires.

Rouen Cathedral

Rouen Cathedral, showing the Butter Tower. The famous spire is obscured by the tree.

Notre Dame de Rouen was one of the subjects which spurred the painter Monet to produce a series of paintings (1892–95), made in different conditions and at different times of day; he is not alone in finding it a building of diverse effects. The present cathedral was begun in 1202, but not finished until 1509, and the overall impression is of a later Gothic style.

The old Norman capital was the seat of an archbishop in the 4th century, and for a long time it was the largest city in France outside Paris. Its historical importance is reflected in the size and splendour of the cathedral, which also reflects the many conflicts in which the city has suffered, most recently from international warfare. Bombs, while wreaking havoc with the existing structure, sometimes reveal

archaeological surprises, and at Rouen revealed traces of a very early church, dating back perhaps to Roman times. The cathedral contains survivals from before 1202, such as the base of the Tour St-Romain on the north-west; but otherwise most of the immense west front is Late Gothic, including the Flamboyant south-west tower, the Tour de Beurre (Butter Tower). Normandy is, of course, a great dairying region; the Tour de Beurre is so named because the cost of its construction was raised by sale of dispensations allowing butter to be eaten during Lent.

Perhaps the most interesting part of the interior is the early 14th-century Lady Chapel. It contains an outstanding example of Renaissance sculpture in the memorial to two cardinals d'Amboise, in black-and-white marble 26-ft (8-m) high.

Although spires were nearly always planned for Gothic cathedrals, few survived long, and the present, enormously tall spire of Rouen – at 512ft (156m) the highest in France – is made of cast iron and replaces the original, felled by lightning in 1822. It has attracted much criticism on the grounds of excessive height and because of the curious lantern-like structure at its tip. But, altogether, Rouen Cathedral is a building with many extraordinary and beautiful parts that do not quite make up a coherent whole.

Münster Cathedral

Münster, the old capital of Westphalia, became the seat of a bishop at the instigation of Charlemagne in 800. The cathedral is basically Romanesque but was largely rebuilt in the 13th–14th centuries and today combines elements of Romanesque and Gothic. Besides the Romanesque twin towers at the western end, the chapel next to the cloisters has a fine Romanesque tympanum, while the porch in the south contains admirable Gothic sculptures of scenes in Paradise.

The people of Münster are said to be more religious than most, and the cathedral today is seldom empty of worshippers who come for a few minutes of private prayer or to pay respects to the tomb of Cardinal Galen, opponent of the Nazis. The cathedral is of relatively modest proportions, solidly rooted in the town, adjoining a square packed with market stalls. There is a pleasing scent of cooking sausages in the air. But for all the appearance of solid conservatism, the religious history of Münster is exotic, for this was the town ruled briefly by an extreme and aberrant group of the otherwise pacific Anabaptists.

By the Reformation, the citizens of Münster had, after years of conflict, acquired some independence of their bishop, and the council was dominated by Lutherans. Two Anabaptist missionaries arriving from the Netherlands received an unexpected welcome, and they saw Münster as the New Jerusalem. Under the leadership of Jan Bockelson of Leiden, who aspired to rule the world preparatory to the Second Coming of Christ, they rapidly gained control of Münster, killing or driving out opponents. Private property was abolished and

all books except the Bible were burned. Since there was a superfluity of women, Münster being a haven for apostate nuns, Bockelson introduced polygamy. In the cathedral, many images were destroyed and, given the violence of Anabaptist rule, it is surprising that any

survived. For a time, the bishop was powerless, but besieged by the combined forces of the Catholic bishop and the Lutheran landgrave of Hesse, resistance collapsed, and the Anabaptists were destroyed with a cruel efficiency that more than equalled the ferocity of their regime.

Münster Cathedral is basically Romanesque but today contains elements of Romanesque and Gothic.

Regensburg Cathedral

The Bavarian city of Regensburg, sometimes called Ratisbon, is situated at a crucial crossing of the River Danube and was the site of a Roman military base. It became the seat of a bishop in the 8th century, when the first church was built on the site of the cathedral. Its 11th-century Romanesque successor, damaged by fire, was largely pulled down for the present cathedral in 1273, but some remnants survive, notably St Stephen's Chapel and All Saints' Chapel, a little octagonal tower with attached semicircular chapels, which still bear Romanesque murals in fair condition.

Regensburg was prosperous in the 13th century. It was a free imperial city and a major commercial entrepôt; much of the trade of Venice and the East passed across its famous stone bridge which was a century older than the cathedral but also still standing. Given the city's prosperity, financing construction of a new cathedral was not too daunting, and the east end rose quickly. The ground plan closely followed that of its predecessor, but the style was now the High Gothic of Strasbourg. Thereafter progress slowed down. Regensburg was still a famous city, the seat of the imperial diet, but it was suffering from increasing competition from booming Bavarian neighbours such as Augsburg and Nuremberg. Nevertheless, building continued according to the original plan until 1530, when the west side was completed, except that the towers rose only to the height of the nave. Like Cologne, Regensburg had to wait until 1867 for the final element and, as with Cologne, it is arguable that the building would be better off without its heavily and rather monotonously crocketed Flamboyant spires.

The interior was refashioned in the late 17th century in the contemporary style of Bavarian Baroque. The high altar remains an undulating dazzle of gilding, but a disapproving King Ludwig I ordered other Baroque embellishments to be removed in the 1830s. Though now rather austere, at least by Bavarian standards, the cathedral contains some 14th-century stained glass, and in particular, some naturalistic sculpture of ethereal charm by the artist known as the Erminhold Master.

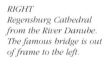

RIGHT
Regensburg Cathedral from the River Danube. The famous bridge is out of frame to the left.

FAR RIGHT
Regensburg is noted for fine sculptures, though these figures are not the work of the Erminhold Master.

Salisbury Cathedral

Most medieval cathedrals were for obvious reasons built over a very long period; that is especially true of English cathedrals. Salisbury is an exception, since the bulk of it, choir, transepts and nave, was completed in a very short time, between 1220 and 1258, in the so-called Early English Gothic style. It is thus architecturally 'pure' in a way that few others are, and typifies English Gothic in the same way that Amiens typifies French.

A Norman cathedral existed in Old Sarum, on the top of a hill with a poor water supply and a royal castle uncomfortably nearby; when the decision to rebuild was taken in the early 13th century, a site was chosen on the plain close to the River Avon. That solved the water supply, but resulted in occasional flooding. The old cathedral was freely plundered for building stone, perhaps a factor in speeding construction. It is a very English setting, and the view of the cathedral from the water meadows, as painted by Constable, is an icon of the heritage industry.

Salisbury is one of the largest English cathedrals, slightly larger than Canterbury, which it resembles in adopting a double-transept plan. The west façade, an out-of-key add-on, the least successful part of the building and not helped by 19th-century replacements for the sculpted figures, was completed in 1266 and the octagonal chapter house about the same time. The perfectly proportioned steeple (tower plus spire), at 404ft (123m) much the tallest in England, was added in 1334.

The interior is cool and a trifle aloof. Many of the images, such as the statues of kings from the beautiful choir screen, disappeared in the Reformation or during other disturbances, and the stained glass was discarded during a disastrous 'restoration' in the 18th century, which also demolished the detached *campanile*. But the dimensions and proportions are impressive and the bold, coloured Purbeck stone of the columns is arresting. The Lady Chapel, with its plunging vaulting, was a structure of special importance because it contained the shrine of a saint. As an example of the Early English style at its best, it is perfect.

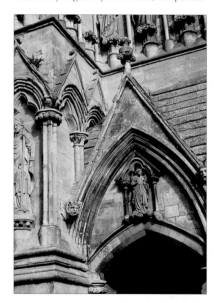

ABOVE
Detail of a side door on the west front.

RIGHT
The well proportioned steeple, seen from the cloisters.

Toledo Cathedral

According to legend, the city of Toledo was founded by Hercules: at any rate, it is a very old city. A Visigothic church was consecrated here in 589, and the early history of the city is closely bound up with the history of the Church in Spain. It was the scene of many early Church councils, and the long struggle between Spanish Catholicism and Arianism was fought out here. The archbishop of Toledo is still recognized as the primate of Spain, though the city itself declined in importance in the 16th century, especially after Philip II decided to make his capital at Madrid. One happy result is that to an unusual degree Toledo has retained its attractive medieval appearance.

The former church, which had served as a mosque under Muslim rule, was demolished by Ferdinand III of Castile (St Ferdinand) in order to build the present cathedral, which was founded in 1227. In spite of common misfortunes, such as despoliation by French soldiers in the Napoleonic era, the cathedral is one of the finest and richest in Spain. It follows the double-aisle plan and is somewhat similar to Bourges in plan, although it is much wider in relation to its height. Construction continued into the 16th century, with additions later, and the basic Gothic design is augmented by Renaissance and Baroque features. Except for the tower, the exterior has none of the extravagance of

Burgos, with very little decorative detail on the main body of the church; but it is equally sturdy and seemingly rooted to its site, 'clothed in russet tones, the colour of a browning roast or of a skin tanned like that of a pilgrim from Palestine'. The interior, thanks largely to its great space, is imposing, with much more sculptural decoration. Because of the space, the mass of powerful piers, each made up of 16 attached columns, do not seem to crowd the nave. Light percolates through the blue-and-red filters of the stained glass and gleams on gilded altarpieces, alabaster tombs and the dark wood of the finely carved choir stalls, all adding to the air of solemn luxury.

RIGHT
The south door of Toledo Cathedral.

FAR RIGHT
A view of the medieval city of Toledo, with the tower of the cathedral visible on the left.

Florence Cathedral

The great Gothic cathedrals of northern Europe were created largely by craftsmen whose very names are often unknown. In 13th-century Florence, artists received more credit, and those who contributed to Santa Maria del Fiore included many of the most famous names of the early Renaissance, from Giotto to Michelangelo.

The cathedral (*duomo*) consists of several units, campanile, nave, domed octagon and baptistery, mostly built between 1296 and 1462. The interior is surprisingly plain, not overflowing with masterpieces as might be expected, and with little of the brilliant decorative effects of the marbled exterior. The original plan was by Arnolfo di Cambio, though it was expanded in the course of construction by Giotto, Andrea Pisano and other masters of the works. Giotto designed the campanile, though only the first stage was built in his lifetime, and his planned spire was never built at all. The Baptistery, in the west, is the oldest building of the group and may have originally served as a church in itself. Apart from the great dome, its most famous features are the bronze doors, a staple of any book on Renaissance art, the south door by Pisano from the 14th century, the others by Ghiberti a century later, which represented the winning design in a competition in which he tied with Brunelleschi, who backed out.

Brunelleschi's dome is one of the most discussed and, though itself unique, influential structures in the history of architecture. Brunelleschi had studied ancient architecture in Rome, including the Pantheon, but he was a more practical architect than many of his

successors, more interested in engineering problems than reviving the antique; the pointed and ribbed dome of Florence is basically constructed on principles more Gothic than Classical. Given that the octagon on which the dome would rest could not be changed, and the distance that had to be spanned was nearly 141ft (43m), the general opinion was that the

task was impossible. But Brunelleschi built his dome – strictly two domes, since there is an inner and outer shell of differing curvatures – without exterior buttresses or timber centring by binding the base with timber and iron rods, employing tension to prevent the dome from splitting outwards. The work took 14 years (1420–34).

The Cathedral of Florence, with the detached campanile and Brunelleschi's dome, one of the most emotive structures in the history of European architecture.

Palace of the Popes, Avignon

In 1305 the Bishop of Bordeaux was elected pope as Clement V, although he was not a cardinal and not an Italian. He immediately appointed a number of French bishops, showed no desire to go to Rome, and in 1309 finally settled in Avignon with his papal court. The 'Babylonian Captivity', as it came to be called, a period of absentee popes under French control, was a disastrous period for the authority of the papacy because it was so prolonged. Gregory XI did return to Rome in 1377 but on his death two rival popes were elected, one in Rome and one in Avignon, and the Great Schism did not come to an end until 1417, having done much over the previous century to encourage heretical thinking among disillusioned Christians.

The Palais des Papes in Avignon, now a museum and exhibition centre, is a monument to the near-failure of the medieval papacy. It is a rather severe assembly of Gothic buildings, its cliff-like walls giving it the appearance of a fortress rather than a palace. Inside, the absence of furnishings and lack of natural light make it even gloomier. Still, it does form an impressive setting for Avignon's annual international festival.

The palace, dwarfing the nearby cathedral, dates from the 14th and early 15th centuries and as the former citadel of the papal state of Avignon, it is a huge complex, with numerous public chambers, chapels, courtyards, towers and gardens. Like the famous bridge with its little Romanesque chapel that no longer crosses the Rhône, the palace has suffered severe damage at various times. It was used as a barracks for Napoleon's soldiers, who left nothing movable behind them and, it is said, even hacked off sections of frescoed wall. However, among other frescoes, they missed a remarkable work in the Oratory of St Michael which is attributed to the school of Duccio.

Cathedral of St Vitus, Prague

The site of Prague Cathedral, within the precincts of the castle, was formerly occupied by a Romanesque basilica, some parts of which can be seen in the crypt. The Gothic cathedral was founded in 1344 to mark the promotion of the bishop of Prague to archbishop. This was the city's golden age, when it was the capital of the Emperor Charles IV and the greatest city in northern Europe. The designer of the cathedral was a Frenchman, Matthias of Arras, but he died in 1352, having seen the east end almost finished. Charles then hired a Swabian, Peter Parler, whose statue may be his self-portrait, whose family played an important part in the

adornment of Bohemia and southern Germany in the 14th–15th centuries and made Prague a temple of the late, courtly style sometimes called 'International Gothic'. Building continued until the Hussite revolt in the early 15th century brought it to a stop, with the nave and most of the main tower unbuilt. A temporary wall was built to close off the nave.

Little progress was made for three centuries. The onion-topped tower, which is nearly 325-ft (100-m) tall, was built in the 16th century, though the Baroque roof dates from about 1770. Otherwise, the cathedral had to wait for another period in the 19th century, when national enthusiasm was high and there was the added inspiration of Cologne. Some of the work, such as the bronze doors depicting an episode from the life of St Wenceslaus, is of high quality. The western spires went up in 1892, and the building was completed just in time to celebrate the millennium of the death of St Wenceslaus in 1929.

The cathedral contains a vast collection of treasures; there are, for example, 24 chapels in the cathedral and few do not contain objects of interest. Perhaps the most notable is the statue of the saint himself in the Wenceslaus Chapel, which is a product of the Parler workshop. A pleasant surprise is the stained-glass window in the New Archbishop's Chapel by Alphonse Mucha, master of the art nouveau poster.

The Cathedral of St Vitus was a product of Prague's golden age, when it was the greatest city in northern Europe.

Ulm Cathedral

Ulm, the city of the *meistersinger*, had been a free imperial city, answerable to no one except the emperor, since 1155. Its great church was founded in 1377, partly as a mark of gratitude for a further boost to its prosperity resulting from victory over the rival city of Württemberg. The church was to hold 30,000 people, probably more than the population of the city at that date, but Ulm was expanding, and by the early 15th century the population was nearer 60,000.

The advanced German Gothic style known as Sondergotik ('special Gothic') developed partly from the rise of the individual artist-craftsmen who are often known by name and by the buildings on which they worked. The Parler family, encountered also in Prague and elsewhere, were engaged on the choir at Ulm, and the master mason from 1392 was Ulrich von Ensinger, member of another well-known family. He is also known to have worked at Strasbourg and Milan, but Ulm is his masterpiece.

The Gothic style in Germany had developed quite differently from France. The German passion for tall spires led to the custom of building one giant steeple, instead of two, at the west end. Ulm minster is the outstanding example, its spire topping out at 529ft (161m) above the ground, the tallest in Germany or anywhere else. To reduce weight, Ulrich employed elaborate tracery and openwork: from some angles one sees more sky than stone, which helps to prevent the spire from seeming too overbearing. However, Ulrich did not, of course, see it finished. He did complete the first stage of the tower, though even that ran into

problems forcing a change of plan; but the spire was only finished in the 1880s. The roof was then strengthened with iron and, when the brick walls protested, the flying buttresses were installed along the sides.

Inside, the minster's finest treasures are Hans Multscher's realistic figure, Christ as Man of Sorrows (c. 1429), and the fine, humanistic, wood-carved figures of the choir stalls by a renowned Swabian artist.

Ulm Cathedral at night. Its spire is the tallest in Germany or, indeed, anywhere else.

Rambouillet

Rambouillet, about 28 miles (45km) south-west of Paris, belongs to that class of French château that began life as a medieval fort and survived into a more peaceful age to become a luxurious country house or hunting lodge, a function that Rambouillet, with its extensive forest, has fulfilled for kings, emperors and more recently, for presidents of the republic.

The château was built in the 14th century and was owned for 300 years by the D'Angennes family, one of whom, in the 17th century, was the husband of the Marquise de Rambouillet, arbiter of Parisian taste. Though strongly defended, it was more a fortified house than a castle, and it changed hands more than once during the Hundred Years War. The only obvious medieval relic now is the great, machicolated Tour François I, named after that Renaissance monarch because he is supposed to have died there after being taken ill while hunting. Other parts were rebuilt during the Renaissance, but the greatest changes were made in the 18th century when Rambouillet came into the possession of the Comte de Toulouse, a son of Louis XIV. He enlarged the place considerably, and built Classical façades that concealed the medieval walls. An unusual feature for which he was also responsible is the decoration of carved wood, in which oak, though an intractable material, is transformed into lacy patterns almost as if it were plaster.

Rambouillet passed to Louis XVI in 1784, who made some changes required by Marie Antoinette, including a small dairy (though in agricultural history Rambouillet is more famous as an early centre of sheep breeding), and it was fortunate to escape the Revolution if not unscathed, in sufficient order for Napoleon to restore it for his own use. He demolished one wing, rebuilt the main gate and the east turret and had his own suite of rooms built next to the Tour François I. The imperial bathroom is a splendid Neoclassical chamber in which the actual bath may be easily overlooked.

RIGHT
Except for its ivy-covered towers, Rambouillet betrays small sign of its origins as a fortress.

OPPOSITE
The garden front.

Guarda Cathedral

Guarda is the highest town in Portugal, almost 3,280ft (1000m) above sea level in the Serra da Estrela; its breezy climate is said to be healthy and its hospital was founded as a sanatorium for consumptives. The region is rural, sparsely populated, and off the tourist track, but the town contains a ruined castle and several other medieval buildings, of which the most interesting is the cathedral.

The Romans built a fort here, but there is no evidence of substantial settlement until the town was founded by Sancho I in the 12th century. The older buildings, in rough granite, look as if they have been there much longer. As its name implies, the town was a defensive outpost, keeping watch on the borders of Muslim – and for that matter, in later times, on Christian – Spain. It is said that one of the gargoyles looking towards the Spanish border makes a rude gesture, but this is not apparent from ground level.

The cathedral was founded in 1390 and completed by 1540. It derives from the well-known monastic church of Batalha, near Leira, which was inspired by French and Norman examples; but Guarda is an altogether tougher customer, built of harsh, rusty granite, which looks well prepared to withstand a siege. Except for the west door, there is virtually no external decoration. The octagonal west towers are not much higher than the roof and the tower over the crossing was never built. Yet the appearance of plainness is misleading. The building has a subtle symmetry, best appreciated from a raised viewpoint such as the towers of the Baroque church nearby, and the design is both rich and complicated. Inside, the lofty vault is supported by rectangular columns, with the end pair surprisingly in a cable-twist pattern, a familiar device of the Portuguese late Gothic style known as Manueline. The florid furnishings in the Manueline style strike an undeniable note of nationalistic grandeur, issuing a reminder that, when the cathedral was built, tiny Portugal was leading Europe in establishing a worldwide maritime empire.

RIGHT
Statue of King Sancho I (reigned 1185–1211), known as the Builder of Cities, among them the frontier town of Guarda.

FAR RIGHT
The stalwart cathedral, from the north.

Vienna Cathedral

Stefansdom, the cathedral church of St Stephen, is a great monument of godliness and Gothic architecture in a city not especially renowned for either. It predates the Habsburgs, having been founded by Ottokar the Great of Bohemia in the 13th century shortly before he surrendered Vienna to Rudolf I, the first Habsburg emperor, in 1273. However, most of the present building is of a later date.

Like many medieval cathedrals, St Stephen's is architecturally a mixture, and one in which time has not altogether succeeded in achieving a harmonious blend. The cathedral has many beautiful things, but as one critic remarked, it is a building that should be appreciated according to humane rather than architectural standards.

It is basically a very large example of the *hallenkirchen* ('hall churches') of characteristic German Gothic type, with nave and aisles of equal height. In Vienna they are covered by a single, immense, steeply-pitched roof decorated with an audacious zigzag pattern of black, green, white and yellow tiles and, over the

choir, a huge Habsburg eagle rather suggestive of modern advertising hoardings. All this is 19th-century work. Of course, the plan of the building rules out a clerestory, which makes the interior rather dim, though there is light enough to admire the rich Baroque decoration, the magnificent tomb of the Emperor Frederick III, the great organ, and the Late Gothic pulpit carved from a single block of stone by Anton Pilgram, who carved his own portrait below the steps.

The oldest part is the west front, which includes parts of the Romanesque original. The tall main door is flanked by two unusual, rather oddly proportioned, octagonal towers that terminate in spires. The transepts act as entrance porches, and above the south transept rises Vienna's finest feature, the great spear-like steeple, 450-ft (137-m) high, which was raised in the early 15th century, though its intended northern twin was never built. Unusually, there is little openwork, but proportion and filigree modelling prevent a sense of heaviness.

The great steeple of St Stephen's Cathedral, over the south transept, still awaits its twin on the north.

Milan Cathedral is without doubt a magnificent artistic achievement, yet it is also, in its way, a failure.

Milan Cathedral

The Italians tended to remain faithful to their Classical heritage, the Gothic style being less suitable in the south, where large windows are not desirable, than in the north. It is sometimes said that there are no true Gothic buildings in Italy, which is to take too French a view of Gothic, but even those who make that generalization allow one exception, Milan Cathedral. Gothic did offer one advantage that Italian architects recognized – greater interior space – and Florence and Pisa are examples of a new spaciousness. Milan and other cities also produced quite individual styles.

Started under the Visconti dukes in the late 14th century, Milan Cathedral was the largest building project of its time, and its construction was spread over many generations. The project

enjoyed widespread popular support, and on occasions when money ran short the citizens provided free labour. Progress was still slow. The façade was not begun until the 17th century, the 15th-century lantern did not get its spire until the 18th century, and the north side was not completed until the 19th century. What emerged was a building with a decidedly French flavour, although it can also be alleged to demonstrate the Italians' basic lack of sympathy for French Gothic. The usual ingredients are present – flying buttresses, huge windows, a forest of pinnacles; but there is a very unGothic emphasis on horizontals, the pitch of the roof is low, and the building does not soar like the cathedrals of the Île de France. It is a very sophisticated design, with the elevation built on a series of equilateral triangles, a concept alien to the French masters. Besides learned residents like Leonardo, many advisers from north of the Alps came to resolve technical problems at various times, but most stayed only briefly and left in frustration, even rage.

It remains one of Europe's most remarkable buildings. It is built of brick faced with pinkish marble, and its great bulk is offset by the rich and complex exterior decoration – 'lacework in stone'. The lantern is a triumph of Renaissance engineering, the polygonal apse is inspired, and the array of sculpture provides a detailed lesson in the history of European sculpture through five centuries.

Kremlin, Moscow

Most old Russian cities have a 'kremlin', which comes from a word meaning fortress or citadel. The most famous one, in Moscow, consists of a walled enclave covering an area of about 90 acres (36 hectares) on a hillside above the Moskva river, and adjoining Red Square. It has been, besides a fortress, the residence of tsars and patriarchs, the seat of government and the centre of Russian religious and political life. It contains a wealth of ecclesiastical and palatial buildings, and from across the river it is a glittering array of gilded cupolas and stone towers.

First mentioned in the 14th century, when some of the buildings would still have been of wood, it was reconstructed by Ivan III in the late 15th to early 16th centuries. Problems arose when a rebuilt church collapsed before the vault was completed, and Ivan was forced to call in Italian architects. They studied the principles of Byzantine architecture before they began, but more than a trace of the Italian Renaissance made itself evident in their work, sometimes called 'Lombardo-Byzantine' in style, and it proved a persistent influence.

The old buildings are grouped around the cathedral square, several of which are based on earlier churches. The cathedral of the Assumption, for example, was modelled on the 12th-century cathedral in the city of Vladimir, though with Lombard affiliations. The Archangel Cathedral (1505–09), where the tsars are buried, bears signs of the Italian Renaissance, especially in its decorative devices. Of Ivan's Grand Ducal Palace, called the Granite Palace, only the magnificent vaulted hall now survives, along with his 266-ft (81-m) bell tower, the oldest, and tallest, of several.

Three grand palaces in the Russian Baroque style survive from the 17th century, when defence ceased to be a prime consideration and cupolas were added to defensive towers. Construction continued in the 18th century although Moscow had ceased to be the capital. Several older buildings were demolished to make way for the vast Great Kremlin Palace, fronting the river, which was built in the mid-19th century under Nicholas I and later used as a parliamentary assembly. It can hold 20,000 people, surely a reasonable capacity for even the tsar's court. In the Soviet era, two substantial but unattractive buildings were added and some necessary restoration took place. The Kremlin was opened to the public in 1953.

OPPOSITE
The Great Kremlin Palace is said to contain 700 apartments, most of them of substantial size.

BELOW
The gilded cupolas of the Kremlin churches and the old Terem palace (right).

Old Hospital, Beaune

Among the finest masterpieces of the Louvre is a painting known as *Madonna with the Chancellor Rolin*, by the greatest master of the early Dutch school, Jan van Eyck. It is a sumptuous painting, its colours still glowing as richly as they did when freshly painted nearly 600 years ago, thanks to Van Eyck's mastery of the medium he was once thought to have invented, and in particular to the quality of his varnish. Van Eyck was court painter to Philip the Good, duke of Burgundy, from 1426, and spent several years in and out of the wealthy, aristocratic, cynical Burgundian court with which, as a painter, he showed such affinity. His painting of the worldly Cardinal Rolin, the duke's chancellor, is dated to about 1435.

Rolin was a remarkable man, intelligent, rich, powerful, ruthless, feared, but he was a generous patron. He founded the hospital of St-Esprit in Beaune, which was also known as the Hôtel-Dieu, God's House, which was opened in 1452. Rolin owned valuable vineyards on the Côte d'Or, still the mainstay of Beaune's economy, but the town was also the birthplace of his mother, and his foundation may well have been a form of spiritual insurance, an act of retribution, and a gift to the people he had exploited. He certainly showed himself willing to spend freely, and the building, ranged around a broad courtyard, might well today be an expensive resort rather than a refuge for the poor and sick. Its steep roofs are covered with coloured tiles arranged in geometric patterns and pierced by dormer windows. Below is an open gallery supported by neat, faceted columns that form a colonnade for the lower floor. In the courtyard is a well with contemporary ironwork and an outdoor pulpit.

Part of the hospital is still in use, though other wards have been converted into a museum. Exhibits include an altarpiece of The Last Judgement commissioned by Rolin from Rogier van der Weyden, who at the time was an even more popular painter than Van Eyck.

ABOVE
The famous Giralda,
once a minaret and the
most notable feature of
what is possibly the
largest cathedral in the
world.

RIGHT
Seville Cathedral,
because of its structure
and great size, was
responsible for
transforming the later
architecture of central
Spain.

Seville Cathedral

Great size is a characteristic of Spanish cathedrals in general and the most obvious distinction of the Cathedral of Santa Maria de la Sede in Seville is that, depending on what measurements are involved, it is the largest not only in Spain but anywhere else in Europe.

According to legend, the 15th-century builders held the opinion that anyone looking at their finished building would be so amazed by its size and shape that he would think them mad; in spite of such a gloomy forecast, the building was finished in remarkably short time, between 1402 and 1520. There is no reason to doubt the sanity of the builders, if only because the size and shape of the building are difficult to perceive on the congested site without the advantage of a helicopter. One tends to see the cathedral only in glimpses, and the situation is further complicated by numerous additions, including a Baroque parish church north of the cathedral, which disguise the original form.

Overall, the roughly rectangular plan measures about 427 x 263ft (130 x 80m). The height of the nave is 131ft (40m) and of the central crossing 184ft (56m). The unusual overall dimensions result from the fact that the site was originally occupied by a mosque; the cathedral has followed the mosque in choosing area over axis. More concrete signs of the mosque remain, notably the famous campanile or bell tower known as the Giralda, which was once a minaret and still bears Muslim decoration below the elaborately Classical belfry.

The hugely spacious, double-aisled interior, with 32 enormous but finely articulated piers and over 70 windows, contains many rich and artistic objects: paintings by the Spanish masters,

fine Renaissance metalwork and carving, and the marvellous Late Gothic screen of gilded wood with scenes from the Life of Christ. There is also a wooden image of the Virgin with movable arms and hair of spun gold, which was presented to St Ferdinand (Ferdinand III of Castile, conqueror of Seville) by his fellow monarch and saint, St Louis, in the 13th century.

Frauenkirche, Munich

Munich is not a city dominated by a particular style or period, like Romanesque Regensburg. Comparatively modern by Bavarian standards, founded by Henry the Lion in the 12th century, Munich contains a wide variety of different sorts of buildings. Much of their magnificence is due to the enthusiasm of King Ludwig I of Bavaria, though there were many losses to Allied bombs during the Second World War, when about one-third of the city was destroyed, including the Wittelsbach palace, but not, ironically, the large and hideous headquarters of the Nazi party. The Frauenkirche, a cathedral since only 1817, also survived, though was seriously damaged; however, most of its valuable furnishings had been removed and stored somewhere safer for the duration.

Rather unusually for Munich, the Frauenkirche, built in the 15th century, is an indigenous building, designed by a local architect, Jörg von Halsbach, known as Ganghofer, who is otherwise unknown. Nor can it be said that he was particularly inspired, though he was certainly more than competent. He was a follower of Hans Stetthaimer, builder of the earlier St Martin's Church at Landshut with its 436-ft (133-m) brick tower. The Frauenkirche is fairly typical of the large south German hall church, which always tends to achieve its spacious interior at the cost of a rather dull exterior. The main structure was complete by 1479, when the vast roof, whose timbers must have depleted the Bavarian forests, was finished. The towers were added later, and they are far the most important feature, responsible for the familiarity of the Frauenkirche as a symbol of the city. As in other examples of architectural landmarks, the appeal is not easily accounted for in architectural terms, for the twin red-brick towers, though matching the rest of the building in mass, are not in themselves particularly spectacular despite their individual bulbous cupolas. They are, however, unmistakable, and that must account for their symbolic status.

BELOW LEFT
Munich's cathedral is a fine example of a south German hall church, a design that gains in interior space but loses in light.

BELOW
Detail of the unusual towers.

OPPOSITE
The Palacio da Pena.

BELOW and BELOW RIGHT
The Palacio Nacional de Sintra.

Palaces of Sintra

The attractive little town of Sintra is set among the hilly woodlands of the Sierra de Sintra, about 15 miles west of Lisbon. Its charms were celebrated by the great Portuguese national poet Camoes, and later by Lord Byron in *Childe Harold's Pilgrimage.* For centuries it was the summer refuge of the Portuguese royal family. Among their memorials are the royal palace in the Old Town, partly wrecked in the earthquake of 1755 but afterwards restored, and the spectacular Palacio da Pena, which crowns a hilltop.

The royal palace, brusquely described by one writer as Moorish and debased Gothic, and by an 18th-century English visitor as this confused pile, is not a prepossessing building from the outside. The first one is likely to see of it is the enormous conical chimneys of the kitchens. It was once thought to be an old Moorish palace, but it seems to have been built from scratch in the reign of John I (1385–1433), though with many Muslim characteristics and on the site of a Muslim building. It has also many features of the curious Portuguese late-Gothic style known as Manueline, which itself owed something to Muslim tradition.

The extraordinary Gothick Palacio da Pena incorporates the Monastery of Our Lady of Pena, which was built about 1500. The monastic ruins were bought in 1839 by Ferdinand of Saxe-Coburg-Gotha, first cousin of both Queen Victoria and Prince Albert, who had married Maria II of Portugal in 1836, receiving the title of king-consort. With the advice of a Prussian engineer, Ludwig von Eschwege, he greatly enlarged it and turned it into a Romantic medieval, palace, part monastery part castle, as a gift for his wife. Opinion on such a building is bound to be highly subjective, but Ferdinand's project, judged on his terms, is a dramatic success. The intensely Romantic atmosphere is heightened by the richly exotic furnishings and, in the chapel, a fine Renaissance altar piece. Today, the palace is the scene of concerts and other cultural activities.

Christiansborg

Christiansborg, the royal slot (castle) in Copenhagen, has been rebuilt at least five times in the course of over 800 years of stormy history, and although it still contains traces of the original 12th-century building, most of what one sees today is less than 100 years old.

Bishop Absalon, founder of Copenhagen, erected his 'harbour castle' in 1167. It played a vital part in the development of the little fishing and trading port during the Middle Ages as it strove to exploit and control the prosperous Baltic trade. The castle was captured twice in the 13th century, when Denmark was weakened by constitutional conflict, and was destroyed and built again. The growing strength of the Hanseatic League, which did not believe in free competition, resulted again in destruction in 1370, when the Danish king was forced to sign the Treaty of Stralsund confirming the dominance of the Hanse. It rose again, and by 1500, with the power of the League fading, Denmark regained its position as the leading North European power. Under Christian III (reigned 1534–59) the castle was much enlarged and became a royal residence. The first tower was added by Christian IV in the 17th century.

In the 18th century much of the existing castle was demolished, and a new one, the first to be called Christiansborg, arose between 1731 and 1745. The Rococo remains suggest a splendid palace, but unfortunately they are few, as it burned down in 1794. Its successor was in Neoclassical style, but lasted only a short time longer and perished by the same means in 1894. The present Christiansborg, founded in 1907, is the work of Thorvald Jörgensen. It is an unpretentiously elegant building, mainly of granite with a copper roof and with an unconventional central tower, which is about 330-ft (100-m) high and is a famous landmark in Copenhagen. As well as being the official residence of the monarch, Christiansborg contains parliament, the supreme court and ministries.

RENAISSANCE TO BAROQUE

CHAPTER FOUR

Medici-Riccardi Palace, Florence

Pitti Palace, Florence

Ducal Palace, Urbino

Quirinal Palace, Rome

Barberini Palace, Rome

Ducal Palace, Mantua

Wawel Castle, Cracow

King's College Chapel, Cambridge

Segovia Cathedral

Fontainebleau

Château de Chambord

Hampton Court

Château de Chantilly

Saint-Germain-en-Laye

The Louvre

Longleat

Villa Rotonda, Vicenza

The Escorial

Rialto Bridge, Venice

Teatro Olimpico, Vicenza

Saint Basil's Cathedral, Moscow

Saint Peter's, Rome

Il Gesù, Rome

Santa Maria della Salute, Venice

Mexico City Cathedral

Saint Paul's Cathedral, London

Versailles

Royal Palace, Amsterdam

Royal Palace, Turin

Drottningholm Palace

Charlottenburg

Nymphenburg, Munich

Schönbrunn, Vienna

Blenheim Palace

The Belvedere, Vienna

Superga, Turin

Royal Palace, Stockholm

Saint Nicholas, Prague

The revival of Classical learning and Classical values in the Renaissance was one aspect of fundamental changes in European society which happened, more slowly than appears in retrospect, over the course of many generations. No new development was more important than the invention of printing, which allowed ideas to spread more quickly and to more people. Printed books helped to undermine the totalitarian authority of the medieval Church and promote the growth of humanism, again inspired by ancient – and of course pre-Christian – civilization, which the humanists saw as a cultural golden age. Printing also made widely available two written works which, together with the discovery of the law of perspective (perhaps by Brunelleschi, the first true Renaissance architect), had enormous influence on architecture. The treatise of Vitruvius, De architectura, written in the 1st century BC and almost unknown even to scholars until the 15th century, was printed in Rome in 1486. Leon Battista Alberti's equally famous, and more lucid, book on architecture, De re aedificatoria, clarified the mathematical principles of design and proportion which, correctly followed, lead to perfect harmony. Though written in about 1452, it was not printed until 1485. It had many successors, notably Vasari's Lives (1550–68) and Palladio's Four Books, I quattro libri di architettura (1570). For the first time, architecture became, if not yet quite a profession, a serious occupation and an admired art,
with established theoretical texts.

Renaissance art and architecture began in Italy in the early 15th century and did not spread to other countries until the 16th. Elsewhere it took different forms, and the first result of the spread of Italian ideas and Italian artists was usually some kind of mixture of Medieval and Classical, as in the châteaux of the Loire, or the elaborate Spanish style known as Plateresque. The influential School of Fontainebleau encouraged a further proliferation of complex styles in different countries; the great houses of Elizabethan-Jacobean England are one example. They were akin, if at some distance, to Italian Mannerism, a more self-conscious style exemplified by Michelangelo in Rome and Giulio Romano in Mantua, which emerged from Classicism in the mid-16th century. Great houses and palaces rose to challenge churches as the pre-eminent buildings of European civilization.

In the 17th century Mannerism, always more of a variant than a distinct style, gave way to Baroque. Like 'Gothic', this was originally a term of abuse, meaning 'misshapen', for a new, vigorous, often emotional interpretation that, while recognizing the authority of the antique, offered greater freedom to the individual artist. Outside Italy, it resulted in so rich a variety of styles (e.g. very restrained in England, very ornate in Spain) that the name 'Baroque' is more apt as a description of the age than as a specific style.

Medici-Riccardi Palace, Florence

Generally known as the Palazzo Riccardi, after its more recent proprietors, this rather forbidding building was the home of the Medici rulers of Florence in the 15th and 16th centuries. It was commissioned by Cosimo the Elder (1389–1464), who ruled as a despot without holding any major office, and was built between about 1444 and 1460. Here beat the heart of the Florentine Renaissance, where Lorenzo the Magnificent kept his brilliant court, Michelangelo first tried out his sculptor's chisels and the Platonic academy was lavishly entertained. It was also the headquarters of the Medici commercial empire.

These Italian Renaissance palaces, built around a courtyard, derived from ancient Roman forms. In the Palazzo Rucellai, built at the same time by the most influential contemporary architect, Leon Battista Alberti, the three Classical orders were employed as pilasters on the three floors in the manner of the Colosseum, though this example was not widely followed as it posed problems of proportion. The huge Medici palace was designed by Michelozzo di Bartolommeo, a follower of Brunelleschi, and is his best-known work. Elsewhere, Michelozzo is renowned for the lightness of his style, but that is certainly not evident here. The impression the palace makes is one of immense strength, emphasized by the pronounced rustication of the lowest storey. These early princely residences were almost fortified houses: they were not expected to withstand a siege, but angry, stone-throwing mobs were a more likely hazard. The second storey is faced with lightly channelled stone, and the top storey is smooth.

The building is crowned by an elaborate cornice incorporating Classical motifs.

The interior is more gracious: the rooms are arranged around an open, arcaded courtyard and the main apartments are on the *piano nobile*, the principal floor (second storey), reached by a splendid staircase. Among the treasures of the palace are the frescoes by Benozzo Gozzoli, painted in 1463, in the little chapel, which illustrate the Journey of the Magi and incorporate several Medici portraits.

The palace was sold to the Riccardi in 1659 and was later altered and extended (there used to be ten, not 17, windows on the second storey). It became state property in the 19th century.

The palace, commissioned by Cosimo the Elder, was once the home of the Medici rulers of Florence in the 15th and 16th centuries.

The rear façade of the Pitti Palace by Ammanati, with the octagonal Fountain of the Artichoke in the foreground.

Pitti Palace, Florence

Formerly the residence of the grand dukes of Tuscany, the Medici and their successors of the house of Lorraine, the Pitti now houses one of the world's great collections of Renaissance art, second only to the Uffizi across the river. The palazzo was built on rising ground near the Ponte Vecchio for Luca Pitti, an ambitious adherent of Cosimo de' Medici, beginning in 1458. Tradition says that the original plans were by the great Filippo Brunelleschi, best known for the dome of Florence cathedral, which is possible although he was dead before work began.

Luca Pitti had chosen an inauspicious moment to commemorate the prestige of his family; within eight years, with the building barely half finished, the decline of the Pitti put an end to its construction. Having passed to the Medici, it was completed and enlarged 100 years later in the time of of the Medici Grand Duke Cosimo I, on the initiative of his wife, Eleanor of Toledo. The architect was Bartolommeo Ammanati, perhaps best known for the charming Ponte S.Trinità over the Arno. He built the slightly grotesque, though often copied, rusticated façade of the Pitti that overlooks the famous Boboli Gardens. Further minor additions were made in the 17th century, and in the 18th century the projecting outer wings were added. They rather spoiled the symmetry of the building but contributed to its appearance as probably the largest and the most imposing palace in Italy outside the Vatican.

The fame of the Pitti as an art gallery dates from the late 18th century, when the public was first admitted to view the paintings. The gorgeous rooms of the Galleria Palatina, each named after one of the planets, contain some 500 Renaissance paintings, mainly Florentine, naturally, but include many of the finest Venetians, several Raphaels and Rubens. There are really five museums in the Pitti, which also contains the treasures collected by the Medici grand dukes, a gallery of modern Tuscan art, and a coach museum.

Ducal Palace, Urbino

The most attractive of all early Renaissance palaces, Urbino is a monument to Duke Federigo da Montefeltro, a model 'Renaissance man' whose hooked nose and square, intelligent head are familiar from several contemporary paintings. His court at Urbino was perhaps less glamorous that those of the Medici in Florence or the Este in Ferrara, but it was one of the liveliest centres of Renaissance culture in Italy.

The palace is very large, spacious, and irregular in plan, largely due to its adaptation to a hilltop site. The transformation of the original medieval building began in 1468 and, thanks to the tall, turreted towers that flank the entrance, and notwithstanding their rather unconvincing machicolation, the first appearance is Gothic. There are also medieval inclusions in part of the east wing and elsewhere, but within the great courtyard, surrounded by its graceful Corinthian colonnade, all is cool Classicism. The architect was the Dalmatian Luciano da Laurana, whose command of delicate detail was unrivalled. He had numerous assistants and advisers, not the least of them perhaps the man responsible for the basic conception, the Duke himself; but they also probably included Piero della Francesca, to whom is attributed the well-known painted panel of an ideal city, and possibly the young Bramante, who was born near Urbino in 1444.

The ducal apartments were beyond the towered west façade, and a passage led to Laurana's 'secret garden', with geometric flower beds and a central fountain. The largest room is the Throne Room in the east, where all the windows face north to provide a pure but subdued light. The decoration everywhere – sculptures, friezes, paintings – is all of a very high order. But perhaps the most fascinating room is a quite small one, the study of Duke Federigo, with its brilliant, illusionist marquetry, said to be based on designs by Botticelli, its carved and pierced wooden panels and brightly coloured ceiling.

View of Urbino, with its twin towers on the right, shows the rather cramped site that partly dictated the plan of the palace.

Quirinal Palace, Rome

The former summer home of the popes is only about 15 minutes' walk from the Vatican, but as it is set on the Quirinal hill, it is usually appreciably cooler, and commands a fine view of Rome. The palace, which is very large and rather complex, was begun by Pope Gregory XIII in 1583 and continued under his immediate successors. The finest Roman artists of the Mannerist and early Baroque periods were employed in its construction and decoration, and it also includes antique and Renaissance works, such as the Classical figures of the Horse-Tamers, found originally in the Baths of Constantine.

The original buildings are mainly the work of Carlo Maderno and Domenico Fontana, who built the main front and the façade overlooking the piazza (except for the entrance portal, designed by Flaminio Ponzio with later embellishments by Bernini). Ponzio also designed the Pope's private chapel (Capella del'Annunciata), which contains beautiful paintings by Guido Reni and other members of the Bolognese school. The highly elaborate Sala Regia (or Sala de Corazzieri) designed, together with the adjoining public chapel, by Maderno, is without doubt the most arresting chamber. It contains ornamental contributions by Bernini and Agostino Tassi, and its marble floor reflects the gilded stucco ceiling and Tassi's painted frieze, in which human figures appear to be leaning out of windows overlooking the room. Among other rooms of special interest are the 18th-century Mirror Room in the Chinese style and a beautiful little library of the same period with inlaid ivory and mother-of-pearl in a delicate Rococo arrangement.

The gardens, little changed since the early 17th century, have statues, fountains, palms, orange trees and lawns enclosed by box hedges cut with military precision, as well as a little Palladian coffee house and an organ played by water.

The Quirinal palace was used by popes hoping to escape the heat and malaria of the Vatican until the late 19th century, when it was appropriated by the King of Italy. Today it is occupied by the president of the Republic.

The former summer palace of the popes on the Quirinale.

The Sala Regia.

Details of atlantes,
Barberini Palace.

Barberini Palace, Rome

The Palazzo Barberini, now the Italian National Gallery, though popularly still known as the Barberini Gallery, is in terms of ostentatious Baroque splendour, one of the most magnificent palaces in Rome. And so it should be, given the reputation of the architects who worked on it. The Barberini family was established in Florence in the 14th century and settled in Rome in the mid-16th century (it seems very profitably). In 1623 Mafeo Barberini was elected pope as Urban VIII. He was an effective ruler but notorious for nepotism and plunder. He was responsible for removing the bronze beams from the Pantheon, provoking the acid witticism, *Quod non fecerunt barbari, fecerunt Barberini* ('What the Barbarians did not do, the Barberini did').

The Palazzo Barberini, opposite the Quirinal Gardens on the Via delle Quattro Fontane, was begun during Urban VIII's pontificate. Three architects are primarily associated with it, Maderno, Bernini and Borromini, which, as someone remarked, is like having a baptism conducted by the Holy Trinity. Exactly who was responsible for what is a matter of argument, but the general consensus is that the original plans of Maderno, who died in 1629 when construction had barely begun, were carried out fairly faithfully by his exalted successors. The most notable feature, however, the great central portico with its two upper rows of large arched windows, is probably the work of Bernini, as is the more orthodox, rectangular staircase. The subtle oval staircase on the other side of the building is likely to be one of Borromini's contributions.

The basic plan is unusual for a Roman palace, since it is in the form of an H, like a country villa, thus lacking a central courtyard. The famous ceiling fresco of the great hall, called an *Allegory of Divine Providence and Barberini Power,* in which the figures seem to float above the room, is the masterpiece of Pietro da Cortona, a client of the Barberini and the exponent of illusionist Baroque decoration at its most extravagant.

Ducal Palace, Mantua

The Gonzaga family gained control of the fortified island city of Mantua in Lombardy in the early 14th century and held it for nearly 400 years. Their court was a centre of princely patronage as early as 1350, and in the 15th century it attracted such major figures of Renaissance art as Alberti and Mantegna, who is buried in Mantua. It reached the height of its reputation during the time of Isabella d'Este (1474–1539), wife of the Gonzaga marquess, and his successor, Federigo II (1500–40). He became the first duke and presided over a court that outclassed even the Medici in Florence.

During this period, several palaces and villas were built, notably the Palazzo del Te (1525–35), the summer villa and honeymoon home (hence the erotic frescoes), which was designed by Giulio Romano. Mantua attracted many of the greatest names of the High Renaissance, including Leonardo, Raphael and Titian.

The vast ducal palace contains about 500 rooms and has stabling for 600 horses; some staircases were designed for horses, to spare their riders the fatigue of climbing on foot. The building goes back to the early 14th century, predating the Gonzaga takeover, and still retains its 14th-century Gothic façade. Many additions, and most of the interior, were undertaken under the Gonzaga, especially during the reign of Federigo, by Giulio Romano and his successors. Their frescoes, woodwork and stucco ornament by Primaticcio, busts by Bernini and some fine Venetian glass remain to be admired, though many of the Gonzaga treasures have been dispersed. Among other remarkable features are an enormous roof garden, a highly informative astrological clock, which recommends the best

time to go on a journey or have one's clothes mended, and a group of apartments built to a small scale for the dwarfs of whom the Gonzaga, themselves subject to a hereditary tendency to deformation of the spine, were so fond. Some later decoration is less attractive: the inspired taste of the Gonzaga during the Renaissance declined towards the end of the 16th century and degenerated into mere extravagance.

The palace of the dukes of Mantua is probably the largest and grandest of all the Renaissance princely palazzi. This is the view from the cathedral.

Wawel, home of the Jagellion dynasty.

Wawel Castle, Cracow

When Poland was reunited by Wladyslaw I in the early 14th century, Cracow (Kraków) became the capital, the place where the Jagellion kings of Poland were crowned and buried for over 200 years. The dynasty ended in 1572, the capital was moved to Warsaw soon afterwards, and Cracow entered a decline. The royal castle, which dates from the 12th century, is sited on Wawel hill, overlooking the city and the River Vistula, which seems to have been the citadel in very early times.

Essentially, the building is a Polish medieval castle that between 1507 and 1536 was turned into an Italian Renaissance palace by craftsmen imported from Italy. This gave rise to some odd conjunctions, such as the little tent-like pavilion that rests on a convenient Gothic battlement, but the overall effect is quite harmonious. The large and impressive central courtyard is surrounded by distinctive three-tiered arcades, the two lower stages of which together equal in height the third stage. Interestingly, one of the four blocks surrounding the courtyard is a dummy. There are no habitable rooms behind its façade; it was built for the sake of symmetry alone.

Some of the state rooms were decorated with considerable splendour at no small expense. The Senate Chamber has famous Flemish tapestries illustrating the story of Noah, and the ceiling of the Chamber of Deputies is equally famous for its panels inset with realistically carved and painted heads. Throughout the palace, which is now a museum with an internationally notable collection of armour, there are fine wooden doors carved in the Late Gothic style, and some of the rooms are still heated by handsome tiled stoves.

Adjoining the castle is the cathedral, the third, possibly fourth church on the site. It was begun soon after the castle, though like its secular neighbour it is a blend of successive styles and includes a very fine Renaissance chapel by Bartolomeo Brecci. The cathedral contains many royal tombs, including a fine effigy of Casimir the Great (1333–70) in pink marble, and the ornate Baroque mausoleum of St Stanislaus.

King's College Chapel, Cambridge

King's College was founded by the English King Henry VI in 1440 and work began on the chapel a few years later. Owing to the upheavals of the Wars of the Roses, little progress was made until more secure times, and in 1505 the work was renewed under Henry VII, first of the Tudor dynasty. It was completed about ten years later under his son, Henry VIII.

The chapel is the most successful example of the astonishing English Late Gothic style known as Perpendicular. Earlier Gothic builders had learned how to achieve great height and lightness by supporting the walls with flying buttresses that permitted very large windows, and at King's the windows seem to occupy the entire wall, bathing the interior in the beautiful light filtered through the stained glass, which is still largely original. This extreme effect is achieved by the use of fan vaulting, in which a fan-like cluster of fine stone ribs distributes the weight of the vault.

Regardless of aesthetic judgments, which are not universally approving, this is an extraordinary demonstration of craftsmanship and engineering skill. The master mason responsible for the vaulting was John Wastell, who had worked at the Abbey of Bury St Edmunds, possibly his home town, and at Canterbury Cathedral, where he became master mason in succession to Simon Clerk. He probably died in the year that King's College Chapel was finished.

The Perpendicular style as seen at King's, and in the Chapel of Henry VII (completed 1519) in Westminster Abbey, represents the end of the road. At King's, amid that purity of glass and stone, the hearty vigour of earlier versions of English Gothic seems to be missing.

Significantly, when Wastell became master mason in Cambridge, Bramante was working on his plans for St Peter's in Rome.

King's College Chapel, the west end. Irreverent students have likened it to a sow lying on its back.

Ortega y Gasset compared Segovia Cathedral to a huge mysterious liner, perhaps galleon, or even battleship would be appropriate: here is militant Spanish Christianity in full sail.

Segovia Cathedral

The large size of Spanish cathedrals reflects the aggressive spirit of the successful Crusaders which, when the cathedral of Segovia was being built, was being directed to the acquisition of an empire in the New World. This is the last monumental church in the great age of Spanish building, in which the Late Gothic style mingles with new influences from Renaissance Italy. Perhaps the best view of it is from the north, late on an autumn afternoon, when the sinking sun lights up the golden stone. As travel posters proclaim, there is something quintessentially Spanish in the view of the city of whitewashed houses, the huge stone church, and the towers and pinacles of the Alcázar, against the distant backdrop of the Sierra de Guadarrama.

During the Revolt of the Comuneros in 1520–21, Segovia was besieged and captured and the old cathedral badly damaged. Some items were retrieved – the choir stalls and the figure of the Virgen del Perdón come from the old cathedral – but total reconstruction was necessary. Work began in 1525, and was directed by Juan Gil de Hontañón. He had worked at Salamanca since 1513 and the plan of Segovia closely resembled that of Salamanca. The work was largely completed under his son, Rodrigo, who died in 1577, though due to the speed of its construction Segovia is stylistically consistent.

The site makes the most of the great size of the building, but it is not particularly heavy or overpowering. The Spanish Late Gothic style tends to indulge in a profusion of Plateresque decoration that can look more like an excrescence than an adornment, and although this is not wholly absent at Segovia, the general impression of the exterior is of a relatively plain building. There is little external sculpture and the main, western entrance, which was usually the subject of the most extravagant decoration, is simple and restrained. The great tower, which is nearly 295-ft (90-m) high and about 52ft 6-in (16-m) square, is plain below the domed octagon and lantern. For those energetic enough to climb its 306 steps, the view is wonderful.

RIGHT
The White Horse
Courtyard, with Jean
Ducerceau's elaborate
horseshoe staircase of
1634.

BELOW
General view from the
pool.

OPPOSITE
A 19th-century statue of
Hercules, no doubt
lamenting the loss of the
demolished Gallery of
Ulysses that once stood
behind him, and, on the
right, part of the Gallery
of François I.

Fontainebleau

The rambling palace of Fontainebleau has been described as a group of châteaux that have met by chance. Situated in a large forest only 30 miles (50km) from Paris, the forest was popular with medieval kings for its hunting. The oldest surviving part of the château is the 13th-century tower or keep, now the centrepiece of the Oval Courtyard. Although additions were made in many different periods, often involving demolition of older parts (the famous Gallery of Ulysses by Primaticcio vanished in the 18th century), there was never a total reconstruction. The most crucial period, when Fontainebleau first emerged as a grand royal palace, was in the reign of François I (1515–47), who commissioned the finest artists and craftsmen to decorate the palace in the 1530s.

A general view reveals buildings erected over three centuries but all are in the same local sandstone and appear comfortably related. The old core of the palace, the Oval Courtyard, is only one of five courtyards. The Gallery of François, which links it to the White Horse Courtyard on the south side, exemplifies the brilliance of the decoration for which Fontainebleau is famous. It was built in 1531 and decorated by the Florentine artist, Giovanni Batista Rosso, one of the founders of the School of Fontainebleau, in 1533–41. The scheme is built on a masterly combination of woodwork, stucco and fresco, of mainly mythological subjects. The way in which paintings are combined with sculpture, though not entirely without precedent (Rosso may have known similar work by Perino del Vaga in the Doria Palace, Genoa), is characteristic of the Fontainebleau school and had a powerful influence on French Renaissance art. After Rosso's death in 1541, his work was continued by Primaticcio, whose female figures in stucco that flank the frescoes in the bedroom of the Duchesse d'Étampes express the Fontainebleau ideal of female beauty. Work continued in the next reign, when Primaticcio was aided by a fellow pupil of Giulio Romano, Niccolò dell'Abbate, but fresco came to dominate stucco.

Later additions included new wings and courtyards and the over-elaborate Horseshoe Staircase in the Baroque period, the 18th-century Salle du Conseil decorated by Boucher among others, and the refurnishing in the Empire style when Napoleon adopted Fontainebleau as his chief residence.

Château de Chambord

Chambord is one of the largest, most famous and beautiful châteaux in the Loire valley, a vision of Renaissance splendour in pale stone. Unlike its near neighbour at Blois, or the even larger royal palace of Fontainebleau farther north, it is stylistically uniform; the original hunting lodge was completely rebuilt by François I. Later alterations were comparatively few, and Chambord remains the outstanding building of the early French Renaissance.

Although the Italian influence is strong – the chief designer was Domenico da Cortona – the successive master masons were French, and the basic plan is that of a medieval castle, with the buildings grouped around a large, rectangular courtyard about 525 x 394ft (160 x 120m), and the main block or tower centred in the north-west façade. At each corner of the main building are large round towers, and another pair flank the main façade. A staggering

riot of turrets, towers and chimneys, a final flourish of the Gothic style, breaks out at roof level. François had a moat created by diverting the little River Cosson, a tributary of the Loire, but it proved troublesome to maintain and was later filled in. The park is enclosed by a wall over 18-miles (30-km) long.

Inside the château, the most remarkable feature is the central staircase, which ascends through four floors at the point where four lofty barrel-vaulted halls meet. It takes the form of a double spiral so that a person going up never meets anyone coming down; contained within

four narrow columns, it offers a view of the whole of each floor.

Louis XIV visited Chambord on several occasions and witnessed there a first performance of a play by Molière. His successor gave it to Stanislas Leczinski, the dethroned king of Poland, and later to the victorious marshal, Maurice de Saxe, after the battle of Fontenoy (1745). Chambord survived the Revolution but lost all its furnishings, and despite some restoration, the interior is still rather bare. The entire property, including the village of Chambord, was purchased by the state in 1932.

OPPOSITE
Chambord, seen from across the moat, is perhaps the most successful of François I's architectural projects.

LEFT
The staggering sky line of the château, from the south. Foreshortening creates a misleading impression: there is a space of about 100ft (30m) between the low building in the foreground and the main block or donjon.

FAR LEFT
Detail.

Hampton Court

The palace of Hampton Court, on the River Thames south-west of London, is a comparatively unpretentious building by comparison with its contemporaries in France. The original builder was Cardinal Wolsey, the humbly born minister of Henry VIII, who presented it to the king in 1529 in vain hope of buying back Henry's good will. As enlarged and completed by Henry, it became the grandest residence in England. Henry brought his various wives here, and it was the favourite residence of his successors, enjoying its most festive days in the reign of Elizabeth I.

It is the Tudor palace, with its forest of decorated chimneys, that the visitor first sees on approaching the towered main gateway. Beyond are two courtyards (a third was later demolished) surrounded by buildings which in both style and material (brick) resemble old colleges of Oxford and Cambridge. The building belongs basically to the English domestic Gothic tradition, but some awareness of the Italian Renaissance is evident, for instance in the terracotta roundels of Classical heads set in the walls.

The palace was greatly enlarged in the reign of the Dutch king, William III (1689–1702), who found it healthier than Whitehall and commissioned Christopher Wren to rebuild it. Wren wanted to sweep away most of the Tudor palace, plans thwarted by dwindling finance, and as things turned out, his cool, English version of Baroque complemented the more rugged Tudor palace rather well. However, Hampton Court soon afterwards fell from favour as a royal residence.

Among the most remarkable features of Hampton Court are the early Tudor royal chapel, which has an extraordinary vaulted ceiling of wood aping stone, and Great Hall, with its magnificent hammer-beam ceiling. The 'real' tennis court is still in use, though rebuilt since Henry VIII played there. The kitchens, imaginatively restored, could cater for 500 guests. Gardens, where Elizabeth I worked in the mornings, have been restored to their appearance in the 16th and 17th centuries. The splendid wrought-iron gates were designed by Jean Tijou in about 1690. A colossal vine, planted in 1769, is still fruiting.

OPPOSITE
The main entrance to Hampton Court is essentially Gothic but with Renaissance roundels on the gateway.

RIGHT
View across the restored Tudor gardens, with part of Wren's wing on the right.

BELOW
A view across the lake,
which augments the
calming effect of
Chantilly

BELOW RIGHT
The mythological figure
fronts what is actually a
19th-century building.

Château de Chantilly

A many-faceted Baroque château, beautifully sited on a small island in an artificial lake 25 miles (40km) north of Paris, Chantilly was the domain of the princely Condés, a branch of the Bourbon dynasty who were leaders of the Huguenots during the French Wars of Religion. It was to Chantilly that the Duc d'Enghien, known as 'the Great Condé' (1621–86), retired towards the end of his hectic military career.

Earlier, the lordship of Chantilly belonged to another famous house, the Montmorency. In the 16th century Anne de Montmorency, Constable of France, reconstructed the medieval castle. He also built the *châtelet* ('little castle') nearby, which still survives, but the château itself was again rebuilt, partly by François Mansart, when the Prince of Condé took possession in the 17th century. The gardens were laid out by André Le Nôtre. King Louis XIV stayed at Chantilly in 1676 and hunted a stag by moonlight, but his visit was spoiled by the suicide of the steward who had been told that the fish had not reached the table on time. Louis, surely well accustomed to eating his dinner cold, was distressed and implored his host for less lavish entertainment next time.

The French Revolution brought disaster, and the main building was completely destroyed, along with Le Nôtre's landscape. However, in 1830, with the Condés extinct, Chantilly was acquired by another branch of the Bourbons in the person of Henri, Duc d'Aumale, a son of the Orléanist King Louis-Philippe. He had the means to indulge his zeal for art, amassing not only paintings, particularly of the Italian and French Renaissance and including most of the known court portraits of Jean Clouet (died c. 1540), but also manuscripts, sculpture and tapestries. The château was rebuilt according to Mansart's plans, and the duke bequeathed it and his collections to the Institut de France, to form what is now the Musée Condé.

The famous race course was instituted in 1834, but the great stables of Chantilly, which accommodated 240 horses, date from the 18th century.

Saint-Germain-en-Laye

While Versailles was being built, the favourite residence of Louis XIV was St-Germain, on the River Seine nearly 12 miles (20km) west of Paris, now virtually a suburb though still on the edge of the forest. The move to Versailles was not popular with all of Louis's courtiers, but when James II of England took refuge in France in 1688, the recently vacated St-Germain was made available to the exiled Jacobite court.

The present château, renovated as the national museum of antiquities under Napoleon III, is a fragment of what was once an enormous complex. The original castle was built by Louis VI in the early 12th century. It was destroyed more than once by the English and rebuilt, but was largely neglected under the early Valois kings in the 14th–15th centuries. It was converted into a royal palace by François I (1515–47), who had been married there. A notable medieval survival is the gem-like Chapel of St Louis, which resembles the Sainte-Chapelle in Paris and may have been the work of the same man.

The Renaissance reconstruction was planned by Pierre Chambiges, and although most of the work was not completed until after his death in 1544 (many famous architects worked subsequently at St-Germain), it faithfully reflects his early French Renaissance style. A remarkable feature is the terraced roof of great stone slabs, which had to be supported by large stone buttresses reinforced with iron. The plan follows the outline of the medieval castle, incorporating a 14th-century tower at the north-west corner, which does impose certain limitations. Along the edge of the roof runs a balustrade with slender stone vases between the windows, a feature echoed above the second storey with a pleasingly harmonious effect. The superb terrace planned by André Le Nôtre in the 17th century, 'the finest promenade in Europe' and over 1¼-miles (2-km) long, offers a distant view of Paris across the Seine.

The Château of Saint-Germain-en-Laye, from an 18th-century engraving.

The Louvre

Now one of the world's greatest art museums, the Louvre began as a small fort in about 1100; by 1200 it controlled shipping on the Seine with the aid of an iron chain stretched across the river. As Paris grew, the fort expanded and eventually became a palace, the decisive conversion taking place in the 16th century, when it became the seat of the royal court in the capital, though the court usually preferred to be elsewhere. The artists responsible were Pierre Lescot, whose buildings ranged around a square court influenced the development of French Classicism, augmented by the refined work of the sculptor Jean Goujon. Cathérine de Médicis built the Tuileries palace (destroyed in 1871) to the west and Henri IV completed the gallery on the river

to link it with the Louvre. Two wings of the old chateau were demolished to enlarge the quadrangle, but without jettisoning Lescot's conception. The palace continued to grow in the 17th century, under Louis Le Vau (when he could spare time from Versailles), and the original and impressive colonnaded eastern front was built by Claude Perrault in co-operation with Le Vau and others, and perhaps influenced by a rejected design by Bernini. After the Louvre narrowly avoided destruction during the Revolution, it was turned into a museum, its collections benefiting from the sack of less fortunate palaces and, later, from Napoleon's acquisitions (though most were returned to their former owners). The 'Nouveau Louvre' on Place Napoléon III was built in the 1850s.

Besides the contents that are its chief claim to fame, the architecture of the Louvre embodies work from the Middle Ages to 1993, when the glass pyramid of I.M. Pei was completed. One of the motives for President Mitterand's determined pursuance of this project, which at first aroused ferocious opposition, was to continue the Louvre's tradition of incorporating new construction from each new age. The pyramid, 75-ft (23-m) high, has a network of cables and girders supporting 800 large glass panels, and is situated in the great quadrangle and surrounded by water. It forms the entrance to the expanded 'Grand Louvre', made possible by the evacuation of the finance ministry from its offices, which resulted in almost doubling the exhibition space.

I.M. Pei's steel-and-glass pyramid, which provided the great museum with a new entrance in 1993 and nearly caused a revolution when the plans were published. However, despite some technical problems, it has since gained widespread approval.

Longleat, a Renaissance palace in the English countryside, has survived with remarkable success in the possession of the same family, now headed by the Marquess of Bath.

Longleat

Apart from a few decorative touches, as seen at Hampton Court, the style of the Renaissance made little impression in England before 1550, and even then, in the new Elizabethan country houses, it mingled idiosyncratically with traditional English Gothic into the 17th century.

At Longleat in Wiltshire, though a comparatively early example (begun 1568), Renaissance concepts are obvious. On the long and elegant façade (the third storey and parapet are slightly later than the rest; there was originally a pitched roof), the three Classical orders are prominently displayed, perhaps

based on engravings in John Shute's *First and Chief Grounds of Architecture*, published in 1563, which in turn borrowed from an earlier book by the influential Italian architect, Sebastiano Serlio. The strapwork decoration on the parapet derives from the Low Countries. However, the plan of the house, though Classical in its symmetry, is traditional, the building arranged around two courtyards. The great hall, which is entered directly from the main entrance, was a feature common to medieval castles and did not go out of fashion in England until the 17th century. Yet the house, which almost demands the name palace, is an undoubted success and is now regarded as one of the finest adornments of the Elizabethan age. For all its French, Italian and Flemish connections, it is thoroughly and uniquely English.

It was built by Sir John Thynne, a rich and well-placed courtier who was associated with the design of several other houses. This one, however, was for his own use, and his descendants still live there. His master mason was Robert Smythson, and Longleat is the first recorded commission of the man who became the foremost, if not the only, architect of the period. Among his other so-called 'prodigy' houses are Wollaton Hall and, probably, Hardwick Hall, where the large windows notable at Longleat are even larger, hence the quip, 'Hardwick Hall, more glass than wall'.

Villa Rotonda, Vicenza

Andrea Palladio (1508–80), trained as a mason and bricklayer in Padua, was probably the greatest and most influential architect of the 16th century, who aimed to capture the splendour and idealism of the Classical past. A wealthy patron encouraged his intellectual interests, nicknamed him Palladio after Pallas Athena, goddess of wisdom, and took him to study in Rome, where he also read the works of Vitruvius and Alberti. He became a scholar as well as a craftsman and, many years later, published his own, equally influential *I quattro libri dell'architettura*. Meanwhile, he had acquired great practical experience, designing handsome but practical farmhouses in the Veneto, subtle churches in Venice, impressive public buildings and palaces, and one of the first permanent theatres since Roman times, the Teatro Olimpico in Vicenza.

Palladio represents the epitome of the Classical virtues of balance, harmony and cool clarity, his work combining ancient Roman splendour with his own airy elegance. Those virtues are evident in what is probably his most famous building, the Villa Rotonda, also known as the Villa Almerico-Capra after a later owner, on a small hill outside Vicenza where, as the architect himself observed, 'wonderful views can be enjoyed from every side'. It was built in the 1550s as a country house for a wealthy gentleman, then a novel concept and quite unlike the working farmhouses Palladio had built hitherto in the region, although, like the architecture, the concept recalled ancient Roman models. The villa has four equal façades facing each point of the compass, with a porch like that of a Roman temple – six columns and a pediment, approached by a broad flight of steps. Palladio believed, wrongly, that Roman houses also followed this design. At the centre of the building is the rotonda, crowned by a dome recalling that of the Pantheon, richly decorated with frescoes and stucco and illuminated by indirect light, suggesting constrained luxury.

Imitation is said to be the sincerest form of flattery and Palladio was perhaps the most imitated of architects. During the 18th-century Palladian revival, his buildings were copied in countries as far apart as Russia, England, where Lord Burlington's Chiswick House is partly modelled on the Villa Rotonda, and North America, on which Thomas Jefferson's Monticello is based.

The Escorial

Philip II of Spain founded the Royal Monastery of St Lawrence about 30 miles (50km) from Madrid in 1557 in gratitude for a victory over the French. The setting is stark but magnificent, 3,300-ft (1000-m) above sea level in the Sierra Guadarrama. The complex of buildings includes monastery, palace, seat of learning and mausoleum. They are set within a huge walled rectangle, 655 x 525ft (200 x 160m), internally divided into courts on a grid pattern resembling the plan of Diocletian's palace at Split and dominated by the large church, a domed basilica resembling St Peter's in Rome. The palace acquired its name from the village that housed the workmen, which means 'the slag heap', and it was completed with extraordinary speed between 1563 and 1585. Most later monarchs added something to the Escorial, but without altering its main features.

From the outside, it is easiest to admire it from a distance, assimilated into the landscape. Its austere grandeur is not incidental. Philip demanded 'simplicity in construction, severity in the total effect; nobility without arrogance, majesty without ostentation', and his architects did not fail him. But the result has not been widely admired. Théophile Gautier, predictably unsympathetic, was not alone in remarking its resemblance to a barracks.

The contents are more rewarding. They include paintings by the Dutch masters, of whom Philip was unexpectedly fond, as well as Titian, El Greco and Velázquez. The library, with its wonderful painted barrel vault is, despite losses, probably still the greatest Renaissance library in Europe, and includes many Arabic manuscripts. The Hall of Battles, a

gallery over 165-ft (50-m) long, is painted with Spanish feats of arms and has a vaulted ceiling with 18th-century designs inspired by Pompeii. The Pantheon of Kings contains the remains of Habsburg and Bourbon kings.

The Escorial has survived several catastrophes that reduced its treasures (including a feather from the wing of the Archangel Gabriel). In 1671 a fire burned for two weeks before it was extinguished, French troops looted the palace in 1808 and another fire in 1872 destroyed part of the library. It remains the most impressive monument of Philip II's Spain which, financed by American silver and fortified by the faith of the Counter-Reformation, became the greatest kingdom in Europe.

Rialto Bridge, Venice

Given their vulnerability, especially in time of war, it is surprising how many Renaissance bridges have survived in Italy. (The Ponte San Trinità in Florence was destroyed in 1944 but has been rebuilt with some of the same materials, rescued from the riverbed.)

Bridges naturally assumed special importance in Venice, a city of canals as well as streets, and the earliest bridges were made of wood. Stone began to replace them in the 12th century, when streets began to be paved, though wood remained the preferred material for short bridges into the Renaissance; Palladio designed several on the principle of the truss. The development of the stone-arch bridge is

one of the outstanding engineering achievements of the Renaissance.

The Rialto is the commercial heart of Venice. A wooden Rialto Bridge over the Grand Canal at its narrowest point was built in 1178, on pontoons. It was replaced in the mid-13th century by another wooden bridge carried on beams, which could be raised and lowered like a drawbridge. The present stone-arch bridge was built in 1588–91 by Antonio 'da Ponte' (1512–95), who probably earned his nickname from earlier, now-unknown bridges. It is an ornamental, single-arched span of two segments, covered with shops in the traditional manner. Many features were required by the commission, including the shops (still there), the

open arch in the centre (where earlier bridges usually had a chapel) and the side pavements. The span is 89ft (27m) and the rise is 21ft (6.4m), the dimensions of the bridge dictated by the need to accommodate shipping on the Grand Canal. From the day it opened, the Rialto Bridge became a Venetian landmark.

The architect-engineer faced serious structural problems because of the soft, wet soil. He overcame them by driving in 6,000 wooden piles under the abutments on each side. The masonry was then so arranged that the stones were bedded at right angles to the line of thrust of the arch, a technique that has been used ever since.

The enchanting Rialto Bridge rests on sound engineering.

Teatro Olimpico, Vicenza

No permanent theatres were built during the Middle Ages. Drama, where it existed, was performed in churches, on temporary wooden stages in market square or inn yard, and later in some kind of temporary accommodation in royal courts and grand houses. Even the rise of professional companies of actors did not necessarily imply a permanent, purpose-built theatre.

By 1500 the desirability of a central, self-contained acting space was recognized in Italian courts and elsewhere, but this only required minor modifications to the existing arrangements. A wooden theatre is recorded at Ferrara early in the 16th century, but when it burned down it was not rebuilt. As late as 1556 a book on stage design took it for granted that the stage would be a temporary structure. One catalyst for change was Vitruvius' *De architectura*, which first appeared in an Italian translation in 1531. Vitruvius provided the first description of what a Classical, specifically a Roman, theatre looked like, and provided the basis for the works of theatre designers such as Sebastiano Serlio (1475–1554).

The Teatro Olimpico at Vicenza was one of the first permanent theatres. It opened in 1585 with a production of *Oedipus Rex*, and it is still standing today. Designed by Andrea Palladio for a group of scholarly classicists, like himself, it is his last building. He died in 1580 and construction was supervised by his disciple Vincenzo Scamozzi, who took over several of his projects and may have been responsible for the design of the stage at Vicenza.

Palladio's theatre was intended as a reconstruction of a Classical Roman theatre on a smaller scale, with a curved auditorium, a small orchestra, and a magnificent architectural set pierced by doorways and backing a very narrow stage. Unlike the theatres of ancient Greece and Rome, however, it was roofed, so the ceiling was painted to look like the sky! Although a magnificent building, its influence on theatre design was slight: a more significant innovation appeared in 1618 in the Teatro Farnese at Parma, which provided more acting space and introduced the proscenium arch, a device that was to dominate theatre design for over 300 years.

Part of the vestibule of the splendid Teatro Olimpico, one of the earliest modern examples, but essentially an academic exercise, something of a dead end in theatre design.

Saint Basil's Cathedral, with, centre, the view from Red Square and, right, decorative details of the astonishing towers.

Saint Basil's Cathedral, Moscow

Christianity came to Russia from Byzantium, and along with the religion, the Byzantine style of ecclesiastical architecture was also imported. The standard form was a plan of a Greek cross (equal arms) within a square. It was topped, typically, by five domes. However, the Russians introduced their own variations, notably the onion-shaped dome, adopted after too many normal domes had collapsed under the weight of Russian snow. Early Russian churches were also chunkier, with minimal openings near ground level, since for 300 years they also served as strongholds to protect the people against the attacks of the Mongols.

By the 16th century, when the old principality of Moscow was transformed into the Russian empire, a basically simpler plan, with a tall central steeple, had emerged, and over time became increasingly decorative. St Basil's Cathedral, opposite the Kremlin, belongs to this tradition, but it introduced another novel development. The central tower is surrounded by eight, not (as hitherto) four, subsidiary spaces, or chapels. It was built in the 1550s to celebrate the victories of the first tsar, Ivan IV (the Terrible), with additions in the 17th century and later. The eight chapels are dedicated to saints whose anniversaries coincided with the dates of Ivan's victories against the Tatars; each one is independently treated, and the eight domes have different designs. Nevertheless, like a basket of tropical fruit, they achieve a recognizable unity. The effect is exotic, but the original building looked quite different; it was whitewashed, the brilliant colours of the domes added in the 18th century.

154

By the time St Basil's was built, the Renaissance had already reached Russia. When Ivan III had begun to reconstruct the Kremlin at the end of the 15th century, he had relied largely on Italians. But St Basil's was a thoroughly Russian building, built by Russian craftsmen and strongly indebted to traditional wooden architecture, in which Russian architects were expert. St Basil's itself was to inspire many later churches, such as the great Cathedral of the Resurrection in St Petersburg, built in the late 19th century.

Saint Peter's, Rome

The 1,000-year-old St Peter's, then and now the most famous Christian church and the shrine of St Peter, was in need of extensive restoration or rebuilding in the 15th century, as several popes remarked. The energetic and determined Julius II (1503–13) finally embarked on the task, with the clear intent of creating a symbol of the power of the Christian faith and, no less, of the magnificence of the papacy, which would rival the buildings of imperial – and pagan – Rome. The man for the job was at hand in Donato Bramante, who planned a Greek cross with a very large central dome. Work began in 1506 but had not gone far when Bramante died (1514). Several famous artists were subsequently employed, including, briefly, Raphael, who proposed a plan in the form of a Latin cross. Antonio da Sangallo (d. 1546) produced a curious compromise, attempting to combine Greek and Latin crosses. He was succeeded by the septuagenarian Michelangelo, who returned to Bramante's central plan but in a brilliantly modified form that largely overcame the drawbacks of such a plan in catering for elaborate ceremonies and large numbers of people.

Michelangelo also designed the famous dome, the chief splendour of the whole Vatican complex. It was not built until 25 years after his death, by Giacomo della Porta, and is probably slightly different in form. Carlo Maderno, who took over as architect in 1603, faced ecclesiastical pressure for more space, which resulted in his major revision of Michelangelo's design, which abandoned the central plan and created a long nave and an immense façade. The final addition was the

more successful design of the piazza with its elegant curved colonnades created by Bernini in the mid-17th century.

It is not easy to comprehend St Peter's as a unit, and the exterior offers little guide to what lies within, where there appears to be not one but several churches, and the atmosphere changes from one part to another. Under the

soaring dome, the impression is of lightness and delicacy, and the sheer space in the nave permits Baroque adornments that might seem excessive in a lesser building. Among the works of art, most famous are Michelangelo's Pietà, and Bernini's dazzling throne of St Peter, with its brilliant use of light as a sculptural element.

The demands of prestige, requirements of ceremonial, and the profusion of architects, all combined to make St Peter's, as a building, less than harmonious.

*OPPOSITE
The west front.*

The imposing interior of Il Gesù, a church designed for preaching to a large congregation.

Il Gesù, Rome

The Jesuit Church in Rome was begun in 1568, 34 years after the founding of the Society of Jesus by St Ignatius Loyola, who is buried here, and was the spiritual base of the Jesuits, especially during the missions in the New World. It provided a model for many later churches in Europe as well as the Americas, and probably had more influence on church building during the next four centuries than any other.

The builders, both members of the Jesuit order, were Giacomo da Vignola, who was responsible for the plan, and Giacomo della Porta, who took over on Vignola's death in 1573 and designed the façade. The latter was a follower of Michelangelo, and succeeded him as architect of the Capitol and of St Peter's, being partly responsible for the dome. The façade of the Gesù is well proportioned but rather plain and flat, even severe, predating the dynamic Early Baroque rhythms soon to be introduced by Maderno and others.

The design of the interior is more significant. Vignola was the finest architect in Rome on the death of Michelangelo and the first to build a church (the Tempietto di S. Andrea, c. 1550) on an oval plan. The Jesuit church has some affinity with Alberti's S. Andrea in Mantua, 100 years earlier. (Like Alberti, Vignola was the author of an influential text on architecture.) The Gesù had to fulfil special functions. Jesuit preachers attracted huge congregations, and to accommodate them Vignola's plan, basically a Latin cross, provided a short, very wide nave with no aisles but chapels opening directly off it, with shallow transepts and choir. A central dome provided plenty of light and promoted good acoustics, so that everyone should hear.

The interior of Il Gesù was redecorated with no expense spared in the High Baroque style in about 1670, with elaborate gilding and frescoes by the Genoese master of illusionism, Baciccia (Giovanni Battista Gaulli). The ceiling of the nave bears a staggering *trompe l'oeil* painting of Christ overcoming the Devil, Baciccia's greatest work.

Santa Maria della Salute, Venice

Not all the most interesting Italian Baroque churches are in Rome. Baldassare Longhena's votive church of S. Maria della Salute was the response of the city of Venice to its delivery from an epidemic of plague in 1630, *salute* here conveying the double meaning of 'health' and 'salvation'. This is dramatically conveyed by the sculpture group by Giusto le Corti above the high altar, which shows the Virgin Mary as queen of heaven, with a ghastly female figure, representing plague, being driven off by a *putto*. The figure of the Virgin is also prominent in the rich sculptural decoration of the exterior.

The church was begun in 1633 on a spit of land between the Grand Canal and the Canale della Giudecca, a conspicuous though vulnerable site. This picturesque yet dignified building, with its handsome dome and secondary dome over the altar, is one of the most memorable landmarks of Venice. It is built on the plan of an octagon, suggesting the Virgin's crown. The octagon leads into the chancel with its semicircular apses, and the high altar is set in the archway dividing choir from chancel. From the main entrance, the subsidiary altars in the six shallow side chapels are invisible, due to the inclusion (unusual in centrally planned Renaissance churches though found, for instance, in S. Vitale, Ravenna) of an aisle around the octagon. The eye is irresistibly drawn towards the high altar; drawing nearer, the whole interior comes gradually into view. The use of the Corinthian order throughout, with dark grey columns against white walls, gives unity to the main elements.

Although the church shows some Classical restraint, the 'trademark' of Santa Maria della Salute confirms its Baroque sense of movement. This unique feature is the huge *volutes* that circle the dome. Although decorative, they were originally coloured, in contrast to the white limestone of the rest, but have faded; they also have an important functional purpose, helping to distribute the weight of the dome more evenly.

OPPOSITE
The dome of Santa Maria della Salute from across the Canale della Giudecca.

LEFT
The side chapels (one partly obscured to the right) have their own exterior façades, like separate churches. The unique volutes are here clearly visible.

Mexico City Cathedral

Those of Classical sympathies generally regarded the ecclesiastical architecture of Spain and Portugal as degenerate: in the Spanish empire, things were even worse. Today, the novelty and vigour of an architecture that combines traditional Spanish styles with strong local influence, particularly in its riotous sculptural decoration, its sheer invention, and the atmosphere created by the intimacy of worshippers with their saints, are more appreciated.

The cathedral of Mexico City is the largest church in the country, a formidably imposing structure whose dimensions alone are impressive; 387-ft (118-m) long, 177-ft (54-m) wide, the western towers are 203-ft (62-m) high. Standing on the site of an Aztec temple, it dominates the large expanse of the Plaza de la Constitución, or Zócalo. Basically it is a reasonably typical example of the colonial Baroque style associated with (but in various individual ways different from) southern Spain, which was employed in many other Mexican churches. In fact it is, overall, more restrained and less unorthodox than most. It was begun in about 1560, consecrated in 1656, and not finished until the beginning of the 19th century.

Owing to the long time span of construction, it displays many architectural and decorative features of virtually all the styles of Spanish colonial art. Some of the vaulting is Gothic, while each bay of the side aisles is domed. The western façade, with white marble statues posed against the warm brown limestone, is broadly Neoclassical. This is largely the work of an underrated Creole architect, José Ortiz de Castro, in the late 18th century,

Mexico City Cathedral, whose impressive dimensions make it the largest church in the country.

though much of the decorative work, like the dome and lantern, was designed by Manuel Tolsá of Valencia in the early 19th century. The view of the cathedral from the west, enhanced by the open space of the Zócalo, is the most impressive, particularly when floodlit in the evening.

For sheer ornamental abundance, the altarpiece (c.1730) in the Chapel of the Three Kings is unequalled. A central painting of the Adoration is surrounded by a tropical riot of sculpted and gilded ornament, with exuberant use of a favourite Spanish device, the *estípite*, a truncated, vase-like pilaster.

Saint Paul's Cathedral, London

The old St Paul's, the cathedral of London, was a vast Gothic pile nearly 650-ft (200-m) long. It was the most notable casualty of the Fire of London in 1666, when the heat reached such a pitch that the stones of the old church exploded like shells. But the fire, like other disasters, had certain compensations. It created opportunities for rebuilding at a moment when Christopher Wren was available, though his plan to redesign the City fell foul of special interests.

Though Wren's style is nowadays often described as English Baroque, it is very different in spirit from the work of, say, Mansart or Bernini, though he knew, and was not unmoved by both. But Wren's style is essentially academic, moderate, even staid. The famous spires of his City churches are exceptional, and most were probably designed by others, though Wren approved them.

Gothic was currently despised, and Wren's idea for St Paul's was a domed, Classical building on the plan of a Greek cross. The ecclesiastical authorities, wanting more space for processions, demanded a traditional cruciform plan with a long nave. Two plans were rejected, before a compromise was reached, and even that was later altered by Wren, with the connivance of King Charles II; but the plan was basically a Latin cross. With a huge circular space under the dome, the final result could be said to have possessed the best of both worlds. The foundation stone was laid in 1673 and the building was more or less complete by 1711.

St Paul's is often compared with St Peter's, Rome, and there are obvious superficial similarities, but it is an altogether more harmonious building. The division of the west façade into two tiers is very successful, while the dome, with its supporting drum and even the gallery, forced on Wren against his will, is not only a masterpiece of elegance but also of structural engineering, where Wren's true genius lay. The stone lantern is supported by an internal brick cone which is independent of both the inner and outer shells of the dome. Wren employed a team of artists and craftsmen of high calibre, notably the wood carver Grinling Gibbons, who made the choir stalls.

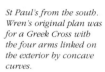

St Paul's from the south. Wren's original plan was for a Greek Cross with the four arms linked on the exterior by concave curves.

RIGHT
Louis XIV's Versailles.

OPPOSITE LEFT
Le Vau opted for low roofs, breaking the hard horizontal of the skyline with statues.

OPPOSITE RIGHT
The north wing, flanking the main approach via the Cour d'Honneur, with the chapel to the right.

Versailles

The palace of Louis XIV, 'the Sun King', at Versailles, is and was meant to be the grandest in Europe. Foreign visitors were first staggered by its sheer size – it could allegedly hold the entire, numerous, French nobility – then overwhelmed by its magnificence. It was a modest château until the 1660s when Louis decided to make it the home of his court, resisting pressure to reside in the Louvre. Here he planned a new citadel to symbolize the eminence of France which was to be manifested in her monarch.

The grounds, described by Saint-Simon as swampy yet waterless, were planned by André Le Nôtre, greatest of the French landscape designers. Vast engineering works were needed to compensate for the drawbacks Saint-Simon mentioned and to supply over 1,000 fountains, which were turned off when the King was absent. Louis Le Vau was responsible for the building, incorporating the existing château. He opted for terraced roofs, breaking up the stark horizontals of the cornice with grand sculpture, but died in 1670. He was succeeded in 1675 by the capable Jules Hardouin-Mansart who, with his team of talented assistants, contributed most

to the building. He vastly extended Le Vau's palace to the north and south and created, under Louis' personal supervision, the royal chapel and the famous Galerie des Glaces (Hall of Mirrors), still the most splendid chamber in the palace, though Louis was compelled to melt down its solid-silver furniture to pay for his wars.

Life at Versailles was grotesquely formal and ritualistic. The unfortunate monarch can never have eaten a hot meal, and the public were admitted, for a fee, to watch him eat, though he could sometimes give private parties for a few cronies in the pavilion of the Grand Trianon. In his depressed later years, Versailles was rather a gloomy place, but it revived under Louis XV, when many rooms were decorated in the lighter, consciously graceful, Rococo style. It was sacked, but not seriously damaged, during the Revolution. Louis-Philippe turned it into a museum full of dull history paintings. Serious restoration began in the 20th century and is ongoing. Much of the glory of the palace in the days of Louis XV and the attractive Mme de Pompadour has been reclaimed, and Versailles is, as intended, an illustrious memorial to the greatness of the French monarchy.

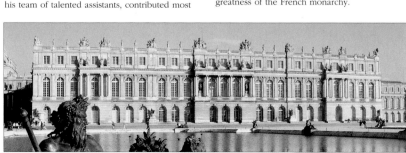

Royal Palace, Amsterdam

What is now the Dutch royal palace in Amsterdam dates from the same period as the Versailles of Louis XIV of France, the huge power that frequently threatened the viability of the little Dutch republic yet, after a Dutch prince had become king of England, came off worse. The symbol of autocratic monarchy in France and the repository of commercial enterprise in Holland are rather different buildings.

Built after the end of the Thirty Years' War in 1648, the Dutch palace was originally Amsterdam's city hall, replacing an earlier building that had burned down. It is a splendid example of Dutch civic architecture in the Classical style, unassertively assured, with minimal Baroque influence. It stands on the west side of the Dam in the heart of the city. Rectangular in plan, it measures about 305 x 245ft (93 x 75m). The architect was Jacob van Campen, the foremost Dutch architect of the period, also responsible for the Mauritshuis in the Hague (1633). The façades are simple and uncluttered and it still looks more like a city hall, though a splendid one, than a palace. However, the pediment is filled with sculpture, representing the Merchant City surrounded by Neptune, tritons and sea nymphs, by Artus Quellin, member of a notable family of Dutch sculptors. The capitals of the pilasters are also decoratively carved, and there are simple swags under the windows. Above the pediment, a tall lantern makes a faintly subversive effort to escape from strict and sober Classicism.

The Dutch were at the height of their mercantile prosperity in the mid-17th century, and everything about this building, from the weather vane in the form of a Dutch cog or trading ship (the badge of the city) to the handsome chimney pieces and the allegorical paintings within, suggests a confident community of wealthy burghers. When Louis Napoleon, brother of Napoleon, became king of Holland, he ordered the city hall's conversion to a royal palace, and it retained that role under the house of Orange.

RIGHT
Detail of the sculpture of the pediment and the lantern.

FAR RIGHT
The palace from across the Dam. Originally the town hall, it was built on boggy ground, supported on over 13,000 piles. To the right is the 15th-century Nieuwe Kerk, where Dutch monarchs are crowned.

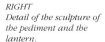

Royal Palace, Turin

The former residence of the kings of Sardinia stands in the centre of Turin. It is a massive building, but its exterior appearance is plain and uninspiring. Inside it is a different matter, for it contains rooms decorated in as luxurious a manner as can be seen almost anywhere else in Europe. It was begun in the mid-17th century, at the beginning of a rich period in Piedmontese art, with Juvarra the outstanding figure; construction continued into the 19th century.

Standing at a distance from the façade, just visible above the roof line is an amazing structure, striking the sort of contrast one might expect if a Martian spaceship landed next to a 1950s office block. This is the dome of the royal chapel, the Capella della S. Sindone where the Turin Shroud is kept, and is the work of Guarino Guarini (1624–83).

Guarini was one of the most imaginative architects of the age, or of any age, beside whom Borromini, whom he admired and borrowed from, seems quite orthodox. He was an intellectual and a well-known mathematician, and his exhilarating but complex designs, with their interlocking spaces, are essentially works of advanced geometry; their appeal is intellectual as well as artistic. Fortunately Guarini's work, which in terms of actual buildings is small, is very well documented, and has fascinated architects of every age since his own. Besides S. Sindone, he is represented by only one church, S. Lorenzo, also in Turin which, though utterly distinctive, has been somewhat spoiled by later additions.

Guarini turned the dome into an object of fantasy. In S. Sindone, the dome is cone-shaped, built up in a series of overlapping segmental arches that decrease in width towards the crown. Filtered light from grids encourages the air of fantasy. Such structures had no obvious precedent in Christian architecture, but something like them appears in certain medieval Spanish churches and is probably of Muslim origin; the vault of the Great Mosque of Cordoba provides suggestive evidence.

The Royal Palace, Turin, formerly the residence of the kings of Sardinia.

Drottningholm Palace

The former summer palace of the Swedish monarchs, on a small island near Stockholm, was inspired, like so many others, by Versailles. Of course it is on a more modest scale, but it is distinctly grand nonetheless, reminding us that Sweden was the major power in northern Europe in the 17th century. The plan of a central block with projecting wings is clearly of French inspiration, and the formal terraced gardens are in the manner of Le Nôtre, but there is evidence of Italian and Dutch influence as well; altogether the palace has a Baroque style of its own.

Construction began on the site of a smaller, earlier building in the 1660s. It was directed by members of three generations of the famous family of statesmen and architects, the Tessins, the original design being the work of Nicodemus Tessin the elder, whose son built the royal palace in Stockholm. The palace contains interesting features, including Gobelin tapestries, fine furniture, a ceremonial staircase with frescoes by D.K. Ehrenstrahl, and a state bedchamber resplendent in blue and gold. There is a delightful Rococo pavilion in Chinese style in the grounds.

But the most interesting part of Drottningholm is the theatre, one of the oldest in Europe. A fire destroyed it in 1762 and the present one dates from 1766. Its most brilliant period was the reign of the theatrically inclined Gustav III (1772–92), himself a dramatist. After him it ceased to function and was used as a store room, which explains how it survived. It was restored to its original state, but with the addition of electric lighting, in the 1920s. It seats over 400, and is still used occasionally.

The 18th-century stage machinery for changing the wings is a unique survival, and still working. Much painted scenery of that time also survives.

Even earlier stage designs can be seen in the museum housed in the royal apartments.

RIGHT
A pavilion in the grounds of Drottningholm Palace.

OPPOSITE
The garden façade of Drottningholm, gleaming brilliant white in the sunshine.

Charlottenburg by night and by day. The unusual dimensions of the drum certainly give it originality.

Charlottenburg

Schloss Charlottenburg stands near the edge of the Spandauer forest about 5 miles (8km) along the Charlottenburger Chaussée from Berlin's Brandenburg Gate. The original building was a country mansion which the Elector, and future king, Friedrich III, a ruler more interested in cultural and courtly affairs than mundane administration, built for his wife, Sophie Charlotte, in about 1690. Its first name was Lietzenburg but when Sophie Charlotte died in the palace in 1705 it was renamed in her memory. The original building was then

enlarged on an E-shaped plan around a large courtyard under a Swedish architect, Johann Friedrich Eosander, who is said to have taken advice from the recently appointed imperial architect in Vienna, the great Fischer von Erlach (1656–1723).

The most striking feature of the building is the dome, which surmounts an unusually high, octagonal drum and is topped by an elaborate lantern and large gilded statue of the goddess Fortuna. Many observers have commented critically on the disproportionate height of the dome, which is slightly exaggerated by the wrought-iron railings that, from a distance, mask much of the ground floor of the comparatively modest central block, but this idiosyncrasy has been sanctified by time. The palace was at its

most splendid in the reign of Friedrich II (Frederick the Great), who was responsible for its magnificent collection of paintings, including masters of the French Rococo such as Boucher and Watteau. Frederick also commissioned the most famous feature of the palace, the Goldene Gallerie, which was carefully photographed as insurance against war damage in 1943, and destroyed in an air raid less than 24 hours later. Later adornments to the park and gardens include the Classical mausoleum by Karl Friedrich Schinkel (1781–1841), and statues of Prussian and German heroes, including a splendid equestrian statue of the Great Elector (father of Friedrich I) by Andreas Schlüter (d. 1714), who, though unsuccessful as an architect, was to Berlin almost what Bernini was to Rome.

Nymphenburg, Munich

The 'castle of the nymphs' on the outskirts of Munich was the summer palace of the Wittelsbach electors, later kings, of Bavaria. Like Versailles, it is essentially a collection of buildings in which some parts are of greater interest than others. The original building, the five-floor central block, was built in 1664 by the Bolognese architect, Agostino Barelli, who introduced the Italian Baroque to southern Germany. In fact it looks vaguely like an Italian villa. The matching blocks on either side, linked by arcaded galleries, were built in the next reign, and the famous gardens were laid out in 1701 by Carbonet, a former pupil of Le Nôtre at Versailles. At about the same time, the original interior was reconstructed to accommodate a great hall three storeys high, for which the arched windows in the façade were installed. The addition of two further buildings on the wings in the mid-18th century, almost matching their neighbours, completed the scheme. The architect chiefly responsible for the final arrangement was Josef Effner, a gardener's son sent to study in Paris by the Elector Max Emanuel.

In the 1720s Effner also built two of the Rococo pavilions in the park, which are more famous than the palace itself. They included the Badenburg, or bath house, more a small swimming pool, and the Pagodenburg, an early example of the taste for 'Chinese' decoration, or chinoiserie. The Magdalenenklause was built about the same time as a kind of hermit's retreat, as a grotto encrusted with stucco seaweed and shellwork.

But the most fascinating of the Nymphenburg's pavilions is the Amalienburg

(1734–39), intended as a hunting lodge. It is the masterpiece of François Cuvilliés, who joined the household of the exiled Elector and returned with him to Munich in 1714 as court dwarf before becoming, with Effner, joint court architect. The Amalienburg is a small building of one storey with a large circular room in the centre. Its vibrant but delicate decoration in gilded stucco and wood seems to float over walls and ceiling. This gem of a building has been described as 'the supreme secular monument of the Rococo'.

Due partly to its longitudinal span, the harmonious assembly of the Nymphenburg is not easily captured in photographs.

171

Schönbrunn, Vienna

Its great size notwithstanding, the Schönbrunn palace is not an intimidating building. That may be due partly to its mellow golden colour, also to the arrangement of the façade, in which the broad wings are brought forward in a welcoming manner. A third reason is the absence of the three imposing domes which the architect, Johann Fischer von Erlach, placed over the main entrance, though their removal plays havoc with the general proportions.

On the outskirts of Vienna, the Schönbrunn was the summer palace of the Habsburgs during roughly the last third of their 600-year reign in Austria. A hunting lodge stood here, where the Emperor Maximilian had his

menagerie in the early 16th century; there is still a zoo, founded in 1752 and one of the oldest in Europe. The house was destroyed during the siege of Vienna by the Turks in 1683, but the Emperor Leopold nevertheless decided to replace it with a palace on a grand scale. Fischer von Erlach was then approaching the height of his fame, but his original design of 1690, which aimed to challenge Versailles, was rejected as too costly even for the Habsburgs. A second plan was put into effect in 1696 and the building was largely completed by 1711. It was subsequently modified somewhat, first by Fischer von Erlach's son, Josef Emanuel, and again by Nikolaus Pacassi, who removed the domes in 1744. Probably its

most famous resident was the Empress Maria Theresa, who spent nearly every summer of her reign (1740–80) here. The palace and grounds were first opened to the public in 1918.

The Schönbrunn contains an alleged 1,440 rooms, most of them of an ornate magnificence striking even by the standards of Austrian Baroque. Among the showpieces are the Great Gallery, with its staggering painted ceiling, huge chandeliers and inlaid floor, the adjoining Hall of Ceremonies, and the sparkling Hall of Mirrors. Smaller rooms, such as the Yellow Drawing Room, are equally splendid in their way and, being on a more human scale, perhaps more attractive to the modern visitor.

Despite its size, the Schönbrunn is not a forbidding building. The sad disappearance of Fischer's domes, however, has not improved its proportions.

Blenheim Palace

Blenheim Palace in Oxfordshire, among the most thoroughly Baroque of English buildings, is a very large and rather pretentious structure designed more as a public statement than a comfortable residence. The means to build it were a gift from a grateful nation to the Duke of Marlborough after his victory over the French at the battle of Blenheim (1704). Although Wren, England's outstanding architect, was at his peak, the Duke chose Sir John Vanbrugh, equally famous as a playwright, to design it, assisted by Nicholas Hawksmoor. Both men had great talent and originality, but did more admirable work elsewhere, Vanbrugh at Castle Howard, Hawksmoor in several London churches.

The plan is of three wings, each with its own internal courtyard, grouped around a larger one and linked by colonnades. The fourth side of the main courtyard was to be filled by a grand entrance front, which was never built. The material is the attractive local stone. Outstanding features are the four bulky towers at the corners of the main block, which hold together the wide and complex spread of buildings, making an impressive sight from a distance, and the arrangement of the entrance where, behind the pediment of the portico, a second, higher pediment appears over the main hall. The skyline is richly arrayed with sculpture by Grinling Gibbons and others, but the formal gardens or *parterre* laid out by Vanbrugh disappeared later in the 18th century when the park was redesigned in the English manner by Lancelot 'Capability' Brown (1716–83). The interior, though grand, is not particularly memorable. The large saloon has frescoes by

Louis Laguerre, one example of the employment of French talent in spite of the context of the structure, and the most attractive room is the Long Library, or gallery.

The project was not entirely a happy one.

The funds proved insufficient and the Marlboroughs were themselves left with substantial bills. Vanbrugh retired in high dudgeon after quarrels with the Duchess, and Hawksmoor was apparently never paid in full.

Blenheim Palace was the birthplace of Winston Churchill, descendant and biographer of the 1st Duke of Marlborough.

The Belvedere, Vienna

It is amusing to go from Blenheim Palace, where guides may mention a loyal ally and subordinate commander of the Duke of Marlborough called Eugene of Savoy, to the Belvedere, residence of Prince Eugene, where the guides are vaguely aware that in his victories over the French the great imperial general had some assistance from an English milord.

The Belvedere is two fine but different Baroque palaces, the unpretentious Lower Belvedere, completed in 1715, where Eugene actually lived, and the Upper Belvedere, completed in 1723, a magnificent showpiece used on festive occasions. The architect was Lukas von Hildebrandt, who had fought in Prince Eugene's army and was the greatest Austrian Baroque architect after Fischer von Erlach, whom he succeeded (1723) as chief architect to the court. Hildebrandt was more Italian than German, having studied in Italy, and the influence of Borromini is evident in the Belvedere, which has been described as 'a rare blend of Teutonic solidity and Mediterranean caprice'. The interior of the Upper Belvedere is a dazzling assemblage in marble, gold and inlaid wood, created by a team of architects gathered by Hildebrandt. Like most Baroque architects, Hildebrandt rubbed his hands when he came to designing a staircase, which was treated as an individual work of art. In the Upper Belvedere, *putti* play around the almost Rococo lamps and vaguely Michelangelesque *atlantes* appear to support the vault and also appear elsewhere. The white marble marvellously lightens the whole structure, which has similarities with an even more attractive

staircase (1711) at Pommersfelden in Bavaria, which Hildebrandt placed within a spacious hall with three tiers of galleries.

The Belvedere later passed to the Habsburgs: Marie Antoinette left from here on her way to become queen of France. The composer Bruckner lived in the caretaker's

lodgings in his last years, and it was the home of the Archduke Franz Ferdinand, assassinated in Sarajevo in 1914. Today it contains the Austrian Gallery (modern art). Medieval Austrian art can be seen in the orangery of the Lower Belvedere.

The Belvedere is perhaps the finest example of the Italian-influenced yet thoroughly Austrian style.

Superga, Turin

Filippo Juvarra (1678–1736) is often seen as the successor to Guarino Guarini in the context of north Italian Baroque, but, although both were based in the same country and both were gifted with extraordinary imagination, otherwise they have relatively little in common. Juvarra, who came from a family of silversmiths and was trained in Rome under Carlo Fontana, was invited to Turin by Victor Amadeus II of Savoy

The Superga, Juvarra's ecclesiastical masterpiece, combines church and monastery in a single unit.

in 1714, over 30 years after Guarini's death. He remained there for 20 years, although he also worked on commissions elsewhere. He spent a year in Portugal, was more briefly in London and Paris, and died in Madrid where he was building a royal palace for Philip V.

Juvarra began his professional career as a stage-designer and continued to carry out work in furniture design and other fields. Nonetheless, as an architect he was hugely

prolific. In the area of Turin he built five large churches, at least eight palaces, besides numerous villas, and redesigned substantial sections of the city itself. His greatest secular work and most original building is the Stupinigi, officially a hunting lodge, in reality a magnificent palace, which balances Juvarra's gift for exciting theatrical design with the restrained Classicism that he learned in Rome.

Juvarra's ecclesiastical masterpiece is the Superga (begun 1716), one of the grandest of all Italian Baroque churches, which stands on a marvellous hilltop site dominating Turin, an indication of Juvarra's keen eye for topographical advantage. Juvarra was thoroughly eclectic, his work gives little sense of a coherent stylistic development, and a notable feature of the Superga is that, besides exploiting many aspects of Italian architecture, it also demonstrates more northerly influences. It is often compared with the great Austrian abbey of Melk (built a decade earlier), and echoes the way in which the body of the church is subsumed in the buildings of the monastery. The church protrudes beyond flanking towers, with a high, elegant dome soaring above the low monastic building, fronted by a grand Classical portico suggestive of the Pantheon in Rome. The commanding position is enhanced by the podium on which it stands, reached by steps on three sides. Inside, Juvarra's sure-footed and sophisticated design is marked by the skilful way in which he handles the transition from octagonal drum to round dome, and the achievement of a simple, spacious, integrated, two-storey structure. As always, he was assisted by some of the most gifted artists and craftsmen in Italy.

Royal Palace, Stockholm

In the middle of the 17th century, Sweden was a great power, and clearly the royal house of Vasa required something more impressive than the ramshackle old castle that then occupied the site of the royal palace, or *slot*, on Stads Island in the heart of Stockholm. A plan to enlarge and extend the castle was put into effect, but in 1694 the whole building was destroyed by fire; the body of King Charles XI, who had just died, was barely rescued from the flames.

There was not much doubt who would design the new palace. Nicodemus Tessin the Younger (1654–1728) had succeeded his father and namesake as Stockholm city architect, and completed his father's work at Drottningholm before moving to France, where he hoped to gain employment from Louis XIV at Versailles or the Louvre. Disappointed, he returned to Stockholm to undertake his finest achievement, and create what has been called the finest monument to French art outside France.

It is a very large, grand, block-like and unbending building with extended wings which, although it certainly manifests a French heritage, also appears to owe something to the *palazzi* of Renaissance Rome. The interior is more thoroughly, and lavishly, French of the Louis Quinze period, and is largely the work of French artists and craftsmen who would be better known had they worked in Paris. Some of the tapestries were designed by Boucher, and imported direct.

Construction did not go smoothly. On the throne from 1697 was Charles XII, the Swedish meteor, who apart from being hostile to everything French, had no money to spare outside his sensational military campaigns. The statues that were meant to decorate the pediment in the manner of Versailles were among the casualties; they would have made the façade less stark. Work petered out entirely after Charles's defeat at Poltava (1709) and was not resumed until after Tessin's death. Subsequent directors of the works were French-trained, and the building was largely completed by 1754, though it has been altered since.

The Royal Palace, detail of the south façade.

St Nicholas is a grand church, skilfully fitted to the cramped and uneven site.

RIGHT
The dome and drum.

OPPOSITE LEFT
Detail of the bell tower.

OPPOSITE RIGHT
Detail of the west front.

Saint Nicholas, Prague

The church of St Nicholas and the Jesuit College in Prague, in the Malá Strana or Lesser Town between the castle and the river, is the finest of all Bohemian Baroque churches. Like others, it owes much to the Italian Baroque of Borromini and especially Guarini. The Jesuits decided to rebuild their Gothic church at the end of the 17th century and the first period of construction lasted from 1703 to 1711. The architect was Christoph Dientzenhofer (1655–1722), a member of the second generation of a famous Bavarian family, settled in Prague. He completed the west façade and much of the nave before work was interrupted, no doubt by money problems. Work resumed in 1737 under Christoph's famous son, Kilian Ignac, who was responsible for the mighty dome and drum and the adjacent tower that dominates the Malá Strana, likened by the irreverent to a fat lady dancing with a thin man. The structure was largely completed by 1755, after Kilian Ignac's death. The reason for building from west to east was to preserve the Gothic sanctuary until the last moment.

Even by the standards of the Late Baroque, this is one of the most dramatic of churches, largely the result of the striking colour scheme of pink, green and cream and the flowing, rhythmic quality characteristic of the whole building. The walls almost disappear in the wealth of galleries, balconies, niches and doorways. There is no insistent point of focus, but the eye is drawn to the fabulous Rococo pulpit by the Prachners, a local workshop, the immense, almost threatening figures of Church Fathers, and the massive high altar with the figure of St Nicholas, a popular church patron

in Prague. Above, the dome over the choir is, in contrast, restrained and ethereal, while in the nave Johann Lukas Kracker's huge illusionist fresco of the Life of St Nicholas, painted in the 1760s (with a self-portrait in one corner), has been described as 'one of the finest expressions of Baroque monumental painting north of the Alps'.

The decoration was only completed in 1775, just two years before the Jesuit Order was, temporarily, dissolved.

BAROQUE TO REVIVALISM

CHAPTER FIVE

The Residenz, Würzburg

Royal Palace, Madrid

Royal Palace of Caserta, Naples

Vierzehnheiligen

Ottobeuren

Die Wies

Sans Souci

Royal Palace, Aranjuez

Royal Palace, Queluz

Spanish Steps, Rome

Tsarskoe Selo, St Petersburg

Winter Palace, St Petersburg

Monticello, Virginia

Syon House, Middlesex

Four Courts, Dublin

Strawberry Hill, Middlesex

Brighton Pavilion

Ducal Palace, Weimar

Iron Bridge, Coalbrookdale

Malmaison

Buckingham Palace

Houses of Parliament, Westminster

Royal Palace, Corfu

Trinity Church, Wall Street

United States Capitol, Washington, DC

Forth Railway Bridge, Edinburgh

Eiffel Tower

Arc de Triomphe, Paris

Washington Monument

Saint Pancras Station, London

Schloss Linderhof

Herrenchiemsee

Sacré Coeur, Paris

Glasgow School of Art

Sagrada Familia, Barcelona

Post Office Savings Bank, Vienna

Secession Building, Vienna

The origins of Baroque were associated with the Catholic revival of the early 17th century and it always tended to be strongest in Catholic regions. Late Baroque grew self-consciously decorative and spawned the Rococo, essentially a decorative style and related to Baroque, much as Mannerism was related to Renaissance Classicism. It seemed a secular, even frivolous style, yet the finest examples of Rococo are to be found among the Late Baroque churches and abbeys of south Germany, notable examples being Ottobeuren and Die Wies.

When it became clear that Baroque and Rococo had nowhere else to go, the result was a revival of Classicism. In some countries, such as England and France, Classicism had never really gone away, but the Neoclassicism of the 18th century was different from the Classicism of the Renaissance. Knowledge had advanced, ancient Roman sites were now the target of upper-class tourists as well as artists, and techniques and building methods had also improved. However, Neoclassicism was also a revival of the Renaissance style: the designs of Palladio were especially influential in 18th-century England and the USA. The Classical style proved adaptable to all sorts of buildings, not only churches and civic buildings, but structures that had no parallel in Classical times.

As a counter to Classicism, other divergent styles emerged towards the end of the 18th century, including the English 'Picturesque', which embraced exotica like the Brighton Pavilion and the monumental Gothic house of Fonthill. Developments in the 19th century were largely dictated by social and economic changes, which required new types of building (hospitals, hotels, factories) and by the new materials and techniques made available by the Industrial Revolution. A dramatic example was the Chicago School and the rise of the skyscraper. Meanwhile, historical styles flourished. The Greek Revival reflected increasing knowledge and the results of archaeological research; previously, Classicism had been predominantly based on Roman models. The Gothic Revival was strongest in England where, besides being adapted to new types of structure, it came to be the only acceptable style for churches. But virtually every historical style, from Ancient Egyptian to Neo-Baroque, cropped up somewhere, and some models were drawn from non-European sources. Architects were sometimes faithful to the original sources, sometimes not, and quite often two or more disparate styles mingled in the same building, in which case the result was not always dreadful: the Houses of Parliament in London mixed Classical planning with Gothic decoration to achieve a very satisfactory result.

Innovations derived from new materials, particularly iron (later steel) and glass, were perhaps the most interesting aspect of 19th-century developments, but towards the end of the century a reaction against 'historicism' appeared, influenced by movements such as the Arts and Crafts movement in England and the Werkbund in Germany, in the styles known generically as Art Nouveau. Initially a purely decorative style, Art Nouveau, coloured by differing national and political ideas, proved significant for architecture also.

The Residenz, Würzburg

The early 18th century was a fertile period for building, both religious and secular, in the German lands. A religious revival in the Roman Catholic Church prompted the building of new pilgrimage churches such as Vierzehnheiligen. The wealthy rulers of Germany's numerous principalities competed to build the richest palaces, resulting, as Ian Sutton puts it, in buildings 'that can still astonish by their scale, verve and vitality'. Perhaps the finest secular building in the Baroque style in Germany was the palace of the prince-bishops of Würzburg, begun in 1720.

The splendour of the Würzburg Residenz rests on the work of many people, but chief among them are the architect Balthasar Neumann (1687–1753) and the painter Giambattista Tiepolo (1696–1770). The Czech-born Neumann was a comparative tyro in 1720, so the Prince-Bishop consulted other experts besides his protégé, including Hildebrandt and the Frenchmen de Cotte and Boffrand, who are presumably responsible for the strong flavour of the Rococo at Würzburg. Neumann was an architect of catholic sympathies who seems to have benefited from these influences. He was to gain fame for his new and complex ways of handling space, and the most magnificent feature of Würzburg, the ceremonial staircase, is probably entirely his work.

The structure was completed by 1744, and the decoration of the interior was carefully considered. Unlike Neumann in 1720, Tiepolo in the 1740s was already at the height of his fame, and correspondingly expensive. However, the resources of the Prince-Bishop were considerable, and the great Venetian painter

arrived, together with his two sons, late in 1750. Within three years he had completed the decoration of the Great Hall and the vault of the staircase, where the theme chosen was the Four Continents; some of the sculptures in the gardens amusingly parody Tiepolo's figures. The Kaisersaal or Great Hall has historical scenes, not always particularly relevant to the Würzburg rulers, and comprises a brilliant display of the Baroque artists' combination of frescoes (Tiepolo), stucco (Antonio Bossi) and architecture (Neumann). Tiepolo's brilliant exploitation of light, his magical, fizzing colours, and his ever-fertile imagination were never more splendidly displayed than at Würzburg.

The Residenz, Würzburg, represents the work of the architect Balthasar Neumann and the painter Giambattista Tiepolo, among others.

Royal Palace, Madrid

Although there was a walled town here under Muslim rule in the 10th century, Madrid is comparatively new and comparatively small – more a *villa* (town) than a *ciudad* (city) – as the capital of a major European country. Although several earlier kings of Castile spent some time here, and the Emperor Charles V (Carlos I) found its dry air and high altitude, 2,100ft (640m) above sea level, assuaged his gout, it was not until 1561 that Charles's son, Philip II, moved his court there, and it did not become the official capital until 1607.

The grand and costly Buen Retiro palace was built in the 1630s, rather too quickly, it seems, as the cost of maintenance proved intolerable, and nothing now survives except the park. The original Palacio Real in Madrid was badly damaged by a fire at Christmas time in 1734, and Philip V decided to build a completely new palace in closer accord with Bourbon tastes. A scheme was drawn up by the great Juvarra, chiefly active in Turin where he built the famous Stupinigi and the Superga, but he died a few months after he arrived in Madrid and the building was completed by his former pupil, Giovanni Battista (Juan Bautista) Sacchetti. He enlarged the building and made considerable alterations, deriving to some extent from Bernini's plans for the Louvre in Paris, but the palace is really Sacchetti's work. He also planned the immediate environment of the palace. The huge ceilings were painted by Tiepolo, who spent his last years in Madrid.

It is an impressive, powerful edifice, its great height partly the effect of a sloping site; it is built of a whitish granite that resembles marble. In style it belongs rather to the North Italian Baroque than to any Spanish tradition. Notable among the contents is the library of ancient books and manuscripts. Huge statues of Spanish monarchs were commissioned to stand on the balustrade, but when the time came to erect them, nerves failed, and they were positioned more safely at ground level, around the Plaza de Oriente, created by clearing about 60 buildings, including several religious houses.

OPPOSITE
The elevated site adds a sense of grandeur to the palace.

LEFT
The façade from the Campo del Moro.

Royal Palace of Caserta, Naples

Caserta, north of Naples, is one of those monumental royal palaces that aimed to challenge Versailles. It was built for Charles III of Naples, a great-grandson of Louis XIV. The architect was Luigi Vanvitelli (1700–73), born in Naples of Dutch descent, who had studied with Juvarra and earned a reputation in Rome before returning to his birthplace in response to a royal summons in 1751.

The palace consists of a rectangular block 492 x 623ft (150 x 190m), with four internal courtyards. It is larger even than the Escorial, and the great length of almost uninterrupted façade is slightly depressing. Vanvitelli's original plan, which included towers at the corners and a central dome on a high drum, might have been more attractive but, though somewhat smaller, it was judged too costly.

This is almost the last major building in the Italian Baroque style, and the plain, repetitive exterior already signals the revival of Classicism. Inside there is more evidence of Baroque energy and panache, notably in Vanvitelli's theatre and the great double staircase. There are one or two Rococo rooms, like the Queen's Bathroom, but the state apartments, which are now open to the public, date from much later and, except for the magnificent Throne Room of 1845, are relatively severe. The palace was to be linked with Naples by an avenue 19-miles (30-km) long. The park was designed to be even larger than it is now, with a watercourse and a variety of fountains supplied by an aqueduct 25-miles (40-km) long and with elaborate sculptural groups such as Diana and Actaeon dotted about the sward.

Caserta was conceived as a challenge to Versailles, and though it did not compare is was certainly vast.

In the end, perhaps the most remarkable thing about Caserta is its sheer size. It is said to be possible to walk around it all day without passing the same spot twice. This vastness is the more staggering when one remembers over what a wretchedly poor country the preposterous Bourbon kings of Naples reigned.

Vierzehnheiligen

In the wake of the Counter-Reformation, religious architecture in central Europe in the Baroque period reached a peak only previously equalled in the late medieval centuries and never since. The sheer size of such buildings as the abbey of Melk, commanding the Danube valley west of Vienna, is staggering, and raises problems for conservation in a secular age. In almost every church, it seems, there is a creative striving for something unique in the handling of space and form.

Vierzehnheiligen ('Fourteen saints'), on the River Main in Bavaria, is a pilgrimage church, the site of a miraculous vision in 1445, and which incorporates the shrine. The decision to replace the Gothic chapel with a sensationally grand Baroque church was taken in 1730, but there was a quarrel over who should design it. The bishop of Bamberg, who eventually won, was a Schönborn and therefore an admirer of Balthasar Neumann, to whom the commission was transferred in 1743. Besides the shrine, Neumann also had to adapt to work done by his predecessors.

Neumann is sometimes called an 'architect's architect': his work seems light-hearted, easy, almost instinctive, but was based on extraordinarily careful and complex planning. The connection often made between German Baroque architecture and the music of Bach is particularly apt in Neumann's case.

From the outside, Vierzehnheiligen is largely a building of straight lines; the lofty, twin-towered west façade, though articulated with the Classical Orders, is undeniably Gothic in shape; moreover the basic plan is a Latin cross and there are other debts to the still

unfashionable Gothic tradition. However, the interior is designed on the basis of intersecting circles and ovals, and there is not a straight line to be seen – even the columns are concave. The emphasis is cunningly diverted away from the crossing towards the shrine in the nave by innovatory handling of vaulting and light sources. The Rococo decoration employs columns of coloured *scagliola* (versatile, plaster-based material resembling marble) and sparkling stucco work. The church was not finished until the 1770s, after the death of Neumann and of his former pupil, Jacob Küchel, who succeeded him and was largely responsible for the interior. It was struck by lighting in 1838 and has been restored more than once.

The exterior of Ottobeuren (opposite) is plain, though assured. However, the Rococo interior is somewhat different. Here, Fischer overcame the slightly cramped effect evident in his other building, Zwiefalten.

Ottobeuren

In the early 18th century plasterers enjoyed an unprecedented demand for their services. A vast amount of sculpture was required in the grand new churches springing up in such numbers in southern Germany, and increasingly it was in plaster rather than marble, partly because plaster was much cheaper, partly because it was better suited to the flying draperies and flamboyant poises of Rococo decoration. Sculptors were displeased, and a compromise was arranged (1725) in which for independent sculptures the plasterer had to follow models provided by a sculptor. This seems to have worked well at Ottobeuren, where J.M. Feichtmayr followed models by the sculptor J.J. Christian.

The abbey of Ottobeuren, just south-east of Memmingen in Bavaria, was originally founded in the 8th century. The decision was taken to rebuild the church in about 1730, but the abbey's masons did not give satisfaction and in 1744 Johann Michael Fischer (1692–1766) was called in. Fischer, born in Bavaria, had served his apprenticeship in Bohemia and knew the Dientzenhofers. Although highly gifted, he is considered to be not quite in the same class as Hildebrandt and Neumann, perhaps partly because he was so prolific: he is said to have designed no less than 22 abbeys and 32 churches. His appointment to Ottobeuren followed his work at the abbey of Zwiefalten, though in plan that church, where Fischer had to follow the medieval foundations, is very different.

Ottobeuren has been decribed by James Lees-Milne as 'probably the noblest of all 18th-century German churches'. Here too Fischer was limited by pre-existing foundations, but he altered the design of the interior by increasing the size and significance of the central piers and emphasized the diagonal axes with additional altars. It is an enormous building, with a soaring façade, but is most renowned for its breathtaking decoration. The gorgeous Rococo decorative scheme creates an effervescent riot of coloured *scagliola* (columns in pale-grey and pink), frescoes (by J.J. Zeiller), and plasterwork, all on a dazzlingly white, gold-banded background, in which structural elements seem almost to dissolve.

Die Wies

Whereas J.M. Fischer concentrated on abbeys, the speciality of Dominikus Zimmermann (1685–1766) was pilgrimage churches of which Die Wies is his finest. Zimmermann was originally a plasterer, often working with his brother, Johann Baptist (1680–1758), who became a painter around the age of 50 and was so successful that he was called in to help Cuvilliés at Nymphenburg. The most thoroughly Rococo of south German architects, he established his style at another pilgrimage church, Steinhausen (begun 1727), not far away, which appears rectangular from the outside but inside turns out to be oval, like Die Wies. Such a plan is convenient for circulating pilgrims.

Zimmermann was of peasant stock and appropriately Die Wies (begun in 1745) was built not for some princely bishop or wealthy abbot but for ordinary people. The name means 'the meadow', and the church even today stands isolated among fields. It originated in events that illustrate the deep piety of the times, a piety that Zimmermann shared. For this was not, as was most common, a medieval shrine; in fact the miracle that attracted pilgrims to the little chapel that preceded Zimmermann's church had occurred as recently as 1738. It involved a crude wooden figure of Christ, painted a horrible green, which had been seen to weep tears; the money for the church was raised in a few years entirely from the offerings of devoted pilgrims.

At Die Wies, Zimmermann combines the spacious oval of the 'nave' (customary terms are not so appropriate for Baroque churches), circled by a wide ambulatory for pilgrims, with a rectangular 'choir'. The dominant colours are white and gold, with carved wooden figures and paintings, including Johann Baptist's spectacular vault frescoes, red *scagliola* columns around the high altar, bright blue ones at the opposite end, unusually grouped in pairs, and windows of disparate shapes that admit plenty of light. Colours and motifs are symbolic, their meaning not always obvious in a less religious age. Because the church was based on a solid wooden frame, Zimmermann did not have to worry much about structural restrictions and was free to exploit to the full the freedom of Rococo decoration.

OPPOSITE
The Church of Die Wies retains its isolation in the fields. The tower is attached to the choir, and the clergy houses are to the left.

BELOW LEFT
The vault fresco of Johann Baptist Zimmermann.

BELOW
Detail of the interior.

Sans Souci

Sans Souci is the North German equivalent of
the Amalienburg, and this fanciful summer
palace of the cultured Frederick the Great of
Prussia, who personally sketched at least the
general design, seems a little unexpected in a
stern, northern, Protestant land. It is a one-
storey building with a low central dome but,
because of its hilltop site in Potsdam, it
commands a fine view from the floor-length
windows. Again like the Amalienburg, it is only
one element in a large complex, though not so
large as the more conventional Neues Palais,
also built by Frederick, and set among a variety
of smaller structures, some contemporary some
later. These include some surprises, such as the
whimsical fantasy of the 'Chinese' pavilion, with
columns in the form of palm trees.

Sans Souci was built by Georg Wenceslaus
von Knöbelsdorff (1699–1753), Frederick's court
architect and close friend, and a man of
similarly cultured and eclectic tastes. He was
also responsible for the most intensely Rococo
additions to Charlottenburg in the 1740s, and for
the Classical Berlin Opera House. He began
work on Sans Souci in 1745 but in the following
year quarrelled with the king over the designs,
with the result that he was dismissed from his
post and never produced another building.

Apart from some slightly obtrusive
sculpture, the exterior is attractive and inviting
but not especially striking, so that the brilliant
Rococo decoration of the rooms beyond comes
as something of a surprise. The little library, the

music room, the so-called Voltaire room, display
an unparalleled fantasy of ornament, employing
almost every conceivable material. Delicate leafy
and gilded forms by Johann August Nahl and
others clamber over door panels, around
windows and asymmetrical frames and mirrors,
and across walls and ceilings. It sounds too
much, but the German craftsmen did not
overstep the bounds of good taste. The effect is
undeniably stagy, but not vulgar.

The King's bedchamber and sitting room,
completed after his death in 1786, is in
Neoclassical style, suggesting that in his later
years Frederick was abandoning the French
frivolities of the Rococo in favour of a more
austere style. The armchair in which he died is
still here.

It is easy to sympathize with Philip II's fondness for Aranjuez, after the rigorous formalities of the Escorial.

Royal Palace, Aranjuez

In spite of the magnificent façade of Santiago de Compostela, architectural historians hesitate to describe the style of Spain or Portugal in the 17th–18th centuries as 'Baroque'. Although there are obvious similarities, such as the love of ingenious and spectacular effects, there is no real affinity with the principles of Bernini and Borromini. The ultra-decorative, specifically Spanish 'Baroque' style is often called Churrigueresque, after the Churriguera family of sculptors-architects from Barcelona.

The palace of Aranjuez is on the River Tagus about 30-miles (50-km) south of Madrid. Superficially, it appears pleasingly uniform, though as so often is the case, its history is more complicated. There was a castle on the site in the Middle Ages, held by the Knights of Santiago, a military order active in reconquering Spain from the Muslims. It passed into royal possession around the end of the 15th century, and Carlos I (the Emperor Charles V) converted it into a hunting lodge. Under Philip II it grew into a palace, built by those who had worked on the Escorial, though here they were in lighter mood. It was subsequently seriously damaged by fire, and the present building largely dates from the reconstruction for Ferdinand VI by an Italian architect, Santiago Bonavia, in the mid-18th century.

The long low buildings around a large courtyard, only two storeys high except for the central main block, were built over a longish period. The wings, with terraced roofs and galleries, were completed after Bonavia's time but followed his subdued Rococo style quite faithfully. The main block consists of three units, with shallow domes at the corners that suggest the influence of Juvarra. Topped by lanterns and placed on drums pierced with circular windows, they augment the general air of quiet distinction. The interior is more of a mixture, and besides many treasures it contains some odd features such as the pseudo-Moorish smoking room in over-bright colours that was added in the 19th century. Of greater interest is the dazzling porcelain room, with tiles and mirrors from the Buen Retiro factory near Madrid.

Royal Palace, Queluz

The palace of Queluz, north of Lisbon on the road to Sintra, was begun in 1747, and much of it was completed by 1752. This attractive Rococo residence, one of the few royal palaces one would like to live in, was designed for a younger son of the Portuguese royal family and was financed out of the profits of the gold and diamonds produced by Brazil. Although not finished at the time of the great Lisbon earthquake of 1755, it suffered comparatively little. It was badly damaged by fire in the 1930s but subsequently restored.

The palace itself, set amid flower gardens, is the masterpiece of a Portuguese architect, Mateus Vicente de Oliveira (1710–60), and has an unpretentious charm and a sense of easy assurance. The stucco of the walls is pink, with white stonework and lime-green windows and doors. Among the main rooms is the Sala des Mangas, with panels of *azulejos* (decorative tiles) in the 'Chinese' manner covering most of the walls, predominantly in blue and gold. The Hall of Mirrors glitters with glass and gilt. In the Ball Room, also with shimmering chandeliers, the Rococo decoration is most lavish, and the room is planned on an elliptical oval.

Other architects and designers, including a Frenchman, Jean Baptiste Robillon, were engaged on other buildings and features of the gardens which augment Oliveira's perfectly proportioned central block. Robillon planned the hanging gardens; the extensive topiary was the work of a Dutchman, Gerald van den Kolk, and the lead statues, a fashion also stemming from the Netherlands, were by an Englishman, John Cheeve. The extraordinary little western pavilion, reached by the dramatic Lion's Steps, is by Robillon. From a staid Classical colonnade, Rococo statuary breaks into a riot against the sky. The eastern pavilion, with its scrolled pediments, is also interesting, but its designer is unknown.

The Palace of Queluz combines fine proportions with exuberant decoration.

The Spanish Steps are usually submerged beneath a sea of tourists.

Spanish Steps, Rome

In Rome, by about 1700, though palaces were still being built, there was increasing emphasis on public projects, as if to turn the whole city into a Baroque monument.

Except in Venice, Rococo did not make much impact in Italy, least of all in Rome, where it was simply too far removed from the honoured principles of Classicism. However, traces of the Rococo did appear here and there, not only in the window frames of 18th-century palaces, but also in some public monuments, such as the Trevi Fountain and the Spanish Steps, which are based on flowing Rococo curves.

In the 16th century, the only way to climb the steep slope between the Piazza di Spagna, where Bernini would later build a fountain, to the church of S. Trinità dei Monti was by a treacherous footpath (the Spanish Steps would provide firm footing but not safety from thieves and bandits). The long delay before the project was realized was largely the result of a territorial dispute between the pope and the French embassy. Compromise was eventually reached, and the French provided money for construction, hence the presence of the French *fleur-de-lis* on the Steps, though they were named after the nearby Spanish embassy.

The Steps, built in 1723–25, were designed by Francesco de Sanctis (1693–1740), who is otherwise little known. This huge and fabulous monument, which has featured so often in literature (the poet Keats died in a room overlooking it), achieves one of the objectives of Rococo by provoking surprise in the viewer, at first at the sheer scale, then by the diverging curves of steps and balustrades. Walking up,

wrote Michael Kitson, 'it is as if the architecture has taken charge, controlling one's movements in ways that are hard to resist or understand yet are gentle enough to be delightful rather than disturbing.'

Tsarskoe Selo, St Petersburg

Bartolomeo Francesco Rastrelli (1700–71) was the leading architect of the Late Baroque/Rococo period in Russia. Though Italian by birth, he trained in Paris and his style is thoroughly French, which suited the cultural aspirations of the Russian aristocracy, though with a few traces of Russian influence. He arrived in St Petersburg in 1716 as an assistant to Jean-Baptiste le Blond, builder of the massive Peterhof, and was appointed court architect to the Tsarina Elizabeth Petrovna in 1741. He was responsible for many buildings, including the Smolny Convent in St Petersburg, the style of which has been described as 'Russo-Rococo'; but the most successful were the Great Palace of Tsarskoe Selo, 'village of the tsar', later called Pushkin, which became the favourite residence of Catherine the Great, and the Winter Palace. Paradoxically, Rastrelli, remembered for enormous buildings which required so many labourers that the workforce was partly recruited from the army, was at his happiest working on a small scale.

The Great Palace, started in 1749, was built around a colossal quadrangle, and is only slightly smaller than the Winter Palace. The main façade is about 330-ft (100-m) long, and is highly decorative in blue, white and gold, with a powerful, rhythmical arrangement of columns, pilasters, balustrades, balconies, *atlantes* and broken pediments. Few of Rastrelli's interiors survive today, though his delicate little pavilions still grace the grounds.

Under Catherine the Great, considerable alterations were made by the Scottish architect, Charles Cameron (d. 1812), trained in Rome, who arrived in Russia in 1774. He was an admirer of his countryman, Robert Adam, though his own brand of Neoclassicism is less delicate and refined, the plasterwork more elaborate. His interiors at Pushkin are possibly his finest work. He employed rich but delicate materials, the colours mostly pale, pastel shades, with much use of glass and, in some rooms, inlaid Wedgwood plaques specially commissioned from the famous English pottery. Some further changes took place in the 19th century, but they were insignificant compared with the disasters of the Second World War, when St Petersburg was besieged for 900 days and the palace suffered looting as well as fires. It was splendidly restored after the war by the Communist regime.

The effect of the exterior of Tsarkoe Selo is like a highly decorated Rococo version of Versailles.

Winter Palace, St Petersburg

When Peter the Great founded his new capital to give Russia a 'window on Europe', a royal palace was built on the bank of the mighty River Neva. This building was soon replaced, and the Winter Palace (now the Hermitage Museum) that now occupies the site is the result of several later reconstructions of which the most important is that of 1754, by Bartolomeo Rastrelli for the Tsarina Elizabeth. Rastrelli was still involved with Tsarskoe Selo, begun five years earlier, and the two palaces have much in common, besides sheer size.

Rastrelli was remarkably successful both in overcoming planning restrictions and in avoiding monotony. To fit in with the rest of the city he was limited to a maximum height of 65ft (20m). The length, however, is nearly 495ft (150m) on the longer sides. He avoided the monotony of, for instance, the palace of Caserta, by designing a highly ornamental exterior that is broken up by pairs of columns and alternating projections and recessions. The colour scheme, similar to Tsarskoe Selo, is white, greenish-blue and gold, although it seems that Rastrelli originally specified orange and white; during the 19th century, the palace was painted a darker, reddish colour. Work on the interior continued throughout the reign of Catherine the Great and beyond, especially after a fire in the 1830s. As a result, Rastrelli's Rococo interiors have mostly disappeared, although the state rooms have been restored, with gorgeous velvets and marbles, to something like their original appearance; his grand double staircase remains as testimony to his theatrical style.

Besides war, one event that might have been expected to cause serious damage was the coup d'état of the Bolsheviks against the Kerensky government, in the Winter Palace, in 1917. The palace was defended by a handful of army cadets, a women's battalion, and a few half-hearted Cossacks. They were no match for Trotsky's Military Revolutionary Committee, backed by the guns of the cruiser *Aurora* in the Neva, and the Revolution was almost bloodless.

Rastrelli, who went to Russia as a youth, had studied in Paris, and the distinctive, graceful, Rococo style he brought to the Winter Palace was more French than anything else.

OPPOSITE
Today tourist boats, not warships, cruise the Neva.

Thomas Jefferson was largely responsible for the adoption of Neoclassicism as more or less the official style of the USA. It was familiar, yet not too English (i.e. not Georgian, an impossible term in view of recent events). His own Palladian villa, Monticello, was the most distinguished of the colonnaded mansions of eminent American gentlemen.

Monticello, Virginia

Appropriately, the Classical revival of the 18th century took strongest root in the USA, perhaps because it was associated with republican virtues, and it became virtually the only acceptable style for great public buildings. Leadership in this respect, as in others, came from Thomas Jefferson, author of the Declaration of Independence, Enlightenment polymath and third president of the USA. He deserves the credit for establishing what became in effect a national style that lent great distinction to simple domestic architecture – the 'clapboard classicism' of New England and elsewhere.

Jefferson, the son of a landowner who was also a trained civil engineer, took architecture very seriously, was genuinely gifted, and would collect much the biggest library of architectural books in the country. Inheriting a large estate east of the Blue Mountains near Charlottesville, Virginia, he built his own house, Monticello, on a carefully chosen, elevated site. Though begun in 1770, the basic plan came to be derived largely from Robert Morris's *Select Architecture* (1775), modified by Jefferson's study of Palladio's villas. Jefferson altered and greatly enlarged the house after his spell in Paris as minister to France (1784–89), increasing the height of the rooms (eventually there were 35) and building the octagonal dome over the hall. During that period, with some help from the French Neoclassical architect Charles-Louis Clérisseau, also associated with William Chambers and the Adam brothers, Jefferson designed the state capitol in Richmond on the model of the Maison Carrée at Nîmes, but larger and with unfluted Ionic, instead of Corinthian, columns. He would later design the University of Virginia at Charlottesville, the buildings representing several Classical variants and culminating in a splendid pantheon.

Monticello is the result of long thought and careful planning, not only in its adaptation of Palladian design but also in its – some would say – characteristically American concern for comfort. Jefferson incorporated various labour-saving features of his own devising, such as revolving shelves to speed the serving of food, and had his bed in an alcove between dressing room and study so that he could move easily from one to the other.

Syon House, Middlesex

Robert Adam (1728–92), the greatest British architect of the late 18th century, is perhaps best known as a decorator, author of the ultra-elegant, Neoclassical 'Adam style', because in so many cases he was working on a pre-existing building. He represented the opposite pole of Neoclassicism from his contemporary, William Chambers, designer of Somerset House in London, with whom he shared the position of royal architect. Chambers regarded him as frivolous.

Syon House, seat of the dukes of Northumberland, was a 16th–17th-century house around a square courtyard. The Duke was cultured, rich, and prepared to spend, although Adam's planned rotunda proved too much even for his pocket. In reconstructing the interior in 1762–69, Adam, fresh from his researches in Italy and Split, created what Sacheverell Sitwell described as 'among the greatest works of art in England', in which, however, practically everything derives from Classical prototypes. In fact there are only five rooms. The monumental, basilica-like hall in the Doric Order has painted medallions on the curved ceiling of the apse that decrease in size to lengthen the perspective. The spectacular anteroom is a rectangle which is converted to a square by a line of free-standing columns. Huge Ionic columns of green marble line the walls and are topped by athletic figures in gilded plaster, with panels of gilt trophies and a multicoloured *scagliola* floor. The largely white dining room and the red drawing room, with its unusual decorated coving, as well as ceiling, where the pattern of medallions suggested to Chambers dinner plates thrown at the ceiling, offer contrasting examples of Classical splendour that is also comfortable.

The whole of the east side, overlooking the Thames and Kew Gardens, is occupied by a very long and very narrow Jacobean long gallery. Here Adam displayed imagination and finesse in overcoming the tunnel-like appearance with Corinthian pilasters that break the line and suggest depth, while the lozenges that decorate the ceiling are interrupted by the walls as if they continue beyond. The overall impression is of what Adam described as 'a style to afford great variety and amusement'. It is the quintessence of the Adam style.

Syon House retains its original appearance of a 17th-century, square-planned, castellated mansion.

*OPPOSITE
Gardens and conservatory: the house is just across the river from the Botanical Gardens at Kew.*

BELOW
*The most memorable
feature of the Four
Courts is the highly
individual design of
drum and dome.*

BELOW RIGHT
*Gandon's Classical
entrance porch is more
conventional.*

Four Courts, Dublin

Dublin became an elegant, largely Neoclassical city during the 18th century, with the old Parliament Building, Leinster House, the Classical façade for Trinity College, and streets and squares of pleasant Georgian houses. Although the English associations of much of its architecture caused mixed feelings in nationalists, few would now condemn it as a symbol of English imperialism.

Among the finest buildings are the Custom House and the Four Courts building, both the work of James Gandon (1743–1823). English-born, of French descent, Gandon was a pupil of William Chambers. He arrived in Ireland in 1781 to design the Custom House. He had to deal with many difficulties during construction, including the threat of violence, but was not deterred, and in 1786 took over the Four Courts building on the north bank of the River Liffey, begun ten years earlier but with only the west wing already built.

Although Gandon rejected the Adam style as too frivolous, he was not exactly Chambers' disciple either. His style, described by Brendan Lehane as 'Palladian with Baroque and Neoclassical additions', also seems to owe something to his French connections, and he had studied Wren's riverside buildings at Greenwich and Chelsea (London). But his imaginative and original style was essentially personal.

The entrance to the Four Courts is a hexastyle Corinthian portico, but the most distinctive feature is the central colonnaded drum, surmounted by a very shallow dome, originally even flatter than today, which gives the building its striking originality and contributes so splendidly to the Dublin skyline. It is one of those structures familiar because it is so distinctive, indeed unique. Below it is the circular central hall from which radiate, on diagonal axes, the chambers that contained the original 'four courts' (Exchequer, Common Pleas, King's Bench and Chancery).

During the Irish Civil War in 1922–23, mines and artillery destroyed all but the shell of the building, and much of the invaluable and irreplaceable archives of the adjoining Public Record Office. The building was restored in 1932.

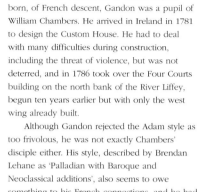

Strawberry Hill, Middlesex

In 1747 Horace Walpole (1717–97), younger son of a British prime minister, leased 'a little plaything house' near the river in Twickenham, south-west of London. Two years later he bought it, and began its conversion into a kind of miniature Gothic castle. Walpole was a cultured, slightly 'precious' bachelor, a dilettante but a learned one. He was the author of an early Gothic novel, *The Castle of Otranto* (1764). His house was a forerunner of the Gothic Revival, but it was conceived in an entirely different spirit, more frolicsome than the studious 'archaeologizing' of the next century, as displayed in the 19th-century addition to Strawberry Hill. It seemed to

Walpole that the Gothic style was well suited to the kind of small country house he required. Completed between 1749 and 1766, Strawberry Hill is a romantic, make-believe place, and Walpole always spoke of it in that way, while privately taking it more seriously than he was prepared to admit.

Walpole was a stickler for authenticity, studying medieval engravings and if possible visiting sites for design sources, and consulting the group of friends he called his 'Committee of Taste'. Among them were the poet Thomas Gray, John Chute and Richard Bentley, who designed a great deal of the house, and for a short time Robert Adam, who designed one of the rooms, although under Walpole's

supervision. The emphasis on accuracy was oddly eclectic. The models for bookcases and fireplaces came from tombs and screens in French and English churches: the chimney piece in the Little Parlour is modelled on the tomb of a 13th-century bishop in Westminster Abbey. The overall effect is neither incongruous nor vulgar, but graceful, delicate and endearing. The whole place is on a small scale: Bentley's delightful staircase would fit in a modern suburban house. After Walpole's death Strawberry Hill was neglected and his furniture dissipated, but the house enjoyed a new lease of life when reopened and enlarged by Lady Waldegrave in the 1860s.

There is somethiong rather precious about Walpole and his Committee of Taste, but his precocious little Gothic villa is a delight. It was expanded in the 19th century, in broadly the same style but in a different spirit.

Brighton Pavilion

On the whole, English monarchs were less extravagant builders than many of their European contemporaries, but one exception was the Prince Regent, later George IV (1820–30), whose expenditure infuriated parliament when called upon to pay his bills. Later generations may be thankful for George's fecklessness, in particular for his greatest 'folly', the fairytale 'oriental' palace known as Brighton Pavilion.

In the mid-18th century Brighton was a

small fishing village on the south coast of England, about 50 miles (80km) from London. The Prince first visited it in 1783 and built a small but delightful brick villa there with the result that Brighton soon became fashionable, and the Brighton Road became dangerously crowded with speeding coaches. In 1806 George decided to extend the villa and hired Humphrey Repton, best known as a landscape gardener, to submit plans. Repton had recently worked on a house for a retired Indian nabob and had 'discovered new sources of beauty and variety in Indian architecture'. His plan was for a building based vaguely on Indian sources. The Prince was delighted, but when work began ten years later Repton had been superseded by the more fashionable, and more gifted John Nash, his former partner.

Nash's building, though indisputably oriental in flavour, mixes Hindu, Islamic and Chinese styles, without being faithful to any. The exterior, with its sparkling white domes (provoking one contemporary critic to remark that 'St Paul's has gone down to Brighton and pupped'), minarets, fretted balconies and arcading, and creamy walls, suggests at first glance a backdrop for a pantomime Aladdin. The relative fragility of the building masks extensive use of iron, invisible except in a spiral staircase. The interior contains the finest display of *chinoiserie* in England, and some of the finest furniture in the style termed (after the Prince) 'Regency'. As well as intense disapproval, the Pavilion, seldom actually lived in, aroused great popular interest in England and elsewhere, and it is said to have been pictured in 19th-century books more frequently than any other English building.

Ducal Palace, Weimar

The medieval town of Weimar in Thuringia became the capital of a duchy in the 16th century under rulers of the Saxon house of Wettin, and though never powerful, Weimar has a distinguished history. After the post-war revolution of 1918–19, the German National Assembly met here and drew up the constitution of the short-lived state known as the Weimar Republic, overthrown by Hitler in 1933. In the history of architecture, Weimar is remembered as the site of the Bauhaus, the most important school of art and design in the 20th century, which originated in the school of arts and crafts founded by the Grand Duke in 1906. He appointed as director the Belgian Henri van der Velde, who was responsible for the policy of teaching through workshops rather than studios; when he left Germany during the First World War, he suggested Walter Gropius as his successor.

But Weimar's greatest period was the late-18th and early-19th centuries, when it was the unrivalled intellectual capital of Germany. Under the Grand Duke Karl August, Goethe, Schiller, Herder and others were attracted to Weimar. The many memorials to them include the Goethe-Schiller Mausoleum and Archives and the bronze monument in front of the German National Theatre, where Goethe was director for many years, though the theatre was later rebuilt.

Schloss Weimar, the ducal palace, is the most important building in Weimar, although not perhaps the most interesting or the most beautiful. An English visitor described it as only 'imposing from its extent'. It was largely rebuilt after a fire, from 1789 until 1803, when the Napoleonic Wars interrupted progress, and was not finished until much later. The major survival from the earlier castle is the tall clock tower, buttressed by adjoining later buildings. Herder, Goethe and Schiller have their own named rooms with scenes from their works, and the gracious private apartments contain Italian Renaissance paintings. The Neoclassical hall is the most distinguished part of the 18th-century building, whose construction, according to tradition, was supervised by Goethe himself.

Schloss Weimar, the ducal palace, is the most important building in Weimar, once the intellectual capital of Germany.

212

Iron Bridge, Coalbrookdale

Iron was used in architecture from early times to strengthen structures, but it was exclusively functional and usually invisible. No one considered it might be beautiful in itself, and that was not widely accepted as such until very recently: some local people considered the Iron Bridge a monstrosity only 30 years ago. Completed in 1779, the Iron Bridge was the first large structure made wholly of cast iron, and signalled the beginning of the end of timber and stone as the materials for bridge construction and eventually for other utilitarian buildings. It gave its name to the village and rapidly achieved worldwide fame.

It was no accident that this innovation occurred in Shropshire, north-west England, a centre of iron founding since the 16th century and a cradle of the Industrial Revolution. The original design was by Thomas Farnolls Pritchard (1723–77), though he died before the final plan was approved. The builder, who probably had a hand in the design too, was Abraham Darby the Third (1750–91). His grandfather, who died in 1717, was one of the first to use coke rather than charcoal in his Coalbrookdale iron foundry, a vital step towards the great industrial take-off.

The bridge is an arch spanning 100ft (30m). The deck is supported by iron ribs passing through vertical pillars set in the stone abutments, five across and in five reducing tiers. They are reinforced by cross-stays and diagonals. The roadway is based on iron plates each 24-ft (7-m) wide, i.e. the width of the roadway, and lined by a cast-iron balustrade. As inevitably happens when new material or new types of structure are introduced, the builders naturally adapted existing techniques. The details of the Iron Bridge thus resemble those of the carpenter and the stonemason – mortise and tenon and dovetail joints, iron keys, screws and wedges rather than rivets and bolts, which were yet to be invented. The iron circles that link vertical pillar, topmost rib and deck reproduce the pierced spandrels of stone bridges, a technique to reduce weight that had only become common a generation earlier.

Coalbrookdale's Iron Bridge lies at the heart of the birthplace of the Industrial Revolution.

Malmaison

Malmaison, 45 minutes from Paris on horseback, is chiefly famous as the home of the Empress Josephine. It barely merits the name of château, being merely a comfortable country house in pleasant grounds. The original 17th-century house was a simple building consisting of a three-floor central block with short protruding wings. It was looted during the Revolution but escaped serious damage. Josephine bought the house and gardens in 1799 while Napoleon was in Egypt, and he was not at first pleased.

It was subsequently enlarged, and the demolition of the original wings weakened the structure and necessitated the unfortunate buttresses topped by vases. Josephine, divorced in 1809, loved the place and lived there for the rest of her life. For Napoleon it had been a relaxing country retreat, where he was able to forget strategy and government and indulge in games of blind man's bluff. He returned, after Josephine's death from a chill caught when showing the Tsar around the park, to contemplate his bleak future after his defeat at Waterloo. He left at five o'clock on 25 June, 'gave a long lingering look at the house and gardens connected with his happiest hours, and left them for ever'.

During the 19th century Malmaison passed though many hands, and most of the park, where Josephine's greenhouses had supplied botanical gardens throughout France, was sold off. The house was presented to the nation in 1904 and was opened as a museum soon afterwards. It remains a monument to the French Empire style; but the pompous furniture contradicts the spirit of the place. Many of Josephine's pictures were bought by the Tsar, perhaps to ease the financial plight of her worthy son Eugène, and found their way to the Hermitage in St Petersburg. One may still feel the presence of that oddly attractive woman under the spreading cedar that she planted to mark the victory of Marengo in 1800, in sympathy with the words of the poet: 'Malmaison is only a sigh ... a place of great languor, an urn for the ashes of the heart ...'

At Malmaison, at five o'clock in the evening of 25 June 1815, Napoleon put on a costume de ville, un habit marron, *tenderly embraced the persons present, gave a long lingering look at the house connected with his happiest hours, and left forever.*

FAR LEFT
The main façade of Buckingham Palace.

LEFT
Detail of the Victoria Memorial (1912), a flamboyant work by Sir Thomas Brock incorporating 2,300 tons of white marble.

Buckingham Palace

Buckingham Palace, in the heart of London, has been the chief residence of the British monarchy for about 150 years. It is not an old building: most of what the public sees today was completed less than 100 years ago, and nothing is left of the original 18th-century building, which was called Buckingham House after its original owner, the Duke of Buckingham. It was sold to King George III in 1762, and when George IV became king (1820), he commissioned John Nash, designer of Brighton Pavilion, to extend it. He estimated that the job would cost £50,000 – nearly three times more than the government was willing to spend and predictably much less than then final cost.

Nash did a great deal to make London more elegant, but Buckingham Palace is not among his greatest successes. His original design was a three-sided court with an ornate triumphal arch forming the entrance. Both style and cost were heavily criticized. Nash was eventually forced to appear before a hostile committee of parliament but, perhaps bored with the project, and certainly with the questions, he returned eccentric answers, and was eventually removed. His successor, Edward Blore, enclosed the courtyard by building the familiar east front, overlooking the Victoria Memorial and the Mall. Nash's far more attractive garden front, despite a rather timid dome, is generally seen only by guests at royal garden parties. Blore also moved

the marble arch from the palace to its present site at the northern end of Park Lane.

Inside, besides Nash's Grand Staircase, probably the most splendid of the 600-odd rooms is the Blue Drawing Room, formerly the Ball Room, containing Napoleon's porcelain table with portraits of military heroes and a clock allegedly designed by George III. Some of the paintings from the royal collection can be seen in the adjacent Queen's Gallery.

The palace was not completed in time for George IV, nor for his successor William IV. But Queen Victoria, succeeding to the throne in 1837, was keen to move in regardless of doors that would not close and windows that would not open.

Houses of Parliament, Westminster

Westminster became the main residence of English monarchs in the 11th century and eventually the capital of England, developing alongside the City of London. Medieval parliaments met in Westminster Hall (1097, rebuilt c.1400). Accommodation was always makeshift, and the fire that in 1834 destroyed most of the old palace (though not Westminster Hall) provided the opportunity to create a purpose-built legislature.

Despite the claims of Classicism, acknowledged, for example, not only in Washington but in nearly every state capitol in the USA, it was agreed that the style should be Gothic, recalling the Tudor Age and the foundations of English liberties. The architect chosen, Charles Barry (1795–1860), was by inclination a Classicist, but he was assisted by the fervent genius of the Gothic Revival, Augustus Pugin (1812–52), a Catholic convert who identified the Gothic style with the Christian religion. He designed everything from the architectural details to inkwells and coat hooks.

Construction began in 1837: the House of Commons was finished by 1847, the Clock Tower, popularly known as Big Ben, by 1858, the larger Victoria Tower by 1860, and the whole complex by 1865. The final result is Classical in plan and overall design but authentically Gothic in appearance, a 'great and beautiful monument to Victorian artifice', and the product of one of the most successful architectural partnerships in British history. It established Gothic as a suitable style not only for parliaments (e.g. Budapest, Ottawa), but for all public buildings.

Encouraged by Prince Albert, the royal consort, no effort or expense was spared on statues and paintings to augment Pugin's gorgeously rich interiors. The Robing Room, a large chamber 54-ft (16-m) long, is a good example of both Pugin's fertile imagination and devotion to 19th-century painting on a large scale with frescoes by William Dyce of the legends of King Arthur. The House of Commons was destroyed by bombs in the Second World War and rebuilt (1945–50) by Giles Gilbert Scott on the original plan but with less rich decoration.

OPPOSITE
View from the river, with the Victoria Tower on the left and the clock tower containing Big Ben in the distance.

LEFT
Detail from New Palace Yard. In a sense the building was more daring than any contemporary example.

The main façade of the Royal Palace in Corfu, with its fine Doric colonnade.

Royal Palace, Corfu

When the Ionian Islands became a British protectorate in 1815, a suitable residence was required for the High Commissioner. At the same time, a meeting place had to be found for the legislative assembly and a headquarters for the British Order of St Michael and St George.

Founded in 1918, its membership was at that time bestowed on those who had performed special service in the Mediterranean region, but which is today more widely spread. The palace was officially known as the Palace of St Michael and St George.

The architect was George Whitmore, at that time a colonel in the Royal Engineers attached to the British garrison in Corfu. A Neoclassical design was inevitable, given the time and place, and the most distinguished feature of the façade is the fine Doric colonnade that marches across it. It is flanked on either side by large arches that are, of course, more Roman than Greek, one of them accommodating what was once the main road; the central pediment of the palace contained a figure of Britannia. The material used was a creamy Maltese stone, which did not weather particularly well. The state rooms on the second storey consist of an elegant central, circular chamber with a dome decorated with plaques of Wedgwood jasperware (white figures raised on a blue ground), and Classical statues.

After Corfu was handed back to Greece in 1864, the palace was sometimes used as a summer residence by the Greek royal family. Corfu suffered during the Second World War from bombing and separate occupation by Italians and Germans, and as a result many buildings and other landmarks were destroyed. The former palace survived both that man-made disaster and the earthquake of 1953. It was rather dilapidated, but it was later sympathetically restored by a local architect and is today a museum of Asian art (founded 1927).

Trinity Church, Wall Street

The Gothic Revival, perhaps stronger in England than anywhere else, first reached the USA as a Romantic fashion but became more serious under the influence of Pugin and others in the second quarter of the 19th century. One of the most enterprising and most active architects of the Gothic Revival in North America was the English-born Richard Upjohn, founder and first president of the American Institute of Architects. His first Gothic building was a picturesque mansion in Maine, but he became most famous as the designer of at least 40 churches, of which one of the earliest and best, and far the best known, was Trinity Church in Wall Street, New York, built between 1836 and 1846.

When it was built, and for many years afterwards, Old Trinity Church was the tallest building in Wall Street, or indeed in Manhattan, and parts of the wall that gave its name to the street and marked the northern boundary of the early Dutch settlement, could still be seen. Though now so thoroughly overshadowed by the looming skyscrapers of 20th-century capitalism that a full view of the steeple is only possible from the middle of the street, it still strives to assert a spiritual presence in the midst of modern materialism.

There was an earlier church on the site, erected, legend says, with block and tackle supplied by Captain Kydd, another kind of pirate, which burned down; when its successor proved structurally unsound it was replaced by Upjohn's building. Upjohn generally followed English models and favoured the Decorated and Early Perpendicular phases of English Gothic (late 13th–14th centuries). Trinity Church is admired for its clean lines and stylistic authenticity, and its stained glass is said to have been among the earliest made in North America. Its capacity is unnecessarily large for today's congregation, though some correlation is said to exist between the number of worshippers and the state of the markets; the church filled up at the time of the Wall Street Crash.

Trinity Church, Wall Street: it is difficult to suppress the feeling that God has been overtaken by Mammon.

219

United States Capitol, Washington, DC

The need for large and imposing government buildings which would replace palaces as the major type of very large secular building, roughly coincided with the return of Classicism in the mid-18th century, not that, in some places, it had ever gone far away. Capital cities increasingly boasted rather similar buildings, with central, columned porticoes, long façades and flanking pavilions. In North America Classicism was firmly established due largely to the influence of Thomas Jefferson, on whose advice the state capitol in Richmond, Virginia, took the Maison Carrée in Nîmes as its model. The prime example, if only on grounds of size, is the Capitol in Washington, D.C.

The competition for the design of the building in 1792 was won by William Thornton, an English-born physician, and the foundation stone was laid by George Washington the following year. Thornton never in fact superintended the actual construction, which proceeded slowly over many years with many modifications by different hands, though on the whole they were sympathetic in spirit to the original Palladian conception. Under James Hoban, architect of the White House, the Senate wing was completed in 1800. Benjamin Latrobe, the foremost American architect of the day, took over in 1803 and within eight years he had completed the House of Representatives wing. In 1814, British troops burned much of Washington, including the White House and the

Capitol, which Latrobe proceeded to reconstruct in a revised form. His plan, with only minor modifications, was completed by Charles Bullfinch by 1830; but before long Congress had outgrown the building, and between 1851 and 1863 the whole complex was reconstructed on a massive scale. Thomas U. Walter's Capitol, which adopted the Greek Revival style and used marble instead of the original sandstone, has overall measurements of 702 x 350ft (214 x 107m). In 1960 the east façade was lengthened by another 33ft (10m). Walter's massive 224-ft (68-m) cast-iron dome, which nods across the Atlantic to St Paul's in London, was topped by a correspondingly massive 20-ft (6-m) statue, Armed Freedom with the inscription *E Pluribus Unum*.

OPPOSITE
The grand approach to the Capitol, an outstandingly distinguished building which shows no trace of its rather turbulent construction history.

RIGHT
Details of the lantern and drum.

Forth Railway Bridge, Edinburgh

The railway bridge across the Firth of Forth just west of Edinburgh is a structure so vast it makes the trains it carries look like toys. A masterpiece of Victorian engineering, it revolutionized bridge-building and still inspires structural engineers today.

The original plan was for a suspension bridge designed by the builder of the Tay Bridge, but when that collapsed in 1879, the plan was hastily dropped. Benjamin Baker, a prominent engineer, then produced a cantilever design, more stable than a suspension bridge, but still relatively novel, though the principle was known and utilized by ancient civilizations.

The main members are tubes 12ft (4m) in diameter and the span of 1,710ft (521m) between piers was a record unbroken for many years. The material was mild steel, not iron as in the Tay Bridge. Use was made of a rocky islet in the middle of the Firth, but otherwise the foundations of the massive piers were built in the turbulent currents of the estuary in caissons, providing a working chamber on the bottom from which water is excluded (the method was used by the Romans and described by Vitruvius). The bridge employed the unheard-of quantity of 58,000 tons of steel, and the total cost of construction, about £33 million, was also a record. The area of painted surface is 653,406sq yd (546313sq m), giving rise to the

common expression for an unending task, 'like painting the Forth Bridge'. Construction took seven years and, after testing with two 900-ton trains, the bridge was opened in 1890. In 1964 it was joined by a road bridge, a suspension bridge with a 3,300-ft (1000-m) span.

Although admired then and since by engineers, the views of others were more mixed. The artist-designer William Morris called it 'the greatest specimen of all ugliness', but few would agree with that verdict today, now that it has become perhaps Scotland's most popular and recognizable image, a Caledonian equivalent of another great monument in steel, the Eiffel Tower.

The Forth Railway Bridge was immediately recognized as a triumph of engineering, but aesthetic approval took longer to achieve.

Views of the Eiffel Tower. It still lords it over Paris and is likely to do so for the forseeable future, a building not for a lifetime, not even for a bicentenary, but for a millennium. The arched base derived from Eiffel's experience of bridges.

Eiffel Tower

International exhibitions that became fashionable in the second half of the 19th century were often the occasion for new ideas, in architecture as well as manufacturing and engineering. The now-legendary Gustave Eiffel (1832–1923), the 'magician of iron', designed the influential Gallery of Machines for the Paris Exhibition of 1867, long before his famous tower.

Eiffel began his career in 1855 working for French railway companies, especially in the design of bridges. By 1880 he was at the height of his powers, involved in projects in a dozen countries, designing dams, locks, reservoirs, casinos, department stores, even churches, and the frame for the Statue of Liberty in New York harbour. Were it not for the tower, his bridges might be better known, especially his masterpiece, the Garabit Viaduct over the Truyère river, in which the viaduct carrying the railway is supported by a parabolic arch, tapering in section towards the peak, which spans 530ft (162m). While being purely functional, is is also artistically satisfying, and the form appears again in the base of the Eiffel Tower, though the arches there are semicircular.

In the competition for a monument to commemorate the centennial of the French Revolution in 1889, Eiffel's plan was accepted ahead of over 100 others. It proposed a tower 984-ft (300-m) tall, by far the highest building in the world, of open iron latticework. Many people thought it was impossible; still more thought it would be hideous. The engineering problems were certainly formidable, but Eiffel's experience, especially in calculating wind forces, in which, along with the builders of the

Forth Bridge, he was a pioneer, and his unrivalled knowledge of the behaviour of iron arches and trusses under the various types of force action produced by loading, ensured the success of the structure. It heralded a revolution in civil engineering and, to some extent, also in architectural design. Aesthetically, it soon came to be accepted and indeed admired, superseding Notre Dame as Paris's most familiar building, its attractions enhanced by the glass elevators which, owing to the arched base, had to move through a curve.

The Arc de Triomphe, derived from ancient Roman examples.

Arc de Triomphe, Paris

The 19th century was a fruitful time for national monuments, a type of structure invented by the Romans. They employed three types – the triumphal arch, the column and the equestrian statue – which were never forgotten, even in the Middle Ages, though they were seldom repeated until the Renaissance. The equestrian statue, such as Giovanni da Bologna's figure of Cosimo in Florence, was preferred then but later, other types were invented, though they were not necessarily built, an example being Étienne-Louis Boullée's colossal monument to Isaac Newton in the form of a globe over 500-ft (150-m) high.

Napoleon was responsible for several monuments in Paris. The Madeleine, a church begun in 1806 in the form of a large Corinthian temple, was at Napoleon's decree turned into a Temple de la Gloire, a military shrine, though it later returned to being a church; the Colonne Vendôme, based on Trajan's Column in Rome, had a statue of the emperor on top, like Nelson's Column in London. The largest and most famous is the Arc de Triomphe de l'Étoile, symbol of French valour, dedicated to 'the glory of the imperial armies'. Designed by Jean François Thérèse Chalgrin, a former pupil of Boullée, it was begun in 1806 though not finished until 1836, when Napoleon was but a memory. It is a vast structure, 162-ft (50-m) high, in the heart of Paris. At the foot of the Champs Élysées, it forms the hub from which 12 avenues radiate like the spokes of a wheel.

It too has a London equivalent in Marble Arch, and the ancestor of both is the Triumphal Arch of the Emperor Septimius Severus in Rome. But the Arc de Triomphe is not merely a copy and in fact is markedly different in that it is more monumental, more bulky and less decorative. The lack of columns and comparatively little relief decoration give it the quality Niklaus Pevsner described as 'blockiness'. Since 1920 it has contained the tomb of France's Unknown Soldier.

Washington Monument

George Washington led the colonial armies that won independence for the United States and became the republic's first president. As a national hero he ranks with Moses or Charlemagne.

Discussion of a public monument took a long time to germinate. The first actual commission was issued by Benjamin West, American president of the British Royal Academy. George Dance, the most original English architect of the age, submitted a design of two large pyramids flanking a vaguely Eastern temple. It got no further. The first monument in the USA was erected in Baltimore in 1815–29. A round column 130-ft (40-m) high and topped by a statue, it belongs to the

tradition of Napoleon's Colonne Vendôme and London's Nelson's Column. The designer was Robert Mills, who claimed to be the first professional, native-born American architect. In 1836 he became official architect to the federal government. He built the Treasury Building, among several others in Washington, and designed the Washington Monument.

Mills forsook his Baltimore column. His original design began with a Doric rotunda, from which arose, unexpectedly, an Egyptian obelisk. The rotunda was abandoned soon after work began in 1848, and all work stopped in 1855. It did not resume until 1877, and was finished in 1884.

The monument is 555-ft (169-m) high, with sides tapering from 15ft (4.5m) at the base to

18in (46cm) at the top, and is the largest in the world. Many other plans, of varying extravagance, in every style and in none, had been rejected, but even Mills' simple obelisk attracted hostile criticism. The architect Henry van Brunt compared it unfavourably with the Giralda in Seville. The sculptor Horatio Greenough, who made the colossal statue of Washington now in the Smithsonian Institution and was also the designer of the monument, an obelisk, at Bunker Hill, objected to that design, though on grounds that actually seem to justify it. 'The obelisk,' he said, 'has to my eye a singular aptitude in its form and character to call attention to a spot memorable in history. It says but one word, but it speaks loud ... It says Here! It says no more.' Exactly.

The custom of celebrating a famous person with a column goes back to imperial Rome, though, in this case, the choice of an Egyptian obelisk aroused lively controversy.

Saint Pancras Station, London

The three great railway terminals in north London displayed a variety of 19th-century styles. Euston, before its reconstruction (or vandalization) in 1967, was Classical, with a tremendous Doric portico (1838) 75-ft (23-m) high and splendid Roman Great Hall (1849). Lewis Cubitt's King's Cross with its simple, misleadingly modern, twin arches and plain 112-ft (34-m) tower, might have been built a century later than it was (1851–52). St Pancras, fronted by the Midland Hotel, now offices, in the form of a medieval castle (1868), represented the Gothic Revival at its most romantic, though some threw up their hands in horror at the whole idea of industrial buildings in the Gothic style.

St Pancras remains one of London's most spectacular sights: a 'great Gothic phantasmagoria ... drawing up with complete confidence into its sky-assaulting range of turrets' (David Piper), the clock tower reaching a height of 270ft (82m). The architect was Sir George Gilbert Scott (1811–78), one of the ablest exponents of High Victorian Gothic, who won the competition in spite of the fact that his was the most costly design. It seems an extraordinarily exotic building for a railway station and hotel, and Scott himself admitted that 'it is possibly too good for its purpose'. Some years earlier he had submitted, unsuccessfully, a design for government offices in Whitehall, and the plans show that it would have borne a close resemblance to St Pancras.

Tucked away behind Scott's fairy-tale façade is an equally remarkable building, the train shed (1868) of William Barlow. It is a great arched roof of iron and glass, 689-ft (210-m long, 242-ft (74-m) wide and 98-ft (30-m) high, held in place by iron rods passing below the platforms. In 1868 it was the world's largest single span. The arch is slightly pointed, as if in acknowledgment of the Gothic front, and although the conjunction seemed distasteful to many at the time, today the two buildings seem a perfect partnership.

An extravagant gilded fountain plays before Ludwig's Linderhof. On windy days the fountain is turned off.

Schloss Linderhof

Linderhof is the most modest of the architectural 'follies' of King Ludwig II of Bavaria. Like Herrenchiemsee, but on a much smaller scale (it is more villa than palace), it can be regarded as a tribute to Ludwig's ideal of Grand Monarchy epitomized by Louis XIV; it was modelled on the Neoclassical Petit Trianon (1762), the masterpiece of perhaps the finest French architect of the 18th century, Ange-Jacques Gabriel (1698–1782), although Linderhof is much more ornamental. It is said to have been Ludwig's favourite residence, and he had plenty from which to choose.

When first built between 1870 and 1879, Linderhof aroused more contempt than admiration, but attitudes have changed somewhat and the excesses of Linderhof, such as the carefully modelled stalactites in the grotto, the strange little 'Moorish' pavilion, the gilded nymphs gallivanting around the fountain, or the lavishly overdecorated rooms, do not prevent it from being seen as a work of art. Its modest size – there are only four windows across the main façade – is an advantage, and it is not merely a slavish imitation of the French Baroque style. No more than at Herrenchiemsee can one imagine finding tranquillity and ease in the royal bedroom, and in general the Rococo interiors owe more to the south German than the French tradition. The craftsmanship is impeccable, and it is difficult to imagine such a building existing in any other time.

Another asset is the site, a wooden valley with mountains rising beyond. Nature, especially the trees, seems to moderate the excesses of Man. A double flight of marble steps rises through terraced gardens to a little

Classical rotunda below the rock face, and the ancient lime tree which probably gives Linderhof ('Lime Court') its name was left in place by Ludwig's builders.

Herrenchiemsee

This is the largest of the never-never-land castles of Ludwig II of Bavaria who, deprived of real power, compensated by building extravagant and redundant palaces where he could indulge his nostalgia for a romanticized past. His indulgence in German myth and legend was most extravagantly expressed in the fantasy castle of Neuschwanstein, but at Herrenchiemsee he pursued another obsession, with Louis XIV of France, the absolute monarch that Ludwig would have liked to have been. He paid several visits, incognito, to Versailles, of which Herrenchiemsee was supposed to be a copy. Building began in 1878 and progress was swift, although the palace was still unfinished when, eight years later, Ludwig was declared insane and his building projects halted.

This dinosaur, though magnificent, is bogus, a palace for a kind of ruler who did not exist, built on an island in a lake, remote and empty. In some ways, it does indeed rival Versailles. The Hall of Mirrors is nearly 330-ft (100-m) long and required an army of servants merely to light the candles. There are many remarkable objects, but it is difficult to contemplate so much anachronistic regal extravagance without a flicker of revulsion. Who could get any sleep in the royal bedroom? In fact, Ludwig only spent 23 nights there. Here is Baroque gone mad, a mass of gilded figures, scrolls, leafwork, emblems, with velvet hangings and various decorative conceits that obliterate the dimensions of the room. In the dining room the table sinks below the floor, so that it can be cleared and replenished without servants appearing in the room, a device copied from Louis XIV. Ludwig dined alone on the 23 nights

Another great fountain fronts Herrenchiemsee, perhaps the most grotesquely inappropriate of all poor Ludwig's excesses.

he spent at Herrenchiemsee, but the table was set for four. The guests who never arrived were Louis XIV, Mme de Maintenon and Mme de Pompadour.

Ludwig preferred his Wagnerian castle of Neuschwanstein (an inspiration for Disneyland) where, amid grand scenes from Germanic legend, he spent his last years alone and mad.

The Sacré Coeur has few admirers, but it is undeniably a landmark.

Sacré Coeur, Paris

Revivalism in 19th-century Western architecture was not entirely new; after all, the Renaissance had been a revival. The chief difference was that 19th-century architects were much better informed not only about earlier European styles but also about those of other civilizations, so a wealth of possibilities were open to them. Arguments between advocates of Classical and Gothic were sometimes fierce, but even the most conservative architects tended to experiment, and some of the most extraordinary buildings of the late 19th century employed a mixture of styles in the same structure (though this was not entirely new either, e.g. Nash's mixture of Chinese and Mughal in the Brighton Pavilion).

The Church of the Sacred Heart (Sacré Coeur) commemorates the pain and suffering endured in the national disaster of the Franco-Prussian War (1870–71) and, though sponsored by private subscribers, it was quickly adopted by the National Assembly. The site is high on the 'butte' or hill of Montmartre and is, in the words of a guidebook, 'only too visible' from any part of Paris. The building, described as 'neo-Romanesque-Byzantine', has not had a good press: 'vulgar and bizarre' is the description of one modern critic, and everyone agrees that the best view of the Sacré Coeur is from a distance, when the dazzling effect of the stone, which whitens with age, is effective. But it seems to lack exactly the quality that this pilgrimage church should have, a sense of soul and spirituality, and instead communicates a strange deadness.

Basically a basilica, it is large – 328-ft (100-m) long and 246-ft (75-m) wide across the ambulatory. The curious dome rises to 272ft (83m). The square campanile contains a bell, the Savoyarde, that weighs nearly 20 tons. The architect was the elderly Paul Abadie (1812–84), and the church is based on his controversial restoration of St-Front at Périgueux. The church is heavily decorated with mosaics by Luc-Olivier Merson and others. Building started in 1876 but it was not finished until 1918, although it was first used in the 1890s.

Glasgow School of Art

The Scottish architect and designer Charles
Rennie Mackintosh (1868–1928) was a man of
singular gifts. His buildings are comparatively
few, in view of his later influence and
reputation, deplorably few in the British Isles,
one of the few complete examples being the
Hill House, near Glasgow, now a museum, and
he is probably remembered first as a designer of
furniture and interiors (e.g. The Willow Tea
Room), usually in collaboration with his wife,
Margaret Macdonald and her sister, Frances. His
universally acknowledged masterpiece is the
Glasgow School of Art, begun in 1897 to
replace the building he had studied in himself.

Some Mackintosh chairs, graceful and
slender, do not look as if they are designed
primarily with comfort in mind, but a notable
characteristic of the School of Art is its
combination of strikingly novel design with
thoroughly practical functioning. The
centrepiece of the building is a highly original
piece of fancy, owing something perhaps to
Scottish tradition, with which Mackintosh was
not in general much engaged; but in spite of its
deliberate asymmetry the plan and the general
exterior form of the building, with its large,
north-facing studio windows, is highly rational.
It is not that far removed from the late 19th-
century Arts and Crafts movement, and the so-
called English Domestic Revival, led by Philip
Webb and Charles Voysey among others.

Mackintosh's interiors were generally more
adventurous. The library has some inexplicable
decorative details and un-library-like features,
but it has gained the approval of generations of
working students. Another aspect of the
Mackintosh style is that, while it belongs

thoroughly in spirit to Art Nouveau, and
employs characteristically languid Art Nouveau
curves, this is predominantly a building of
straight lines and verticals. It is hard to imagine
personal styles less alike than those of

Mackintosh and Gaudí, and Mackintosh has
more in common, in spirit if not in detail, with
Otto Wagner, the designer of the Post Office
Savings Bank in Vienna.

All architecture is derivative, some more derivative than others; but Gaudí's is in a class of its own.

Sagrada Familia, Barcelona

The ultimate exponent of the plant-like curve in the Art Nouveau period was the Catalan, Antoní Gaudí (1852—1926). A devout Roman Catholic, Gaudí reworked the old observation that there are no straight lines in nature: 'The straight line belongs to man, the curve to God'. His extravagant, sometimes grotesque buildings have struck some observers as more devilish than divine, but they are indisputably fascinating and undeniably original. Influences may include Gothic (in the case of the Sagrada Familia), Muslim and Classical, but Gaudí's style was utterly personal and he owed less to any historical style than all previous architects.

Many of Gaudí's most exciting schemes came to nothing, but it seems remarkable that so many of his designs were fulfilled. He was assisted by the faithful patronage of a wealthy industrialist, Eusebio Güell, for whom, besides other buildings, is named the well-known Parc Güell, with its undulating mosaic-collage of a wall that also backs a bench, a probable influence on Picasso, also a resident of Barcelona. Another asset was his identification with the cause of Catalan nationalism; all his buildings are in the Catalan capital. Had he been a foreigner, perhaps Barcelona's wealthy middle class would have been less ready to take up residence in apartment buildings such as the Casa Batlló, in rooms with no straight walls and balconies reminiscent of the jaws of a shark.

The Church of the Holy Family (Sagrada Familia) was originally intended to be a conventional Neo-Gothic edifice, and Gaudí, who took over the project in 1883, retained a Gothic general outline, while introducing Art Nouveau curves; the tall spires ('like the homes of giant termites' says Ian Sutton) are convex and elaborately ornamented. The façade, completed in Gaudí's lifetime, suggests a 13th-century French church overgrown by vaguely vegetable forms. There are some almost 'pure' Gothic features, and some that owe nothing whatever to Gothic or any other style. The building is an important marker in the gradual abandonment of historicism in architecture, and also a testament to Gaudí's craftsmanship and understanding of structure. Only a relatively small part was built in the 1890s, and the project was then practically abandoned for nearly 100 years until another era of intense Catalan nationalism provided the motivation to embark on its completion.

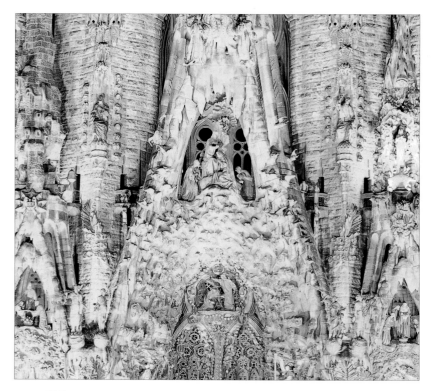

The massive, relatively conventional exterior of Wagner's Post Office Savings Bank bears little relation to the sleek lightweight interior.

Post Office Savings Bank, Vienna

Otto Wagner (1841–1918), one of the apostles of Modernism, was the most influential Austrian architect at the turn of the century, at first as a teacher, later by example. His early work was broadly in the Neoclassical tradition, which remained a presence in his later style. He was appointed professor at the Academy of Fine Art in Vienna in 1894 where, in his inaugural lecture he called for a newer, rational approach to architecture, abandoning historicism and asserting that 'nothing can be beautiful if it is not practical'. He was also head of the city's transport planning department, and designed stations for the Vienna Metro. In 1897 he became the leading architectural influence in the Viennese Secession, a new group founded by mainly younger men, including Josef Olbrich and the painter Gustav Klimt, who were united in rejecting academic art and favoured contemporary movements.

Like Charles Rennie Mackintosh, who exhibited at the Secession exhibition in Vienna in 1900, Wagner, and the Viennese architects he influenced, avoided the undulations of the so-called 'Belgian line' and generally remembered that architecture is supposed to be an art of line and space; but Wagner was not averse to decoration, sometimes rich and exotic. His Post Office Savings Bank (1904) has been consistently admired for a century and is one of those buildings that have never gone out of date, its use of glass making it particularly apt today. It displays with complete success the achievement of clarity, space and expression of function, aimed at by the Secessionist architects. The main banking hall is a large open space with a glass floor, admitting light to the basement, and a vaulted glass ceiling. The aluminium bolts fixing the marble panels to the monumental façade are repeated in the banking hall, where the heads are polished to attract attention to them.

The building escapes the stricture sometimes applied to the architecture of the Vienna Secession that it is too heavy and forbidding, a trait that is not absent from Wagner's second most famous building, the monumental, domed Church of St Leopold at Steinhof, outside Vienna.

Secession Building, Vienna

The outstanding architects of the Vienna Secession influenced by Otto Wagner were Josef Hoffmann (1870–1956), who built the luxurious Palais Stoclet in Brussels, and Joseph Maria Olbrich (1867–1908). They carried further the more geometrical form of Art Nouveau initiated by Wagner and Mackintosh towards an architecture of volumes and masses.

Olbrich studied at the Vienna Academy and, like Hoffmann, worked under Otto Wagner in the 1890s, becoming a founder member of the avant-garde Secession group. He made his reputation by designing their headquarters, the Secession Building, in 1896. This small, blocky, cubic building is surmounted by a curious gilded, openwork, wrought-iron dome, known as the Golden Cabbage, a symbol of the Secessionist journal, *Ver Sacrum*. The whole building could be regarded as an irreverent gesture towards the entire Classical tradition, but the combination of solid, simple shapes with inventive decorative detailing is characteristic of Olbrich's work in general. Much of the decoration was in fact designed by other members of the group, including the painter Gustav Klimt.

In 1899 the Grand Duke of Hesse invited Olbrich to Darmstadt, introducing the style of the Vienna Secession to Germany, and he remained there for the rest of his short life. Darmstadt was the home of an artistic colony, whose members included Peter Behrens, later the architect of the AEG Factory in Berlin, and other distinguished industrial buildings. Several of the artists designed their own houses. Olbrich designed his, and also several others, as well as the Artists' House, the communal building of the

artistic colony. In a ground-breaking event, the whole settlement was presented as a standing exhibition in 1901. Later, Olbrich also built the tower known as the Hochzeitsturm, and the following year began his last building, a department store in Düsseldorf. By then, Art Nouveau had passed its inspirational peak. Hoffmann would move in a different direction, but what direction Olbrich's career might have taken we cannot know.

Olbrich's Secession Building, with the Surrealist Golden Cabbage (in fact foliage) just visible.

THE FAR EAST

CHAPTER SIX

Great Wall of China

Wild Goose Pagoda, Sian

Temple of Heaven, Beijing

Cheng-te

The Forbidden City

Kyongbok Palace, Seoul

Potala Palace, Lhasa

The Horyuji, Nara

The Todaiji, Nara

Himeji Castle

Byodoin, Uji

Golden Pavilion, Kyoto

Katsura Villa, Kyoto

Saint Mary's Cathedral, Tokyo

Great Hall of the People, Beijing

Olympic Stadia, Tokyo

Having developed in relative isolation, the Chinese arrived very early at their preferred basic forms of building, which appear to have altered little in style over the centuries. To some extent this apparent lack of change is merely the view of an alien and inexpert eye; nevertheless, basic forms remained similar from one dynasty to the next, and architecture, which was never seen as a fine art among the Chinese, became highly ritualistic, subject to strict religious or social conventions. Since the structural material was invariably wood, except for pagodas, there are few buildings in China today dating from before the Ming dynasty (1368–1644) although, since the Chinese style spread all over eastern Asia, equivalent buildings of earlier periods can sometimes be seen in Japan where, for instance, the Horyuji pagoda represents the style of T'ang China.

From very early times the Chinese adopted the trabeate style, the architecture of post and lintel as in ancient Greece. Walls were never a structural element, and the outstanding feature of Chinese buildings came to be the roof, usually tiled, with its curving lines and overhanging eaves. Buildings were typically of one storey only, again with the exception of pagodas. Without any form of truss, to make buildings larger it was necessary to increase the number of columns, which thus constricted the open space. This problem was overcome by an intricate system of brackets, which increased the breadth of support afforded by each column and thus reduced the number of columns required for a given space. Carved brackets came to be the chief evolutionary feature of Chinese architecture as well as a major decorative feature. In time, the clusters of brackets, expanding as they ascended and supporting a range

of beams, became extremely intricate, bewildering to the casual observer (about 60 different types are employed in the Yinghsien pagoda), and demonstrating refined carpentry skills – perhaps most notably in Japan. This gave rise to the need for a constant unit of measurement, based on the standard measurement of the bracket and thence the proportionate size and spacing of beams and pillars. This modular system was described by Li Chieh in 1103 in his book on architecture, actually a craftsman's manual, which like all Chinese books on architecture, is silent on questions of aesthetics.

In general, Japanese architecture followed the Chinese example, although Japan had its own traditions, dating from before the advent of Buddhism in the 5th century BC and which continued to exert some influence into the modern age. Broadly, Japanese architecture tends to be less grand and more decorative, with greater empathy with nature, reverence for tradition, and thus continuity of style. The simple, natural, Zen-inspired buildings of the early modern period in particular had a powerful influence on the Modern movement in the West.

The invasion of Western influence in the Far East in the late 19th century introduced dramatic changes, the resulting Sino-European compromise architecture seeming to lose more than it gained. Eventually, International Modernism produced no less thorough a revolution in the East than it did in the West although, in Japan particularly, ancient traditions were not entirely abandoned.

Chinese names are given in either the old Wade system of transliteration or the Pinyin system (or both) according to which is likely to be more familiar.

Great Wall of China

The Great Wall of China (Wanli Changcheng) is often called the largest man-made structure in the world; including all its branches, its total length is about 4,000 miles (6400km). It stretches across northern China from Po Hai on the Yellow Sea (Huang Hai) far into Central Asia.

When the Qin emperor Shih Huang-di united China in 221 BC, some sections already existed, made largely of rammed earth. Shih Huang-di ordered it to be linked up and rebuilt to form a single system. Its purpose was to defend the settled communities of China from the predatory, nomadic Ixongnu (Hsiung-nu). It was often rebuilt, sometimes on a different route, in succeeding centuries. The empire-building Han extended it to the Jade Gate (Yumen) in Gansu, and the present structure belongs predominantly to the Ming dynasty in the 15th–16th centuries. It consists of a complex of fortified walls (a traveller entering by the Xifengkou Pass would actually pass through four gates and three sections of wall), and is constructed of masonry on an earth core, though the original was sometimes faced with brick. Manned signal towers at regular intervals communicated by smoke (daytime) or flame (night). Dimensions vary, but in general the wall is about 30-ft (9-m) high, the towers about 40ft (12m). The wall is up to 12ft (3.75m) across, enabling a column of ten men wide to march along it.

The Qin emperor could conscript vast numbers of labourers for building programmes that exceeded even the pharaohs'. They included a network of roads, for swifter troop movement, a canal through the mountains to the southern coastal region, never completed, and, famously, a posthumous 'bodyguard' of about 7,000 life-size, individualized, clay soldiers and servants.

The effectiveness of the Great Wall is hard to judge. It no doubt deterred raiding parties, but it did not prevent large-scale invasions. The main problem, especially in unsettled periods, was keeping it manned. After the Manchu conquest (1644), the frontier moved farther north and the Wall became redundant. It deteriorated over the years but since China has become accessible to international tourists, large parts have been restored.

*LEFT and OVERLEAF
The Great Wall, wrongly reputed to be the only man-made feature on earth visible from space, but still the world's largest.*

Wild Goose Pagoda, Sian

Sian, or Xian, is the former Chang'an (Changan), ancient Chinese capital. In the 7th century AD, it was the abode of the monk Hsüan-tsang, a hugely famous figure after his amazing travels, also known as Tripitaka, 'Master of the Law'. He crossed the desert and the Hindu Kush into India, where he learned Sanskrit, traversed most of the subcontinent and returned in 645, after 15 years' absence, with 700 books and a large collection of sacred Buddhist artifacts. A few years later he suggested the construction of a stone building, described as a 'stupa', in which to store his treasures, the study of which occupied his remaining years. He stipulated that it should be 300-ft (90-m) high, to be worthy of so great a kingdom and to stand as a monument to Buddhism. According to contemporary accounts, his proposal was put to the Emperor who immediately ordered construction to begin, in or about 652. The Wild Goose Pagoda, more pedantically the Great Gander Pagoda, which has survived to this day, however, is a slightly later building, dating from 701–705 and containing Hsüan-tsang's ashes.

The appearance of the original building has provoked considerable interest, since accounts report that it was built 'in the form adopted in India'. It was actually only 175-ft (53-m) high, had five storeys and was topped by a cupola or stupa. It probably resembled the Indian Buddhist shrines that Hsüan-tsang had visited (there are quite close affinities between some later styles of pagoda and Indian temple towers).

The new building, square in plan (the octagonal plan, eventually universal, appeared in the late 8th century), has seven storeys separated by corbelled cornices, and is 190-ft (58-m) high. The form of construction closely resembles the timber towers of the Han period (206 BC–AD 220), which are known from survivors in Japan. It is built of yellowish brick on a rammed-earth core and has little space inside (it could not have served Hsüan-tsang's original purpose), although there is a staircase with vaulted openings leading off it. The Pagoda is powerful rather than decorative, but the potential tedium of the walls is relieved by dividing them into very shallow bays.

The Wild Goose or Great Gander Pagoda contains the ashes of the monk Hsüan-tsang, also known as Tripitaka, 'Master of the Law'.

BELOW
*The Hall of Prayer,
perhaps the most sacred
building in China.*

OPPOSITE
The Processional Way.

Temple of Heaven, Beijing

The Temple of Heaven (T'ien-t'an) contains probably the most familiar building in China, after the Great Wall. The entire complex covers about 690 acres (280 hectares) to the south of the Forbidden City in Beijing. It illustrates the Chinese love of symmetry, particularly strong in Ming China (1368–1644), and it follows the same symbolically significant north-south axis as the Forbidden City, though in fact slightly off-line, while also duplicating it. The splendid geometry of the whole site is most easily appreciated from the air. From the blue-roofed

Hall of Prayers on its high marble platform in the north, a raised processional way leads via another circular building, 'the Imperial Vault of Heaven', to the larger enclosure in the south of the Altar of Heaven, or Circular Mound Altar, with its circular marble walls encircling ascending terraces and four sets of double gates in the square enclosing wall.

The whole layout dates from 1420; the Altar of Heaven and the Imperial Vault were built in 1530, but the design was older and would have been familiar under the Han dynasty (206 BC–AD 220). Most of what one sees today is actually the result of extensive renovation in the 18th century; in the case of the Hall of Prayer the late-19th-century timber for the pillars came from the Pacific North-West of the USA. Nevertheless, it would have looked no different in Ming times. The three-tiered, drum-shaped Hall of Prayer, housing 'the Altar where Prayer for Grain is Offered', is sometimes described as the most sacred building in China. Its form is dictated by cosmological concepts and it stands on an ancient site where once the emperor offered animal sacrifices. The building is about 125-ft (38-m) high and 100ft (30m) in diameter. It is supported by 28 massive wooden columns, four in the centre symbolizing the four seasons. The remaining 24 form two concentric rings, representing respectively the months of the   year and the old division into 12 of the day and night. There are no structural walls, only latticework partitions. The beauty of the building lies partly in its shape, but also in its intense colours, gold, white and red, with the tiles of the conical roofs a deep midnight-blue, and the topmost roof crowned with a golden ball.

Cheng-te

Cheng-te (Chengde), in rugged countryside north-east of Beijing and not far from the Great Wall, was an old Manchu town, rediscovered by the famous K'ang-hsi (Kangxi) Emperor (1662–1722) of the Manchu or Ch'ing (Qing) dynasty. It offers one of the finest displays of imperial architecture in China.

In 1703 K'ang-hsi, keen to escape the summer heat of Beijing and gain easy access to old Manchu hunting grounds, undertook to build a summer palace there; a subsidiary reason was to impress the Mongol tribes to the north. Work continued under his successors, notably Ch'ien-lung (Qianlong, 1735–95), and by the end of the century the complex included over 70 buildings. In general not a particularly extravagant ruler, K'ang-hsi pulled out all the stops here, drawing craftsmen from every part of the empire to construct a complex of pavilions and palaces, temples and pagodas within a huge, walled park dotted with pools, lakes, islands and ornamental bridges, an assembly that blends perfectly with the natural landscape. Engravings by one of the Jesuit missionaries whom K'ang-hsi both welcomed and employed, reached England in 1723 and are said to have stimulated the 18th-century revolution in garden design. Lord Macartney, who led a humiliating British embassy to China in 1793, remarked, as he waited to be summoned as a barbarian tributary to the Emperor's presence, on the resemblance of his surroundings to the park of an English country house.

The buildings themselves, though they are far more elegant than the Manchurian village that K'ang-hsi is said to have wished to imitate (the palace buildings themselves have 120 rooms!), are much less grand than, for instance, the imperial palaces of Beijing. Some appear quite dark, with little decoration and muted colour. However, K'ang-hsi's successors were less economical, and some interiors, such as the Hall of Frugality and Sincerity, are decidedly sumptuous.

Some fine temples outside the park, whose numbers have been depleted since the 18th century, suggest Tibetan influence, an acknowledgment of the Ch'ing emperors' interest in Tibetan Buddhism; a model of the Potala was made at Cheng-te in honour of a visit by the Panchen Lama in 1786.

Besides the exquisite buildings of K'ang-hsi, Cheng-te includes more utilitarian structures.

The Forbidden City

The imperial palace, or palaces, within the Forbidden City (forbidden to all commoners and foreigners) were built by the Ming emperors in the early 17th century. Though extensively restored under the Ch'ing (Qing) in the 18th century, with some decorative additions, the original style was faithfully repeated in accordance with the tradition, in Beijing particularly, of preserving both the detail of buildings and the symmetry of the city plan, on its north-south axis inherited from Han times. This array of huge gates, terraces, halls, gateways and courtyards, in brick, marble and wood, which has now been restored as a museum, presents an unparalleled display of imperial magnificence.

The main entry is via the monumental Meridian Gate (Wumen), formerly reserved for the emperor alone, which also served as a platform for imperial announcements. Beyond is a vast courtyard, crossed by a balustraded stream with five marble bridges, and the Gate of Supreme Harmony, guarded by an imperious row of bronze lions and flanked by galleries and pavilions. It leads into another, even larger courtyard, about 656-ft (200-m) wide. On the far side is the greatest of the three ceremonial halls, the Hall of Supreme Harmony, where the Emperor presided from his golden Dragon Throne. It stands on a three-tiered platform and is approached by stairways and ramps in white marble. Here, as throughout the Forbidden City, while the decoration is sumptuous almost beyond belief, the basic plan is very simple. It is rectangular in plan, with the supporting columns arranged in double rows. The overhanging, tiled roof protects the open colonnade and is surmounted by a second roof, more steeply curved.

Farther along the axis stands the Hall of Middle Harmony, a lesser audience hall, and the Preserving Harmony Hall, used for the famous civil-service examinations, which contains carvings of dragons on a marble block weighing 250 tons, brought to the site by skidding it along roads artificially flooded in winter so that they froze. Farther north are the imperial living quarters, buildings of mind-boggling extravagance but on a smaller scale.

Within walls 2.5-miles (4-km) long, the buildings of the Forbidden City are said to contain 9,000 rooms, the sort of statistic that no one can confidently contradict.

A temple in the extensive and beautiful gardens of the Kyongbok Palace. This is a modern reconstruction, but a faithful one.

Kyongbok Palace, Seoul

In spite of a sprinkling of stone pagodas over 1,500-years-old, historic buildings in Korea are rather few, not only as a result of perishable materials but also of the wars and invasions that have ravaged this peninsula over the centuries.

Historically, Korean architecture is an amalgam of chiefly Chinese, Japanese and native traditions. Differences are due partly to climate but mainly to different sensibilities. Simplicity and naturalism are the key to Korean architecture, which avoids the excessive decoration sometimes found in China; indeed the influence that flowed from China and Japan also moved in the opposite direction.

The Choson dynasty, also called Yi, after its founder, seized power in Korea in 1392, and unified the country under its rule, which lasted until the Japanese annexation of 1910. The early kings established Confucianism as a kind of state religion, which encouraged a period of artistic renewal. The oldest of five palaces in Seoul, the Kyongbok Palace (Kyongbokkung) was begun in 1395 as the seat of government and the royal residence. It is a collection of graceful and varied pavilions and other buildings set among beautiful gardens and pools, and lies at the north end of the broad avenue of Sejongno in central Seoul. There are few finer examples of man's sensitive awareness of the beauties of nature.

The Japanese invasion of 1592 resulted in the burning of the palace, and the royal family moved to the Changdok Palace (begun 1405). They did not return to Kyongbok until after the reconstruction of 1867, and were driven out for good in 1910 when Japanese annexation was confirmed. The Japanese authorities tried to obliterate Korean culture and of the 200-odd buildings that made up the Kyongbok Palace, all but about ten were ruined, and a vast concrete Japanese headquarters was built in its southern courtyard. This building was demolished when a major restoration, scheduled for completion in 2020, was begun in 1995. Within five years the royal residences had been completed and the complex was on the way to reclaiming its former glory.

Potala Palace, Lhasa

Named after the sacred Mount Potalaka, the Potola Palace was the official summer residence of the Dalai Lama, the spiritual and political leader of Tibet. Under the current Chinese regime, which is hostile to Tibetan culture, the Dalai Lama is in exile, his summer palace has been turned into a 'Pleasure Park', and the Potala itself is a museum. Its 13 storeys, which once made it possibly the world's tallest building, compete with ugly concrete tower blocks, though it still dominates Lhasa, and its golden roofs greet the approaching traveller from afar.

The first palace was built in the 7th century, and at least one small chapel in the Red Palace is believed to date from that period. It was entirely rebuilt, on the same site and two storeys higher, in the 17th century by the Fifth Dalai Lama (1617–82) in a style that blends Chinese, Indian, Central Asian and Tibetan traditions although, in Tibet more than anywhere else, architecture is subordinate to religion. Considerable renovation and restoration has taken place since, most recently under Chinese authority. The building is 387-ft (118-m) high, and the area of the interior has been calculated at 155,500sq yd (130000sq m). Altogether it contains about 1,000 rooms and about 200,000 works of art, including murals, sculptures, tapestries as well as scrolls, books (the Potala contains a printing press with 18th-century wood blocks), sacred relics, painted banners (*tanka*) and religious images, especially of the eleven-faced Avalokiteshvara, the *bodhisattva* of mercy associated with Mount Potalaka.

The outer section, known as the White Palace, contained the Dalai Lama's residence, the offices of government, as well as a school and living quarters for the monks. The inner section, the Red Palace, which rises from the centre of the White Palace, contains religious buildings, including the tombs of former Dalai Lamas in the form of golden stupas. The largest chamber of the White Palace is the hall where the Dalai Lamas were enthroned, with murals illustrating scenes from Tibetan history and the lives of the Dalai Lamas. Still larger is a pillared chamber in the Red Palace, with 17th-century murals depicting the Fifth Dalai Lama and Tibetan kings. Murals on the second floor of the Red Palace are of particular interest since they portray the construction of the Potala in the 17th century.

BELOW and OVERLEAF The Potala Palace was once the home of the Dalai Lama, the spiritual and political leader of Tibet, before he was forced into exile.

The Horyuji, Nara

Chinese culture and Buddhism arrived in Japan, via Korea, in the 6th century and received a powerful impetus from Prince Shokotu (572–622), whose reforms were largely responsible for transforming a basically tribal society into an imperial state, based on the model provided by T'ang China. He is also credited with the construction, close to his palace, of the monastic complex of the Horyuji, the earliest in Japan, which became the centre of a popular cult identifying Prince Shokotu with the Buddha. The Horyuji, built mainly in 601–607, was burned down in 670 but promptly rebuilt. Not everything was destroyed: among the many treasures of the Horyuji are early 7th-century bronze Buddhas of Korean workmanship. The monastic buildings in 670 were confined to the present western precinct, the Teaching Hall in the north being later. The eastern precinct, containing the octagonal Hall of Dreams dedicated to Prince Shokotu, dates from the Nara period (8th century).

The main enclosure is surrounded by a gallery or cloister, open but for lattice panels between the outer pillars. It contains two main buildings, raised on masonry platforms. The Golden Hall, which was equipped with its huge mural paintings during the 670 reconstruction, has columns showing slight *entasis* that some scholars rather improbably ascribe to distant and indirect Western influence (support for the roof is supplied, of course, through brackets, not capitals!). The other, outstanding building, known to millions through photographs, is the five-storeyed pagoda (Gojunoto). It is the oldest surviving pagoda in Japan and valued all the more as an example of the T'ang style, of which none comparable remains in China itself. Square in plan, it is 105-ft (32-m) high, with deeply projecting eaves. Each ascending storey is slightly smaller than the one below, giving it a sense of balance and stability. At the top is a tall pinnacle of bronze rings, deriving ultimately from the umbrella symbols of Indian temples.

One of the buildings in the Horyuji complex, which dates back to the time of Prince Shokotu.

The Todaiji, Nara

During the Nara period (710–784) in Japan, a permanent capital was established for the first time at Heijo (Nara), modelled on the T'ang capital of Chang-an. Buddhism became more strongly established, due to court patronage, and numerous monasteries were built or rebuilt.

In 745, prompted by an outbreak of plague and other disasters, the Emperor Shomu called for the founding of a new monastery, the Todaiji or Great Eastern Temple, which would house a massive new Buddha figure, the Daibutsu, (Great Buddha) or Buddha Vairočana, an enormous cast-bronze figure over 53-ft (16-m) high, and also serve as the headquarters and training centre of the numerous provincial monasteries and nunneries that the devout Emperor had founded at state expense all over the country – a Japanese Cluny. With the aid of many people – the Emperor had called upon everyone to contribute 'at least a twig' – much of the vast complex of the Todaiji was completed by 752, when an Indian monk, with a brush attached by a cord to the hand of the Emperor below, painted in the irises of the eyes of the Great Buddha, thus giving the statue life. The total area of the Todaiji covered an area about 2,460-ft (750-m) long and 1,970-ft (600-m) wide. It included two pagodas and living accommodation for thousands of apprentice monks. The whole place was destroyed in one of the wars of Minamoto and Taira in 1180, and over the years fire and other disasters wreaked havoc. The only substantial building left today is the Hall of the Great Buddha, which itself has been rebuilt several times. Most of the present structure dates from 1709, the roof from 1980. It is said to be the

world's largest wooden building, 225-ft (69-m) long and 150-ft (46-m) high, and derives from the typical T'ang palace, although with a recognizably Japanese aspect. The Great

Buddha has also survived, an immense and calming presence, although not a scrap of the material of the original statue remains.

Japanese temples, like the Todaji, usually consist of a number of buildings, with the main one in the centre of a series of enclosures.

*LEFT
The interior of the Hall of the Great Buddha.*

Himeji, the 'White Heron Castle', was originally built by a warlord in the 14th century, but it was rebuilt and greatly enlarged from the late 16th century.

Himeji Castle

With the virtual collapse of the authority of central government in medieval Japan, those who could carved out their own domains and prepared to defend them; even the great monasteries had large armies of fighting monks. The *daimyo* or warlords who dominated medieval Japan built their forts or castles on easily defended hilltop sites These medieval castles were of course built of wood, but with the arrival of guns and cannon, they became suddenly vulnerable. At the same time the civil wars of the 15th–16th centuries, in which the constant strife between warring *daimyo* was finally ended and the Tokugawa shogunate established, encouraged the building of large castles (*hirajiro*) of stone, at least the lower storeys, often on artificial mounds commanding the valleys. Eventually, these castles served other purposes besides war, notably for encouraging trade and serving as centres of local government; they were often decorated with painted screens and other furnishings of great magnificence.

Japanese castles, which have no equivalent in China, were unique in adapting the style of a one- or at most two-storey building, with its curved, projecting eaves and gables, to a building six- or seven-storeys high. Several examples of these buildings, which so impressed visitors from Europe, still remain, including Himeji, Kumamoto and Matsumoto, which was built by Hideyoshi in about 1595.

Himeji, the 'White Heron Castle', was originally built by the Akamatsu *daimyo* in the 14th century. It was rebuilt and greatly enlarged from the late 16th century by Hideyoshi and later owners. It is set on a lowish hill and

protected by a moat, in some sections by double moats, and a complex of earth ramparts. The lower parts are protected by a formidably battered, inward-sloping wall. From the outside, the main keep or donjon has five storeys, but from the main enclosure on the inward side it

has seven. It is linked with several other, smaller blocks. Altogether, the castle, which dominates the modern city of Himeji, looks impregnable, yet its upper parts, in gleaming white with grey-green roofs, manifest considerable elegance.

Byodoin, Uji

One of the many aspects of Japanese culture that profoundly impressed Westerners was the art of the garden. They were intrigued by the aesthetics of landscape-garden design as illustrated in the medieval Zen Buddhist temples of Kyoto, particularly the famous drystone gardens typically consisting of raked sand with strategically placed rocks and few if any plants. But there were other traditions, some of them older than Zen, that influenced the art. One was the cult of Amida known as the Pure Land Buddha, who originated in India and later flourished in China from the 5th century AD, reaching Japan by the 11th century. Pure Land Buddhism has some obvious parallels with Christianity, for instance in its emphasis on enlightenment, or salvation through the intervention of the compassionate Buddha Amida (Amitabha), a name that can be translated as Eternal Life, and the promise that eventual access to the Land of the Western Paradise (the Pure Land, Gokuraku) requires only faith and devotion.

The Byodoin at Uji, a few miles south of Kyoto, is a temple and garden that represents an earthly representation of the Pure Land. It was originally a Fujiwara palace, converted into a temple in 1053, a generation after it was first built. The main construction, built on an island, is the Phoenix Hall, one of the most elegant buildings in the whole of Japanese architecture. It is the only original building among the whole assembly of the Byodoin, and is named after the two gilt-bronze birds that stand on its roof. Viewed from across the tranquil lily pond, there is something bird-like about the whole building, with its swooping roof apparently preparing for

flight, and wings on each side that culminate in smaller, projecting pavilions, a plan deriving from the typical aristocratic palace. The whole façade is nearly 160-ft (49-m) long, although from a distance it does not appear so large. Inside is a gilded wooden Amida figure by Jocho, the most famous sculptor of the Heian

period (784–1185), who developed the versatile technique of joining several blocks rather than carving from a single piece of wood.

The swooping roofs of the Amida, or Phoenix Hall, Byodoin.

Golden Pavilion, Kyoto

Columbus's men, sailing west from Europe in
1492, expected to find their way to the fabled
lands of Cathay (China) and Cipangu (Japan)
where, they had heard, the very roofs of the
houses were made of gold. Possibly the origin
of this tale was a rumour, passed to the West by
who knows what mysterious means, of the
Golden Pavilion.

Like the earlier Phoenix Hall at Uji, the
Temple of the Golden Pavilion (Kinkakuji) is an
elegant building on a lake in an exquisite
setting. The gardens here are on a magnificent
scale, and include aspects of the typical Zen
garden as well as the water gardens of the
Heian period associated with the villas of the
aristocracy, who liked to do some fishing from a
comfortable lodge. They offer several carefully
calculated views of the glittering pavilion, in a
manner associated with the Zen monk Muso
Soseki (1275–1351) who built small shrines with
'natural' gardens on his wanderings through the
countryside, until he was taken up by the
Ashikaga shoguns. The Golden Pavilion was
built in 1397 and was originally part of the
palace built after his official retirement by the
Ashikaga shogun Yoshimitsu, the most powerful
governor of the dynasty and patron of the Noh
drama. He received visits from the Emperor
here, and it was converted into a temple after
his death. It has three storeys, the top one
smaller, and its light, airy, even joyful
appearance, with wide balconies under the
extending eaves, is enhanced not only by its
reflection in the lake, on which it seems to float,
and by the lovely setting, but also by the glitter
of the gilding. (It proved influential: one of
Yoshimitsu's successors built a Silver Pavilion.)

With occasional restorations, the building
survived wars, bandits, earthquakes and other
threats for over 550 years, only to be burned to
the ground in 1950. It was reconstructed
immediately and, after some delay, regilded.

The Katsura Villa complex celebrates the poetic marriage of house and gardens in the intimate sukiya *style.*

Katsura Villa, Kyoto

A number of splendid residences were built in or around Kyoto towards the end of the 16th century. One of them gives its name to the brief Momoyama period (1573–1615), which roughly coincided with the ending of the wars between the *daimyo*, the unification of Japan, and the establishment of the Tokugawa shogunate, marking the beginning of the Edo period, when the capital moved to the future Tokyo. Probably the best-known is the Katsura Rikyu, named after the river on whose bank it stands, southwest of Kyoto. It was originally authorized by Hideyoshi in about 1590 for Prince Toshihito, brother of the emperor, and after his death in 1629 it was enlarged further by his son, Prince Toshitada. The original designer of the beautiful gardens and the layout of the villa was Kobori Enshu, a master of the tea ceremony.

Both princes, not to mention Hideyoshi himself, were enthusiasts of this hugely influential convention. With its emphasis on rustic simplicity, it did not encourage artistic innovation, though Hideyoshi built himself a large and luxurious tea house. Katsura's tea houses (there are no less than four) are made of simple materials – plain wood, thatched roofs, etc., used in a sophisticated way.

The whole complex, on a sloping site, covers about 16 acres (6.4 hectares) and is surrounded by a high bamboo hedge. There are three main, interlinked buildings or halls and many other smaller, pavilion-like buildings, self-consciously simple with an almost total lack of furniture and ornament, designed to admit a maximum of light and set in a largely artificial landscape. The older ceremonial *shoin* style is still evident in the main Old Hall; otherwise, the villa represents the more domestic *sukiya* style, in which house and garden are one, of the Edo period. Interior floor space is variable, thanks to sliding paper screens, and is based on the fixed unit of the straw floor mat (*tatami*). The buildings are connected by paths which wander among streams and pools supplied by the Katsura river, with a constant provision of well-calculated views from the open pavilions and verandas, Japanese gardens, of course, being designed to present a view, not for strolling around.

Saint Mary's Cathedral, Tokyo

Modernism finally swept away historical styles even in the ecclesiastical field, and one result of the globalization of architecture in the mid-20th century was that the best architects were commissioned to design buildings for societies of a different culture from their own, often with highly satisfactory results. It could be said, for instance, that many of the best modern Christian churches were designed by non-Christian architects.

The cathedral in Tokyo, designed by the great Japanese architect, Kenzo Tange, was built between 1961 and 1964 and is therefore contemporary with his more famous Olympic buildings. It combines a novel concept of structure with traditional symbolic form, being on a cruciform plan. (This was partly dictated by the site, since it replaces the former cathedral destroyed by bombing during World War II.)

The cathedral dominates the low-rise houses of the Bunkyo district of Tokyo like a huge silver bird. It hardly has conventional walls or roof, but vast, shimmering sails or shells, clad in ribbed stainless steel, which rise to repeat the cross form at roof level, angling upwards from the centre, more sharply so over the chancel. A broad ribbon of skylight runs along each arm, interspersed with cross-beams bracing the shells. When it reaches the peak at the end of each arm of the cross, it descends as a long vertical window to the ground. The architect has made something almost abstract out of a traditional Gothic form, and this impression is strengthened by the lack of sculpture and the tall, tapering concrete needle of the bell tower, 197-ft (60-m) high and set well apart from the cathedral, from

which one might expect to hear electronic music rather than bells. People enter through two low annexes that skirt the nave like aisles. Inside, the light is muted by louvres on the skylights. The soaring concrete shells still bear the marks of the shuttering, perhaps surprisingly in view of Tange's identification of beauty with function, but their clear if dizzying upward sweep recalls the ideals of medieval builders.

St Mary's is the creation of the great Japanese architect Kenzo Tange and is contemporary with his famous Olympic buildings.

The Great Hall of the People contrives to fulfil the conflicting demands of several sharply contrasting traditiions, and does so with more success than might have been expected.

Great Hall of the People, Beijing

During the second half of the 19th century, foreign, mainly Western, influence threatened to swamp China culturally, as well as economically and politically. The buildings of the foreigners were in their own style, and few were distinguished. Chinese imitations were even

worse, giving rise to the hybrid style of the so-called Chinese Renaissance or Revival. Progressive, reform-minded Chinese recognized that traditional architecture had to adapt to modern needs, and that reform implied Westernization. But the 'Eclectic' buildings of the interwar period were essentially Western – 'foreign buildings with Chinese roofs on', as one famous scholar called it, or 'pigtail architecture'. Political disarray and economic weakness did not help matters.

After the Communist victory of 1949, Russian influence was understandably strong, but the 'Soviet wedding-cake' style was no great improvement, and eventually ideological differences made it less popular. The alternative was a slow and cautious move towards the International Modern style, though there were ideological difficulties there too, as it was strongly associated with the USA.

The most memorable building that resulted was the Great Hall of the People (1959), a gigantic edifice on the south-west side of Tiananmen Square in Beijing. It is chiefly memorable for its size rather than its beauty, though it has a certain almost Classical sense of order and, built within one year, was an impressive symbol of the strength of the Communist Republic. It is an immense, flat-roofed building, 1,100-ft (335-m) across the façade, capable of seating 10,000 people, and surprisingly colourful, with grey marble columns set in red bases, a gold cornice, the lower parts of the building in pinkish stone and the walls a warm yellow. Inside, walls and ceiling are rounded and the main light source is a red star set in sunflowers. The main floor space, over 6,050sq ft (562sq m) in area, could

house all the buildings of the Forbidden City.

More recently, the Chinese in their mushrooming industrial cities have abandoned the ancient tradition of building spaciously but horizontally, not vertically. The pagoda was the only exception and that has now been replaced by the tower block.

Tange's audacious twin stadia, or sports halls, for the Tokyo Olympic Games of 1964 were perhaps his greatest masterpiece.

Olympic Stadia, Tokyo

Japanese architecture was extremely lively and imaginative in the post-Second World War era, with Kenzo Tange as its outstanding exponent. He took a leading part in the debate concerning tradition in the 1950s and was the dominant influence on, though not really part of, the movement called Metabolism, propounded by a group of young Japanese architects who produced some highly futuristic buildings in the 1960s, though they soon broke up and went their separate ways.

Tange was more adept than most at combining tradition with the International Modern style. He expressed his hope or belief that the belated achievement of a democratic society in Japan would release great national energies and create something new and exciting. Sympathetic to Shinto and Buddhist tradition, in his Tokyo City Hall he imitated, not altogether convincingly, the techniques of the very early Jomon culture in Japan, which ended in about 300 BC. More successful was his widely praised Kagawa Prefecture building in 1955–58, which mingled concepts drawn from the Heian period (9th–12th century) with the characteristic forms of the International Modern style, reworking details of traditional wooden architecture in concrete.

His hugely audacious twin stadia, or sports halls, for the Tokyo Olympic Games in 1964 were perhaps his greatest masterpiece. Their sweeping, curved, steel-covered concrete roofs, forming vast ellipses suspended like tents above the arena, seemed in line with Japanese tradition, not because of any direct borrowing but through their brilliant asymmetrical arrangement and siting, a demonstration of how

thoroughly Tange had comprehended historical aesthetics, not to mention the latest engineering techniques. These buildings proved as 'functional' as they were spectacular and set a high standard for future designers of such Olympian structures. They showed, too, that

modern architecture did not necessarily have to be Western, although this particular road did not take him very far; Tange's interests subsequently changed as he became absorbed by urban planning and he largely abandoned his concern for preserving tradition.

SOUTH ASIA

CHAPTER SEVEN

The Great Stupa, Sanchi

Ajanta

Kailasanatha Temple, Ellora

Mamallapuram (Mahabalipuram)

Bhubaneswar

Temple of the Sun, Konarak

Khajarao, Madyha Pradesh

Jama Masjid, Fatehpur Sikri

Humayun's Tomb, Delhi

Udaipur, Rajasthan

Gul Gunbad, Bijapur

Golden Temple, Amritsar

Red Fort, Delhi

Taj Mahal

Badashi Mosque, Lahore

Victoria Terminus, Bombay

Viceroy's House, New Delhi

Chandigarh, Punjab

National Assembly Building, Dhaka

Borobudur, Java

Angkor Wat, Cambodia

The architecture of the Indian subcontinent, reflecting historical conditions, is unique in several respects; in spite of centuries of conflict and upheaval, there is overall a remarkable sense of continuity. It can be broadly divided into three periods. The first is that of the 'native' tradition, sometimes called 'Hindu', a term that is strictly speaking both anachronistic and inaccurate, although it does describe most of the great surviving monuments. It began well over 2,000 years ago and continued up to about the 12th century (longer in some regions), spreading beyond the subcontinent to Indonesia and south-east Asia. The second is the era of Islam which dominated North India, and under the Mughals most of the subcontinent, when it produced perhaps the most beautiful buildings in the world. After the collapse of the Mughal empire in the 19th century, the British became the dominant power in India. Imperial European powers generally followed their own architectural styles, and the British were no exception although, in the late 19th century, many British architects endeavoured with varying success to incorporate local traditions in their still essentially Western buildings. By the time India and Pakistan became independent (1947), they, like practically every other ex-colony, attempted to establish a new identity under the ubiquitous influence of the International Modern style.

The earliest architecture was wooden, but nothing survives. The earliest surviving buildings are the Buddhist stupas, which, like later

Hindu temples, betray their origin in wooden structure and carving. The first stone temples were excavated or rock-cut, as at Ellora and Mamallapuram: those built by the more common method, by assembling stone blocks, first appeared in the 7th century. Styles steadily evolved, though they continued to suggest the tradition of woodcarving, being more sculpture than architecture. Not until quite late in the period did Hindu architects learn how to create large internal spaces.

Muslim attacks, and eventually conquest, from the north-west resulted in the destruction of Hindu temples throughout northern India, although a few regions, such as Orissa, escaped. But Muslim rulers, whose architectural traditions came from Persia and Central Asia, naturally employed Hindu workers and adopted Hindu architectural features. The Indo-Islamic style existed long before the arrival of the Mughals, but reached its peak under Shah Jahan (1628–58), builder of the Taj Mahal. Nor was this exclusively a Muslim style. Hindu princes in Rajasthan built their palaces in the same style as the Mughal emperors in Delhi.

The British created some strange buildings in what was called the 'Indo-Saracenic' style, but eventually achieved a fairly successful blend in Viceroy's House, New Delhi. Independent governments, seeking a new, national style, perhaps inevitably tended to employ top Western architects, notably Le Corbusier (Chandigarh) and Louis Kahn (Dhaka).

The Great Stupa, Sanchi

The monuments at Sanchi, on a hill in Madhya Pradesh, form one of the most important Buddhist sites in India. Together they represent a potted history of Buddhism and a museum of the development of techniques in architecture and sculpture, encompassing the transition from wood to stone.

The stupa is not intrinsically a structure of commanding architectural interest, and the Great Stupa at Sanchi is not the most impressive. Although it is one of the largest in India, measuring 121ft (37m) in diameter and 52ft (16m) in height, the stupas at Anuradhapura in Sri Lanka are far larger. It is not one of the eight stupas to which the ashes of the Buddha were distributed, but its core dates from the time of the Maurya emperor, Asoka (273–232 BC), the wise ruler who adopted Buddhism without threatening its egalitarian appeal.

The Buddhist stupa derived from the funeral mounds of earlier times, and had a similar function in that it contained Buddhist relics (one of the smaller stupas at Sanchi contained relics of famous disciples of the Buddha); but eventually the stupa itself became an object of worship. Early Buddhism was unconcerned with appearances, the structure itself was not important, and the Great Stupa was originally much smaller and plainer – a mound of earth and stone covered with bricks and plaster, with a small space in the centre for the relic, niches for lamps set in the dome, and a circling ambulatory. As Buddhism grew in wealth and the monks in influence, the material world intruded. The Great Stupa doubled to its present size in the 2nd century BC, wood was replaced

by stone, and sculpture made its appearance, reaching its peak around 50 BC with the four magnificent *toranas* (gates) of the Great Stupa, one of the glories of Indian art.

Neglected for 600 years, Sanchi was rediscovered by a British officer in 1818.

Unfortunately, treasure-hunters and amateur archaeologists caused considerable damage (Asoka's pillar was used in a sugarcane press) before the British government took steps to protect it.

The Great Stupa at Sanchi is India's most famous Buddhist monument.

Ajanta

A year after the 'discovery' of Sanchi, a British hunting party stumbled on the rock-cut Buddhist sanctuaries (*chaityas*) and monks' houses (*viharas*) of Ajanta, in the Sahyadri Hills about 230 miles (370 km) north-east of Bombay and not far from the later site of Ellora. Overgrown by dense forest, they had apparently been undisturbed for centuries. There are 29 caves at Ajanta, dating from the 2nd century BC to the 8th century AD. Cut in a U-shaped hillside above a ravine, they would have originally been reached from the river by steps.

Strictly speaking, these are works of sculpture rather than of architecture, since they were carved from solid rock, a volcanic lava comparatively easy to cut; but they are of special architectural interest because the freestanding buildings on which they were modelled were made of wood and have therefore long disappeared. One of the oldest, Cave 10, from before 100 BC, measures 98 x 41ft (30 x 12.5m) and is 36-ft (11-m) high. The method of work was to start at the top, the roof being completely finished before moving down, thus avoiding the need for scaffolding. Covering such a long time span, the caves also show how the skills of the 'builders' advanced. Whereas the early sanctuaries closely follow existing models, the later ones show the development of more inventive design. The impressively sculpted façade of Cave 19, a large *chaitya* hall which belongs to the Gupta period (early 6th century), although it retains the customary large, almost-circular opening, the only source of light, is unlikely to have duplicated a freestanding building.

The greatest glory of Ajanta, however, are the paintings, which besides the life of the Buddha, depict life and culture in almost every imaginable aspect, with buildings, street scenes, court and domestic life, as well as astonishingly realistic paintings of animals. Some, like the famous Bodhisattva Padmapani in Cave 1, are of unsurpassable quality, which is extraordinary given the working conditions, with the only light reflected from metal mirrors mounted outside.

OPPOSITE
Overall view of the cave sanctuaries of Ajanta in the cliffs above a curve of the River Waghora.

LEFT
One of the Gupta façades. The circular opening is the main source of light.

Kailasanatha Temple, Ellora

The earliest rock-cut sanctuaries at Ellora are contemporary with the later ones at nearby Ajanta, but work continued much later, well after the time when freestanding temples were first built in stone elsewhere in India. There are 34 caves: from south to north, 12 Buddhist, 17 Hindu and 5 Jain. Chronologically, they were made in roughly that order, but some Buddhist and Hindu work was going on simultaneously, although there are also signs of a Hindu takeover in places: the Hindu Cave 15 was probably originally a Buddhist *vihara*, or monastery. Of the Buddhist caves, the most impressive is the Tin Thal ('three-storeyed') Cave 12, with its rich sculpture, but on the whole they are less impressive than those at Ajanta.

The outstanding work at Ellora is the Hindu Kailasanatha Temple which, although cut from the rock, is not enclosed but open to the elements. Work started with trenches cut in the top of the cliff, eventually isolating an immense block of stone over 200 x 150ft (60 x 45m) in plan and over 100-ft (30-m) high. The top was completed first, with the main shrine on what became the upper storey, as work continued steadily downwards. Other large blocks were left intact, to be fashioned later into separate shrines and pillars, and a life-size carving of an elephant. The temple, which as a giant sculpture has been called the most impressive single work of art in India, is dated to the late 8th century, but work must have continued for many years. The name of the temple means 'Lord of [Mount] Kailasa', and it is supposed to represent the sacred mountain beyond the Himalayas that was the home of Shiva. As elsewhere, Shiva himself is represented in an inner sanctuary in the form of a large *lingam* (phallus).

The whole creation, a marvel of craftsmanship and imagination, is a proclamation of Hinduism resurgent and, by implication at least, a symbol of its victory over Buddhism. Because of its situation, closely hemmed in by the surrounding rock face, it is difficult to appreciate its magnificence as a whole, and it is notoriously impossible to photograph effectively.

*Detail of the
Kailasanatha temple.*

*Some of the rock-cut
temples at Ellora.*

Examples of the rock-cut temples of Mamallapuram, one of the most important sites of Indian art.

Mamallapuram (Mahabalipuram)

Mamallapuram, on the coast of the Bay of Bengal south of Madras (Chennai), was established as a major port by the commercially minded Pallava dynasty in the 7th century. Besides merchants, it also became, and remains, an attraction for pilgrims. Nothing of the old port has survived except for the magnificent collection of rock-cut temples in the Pallava, or early Dravidian, style, which was to be influential throughout India and in Cambodia and Java. Most of the temples were carved from outcrops of rock on the seashore. For architectural historians, they provide evidence of the influence on Hindu temples of earlier Buddhist architecture, particularly the *chaitya* hall.

The rock-cut architecture consists of ten *mandapas* (open halls, or 'caves'), and eight *rathas* (monolithic temples whose form suggests a chariot, i.e. *ratha*). Five of the *rathas* are named after the Pandava heroes of the Mahabharata and their wife, Draupaudi. Among the most interesting are the Arjuna *ratha*, with its curious tower, and the Bhima *ratha*, rectangular and barrel-vaulted, clearly deriving from the Buddhist *chaitya* hall. The *mandapas* are comparatively small, none more than 25-ft (7.6-m) deep, and are like open art galleries, where pilgrims can contemplate in shaded leisure the accomplished sculptures of gods and mythological scenes.

The sculpture of Mamallapuram is its greatest glory. It includes one of the world's most famous bas-reliefs, called the Descent of the Ganges (the precise subject is a matter of argument), carved in the serene yet vigorous

Pallava style on the surface of two large, adjacent rocks, 95-ft (29-m) long and 23-ft (7-m) high.

The most striking architectural feature is the Shore Temple, built – and it is 'built', not cut – in the early 8th century, after work on rock-cut temples petered out. Its square towers, rising in

diminishing horizontal bands like a ziggurat, are an early example of the typical southern Indian temple tower (*vimana*), which is distinct from the smooth and rounded *sikhara* of the north. The towers of the Shore Temple clearly derive from the earlier, carved Dharmaraja *ratha*.

Bhubaneswar

Bhubaneswar, the great temple city of Shiva in Orissa, eastern India, bears much the same relationship to medieval north Indian architecture as Mamallapuram does to the south Indian style.

The temples that survive today, out of the hundreds, even thousands, that tradition asserts were once present, date from the late 7th to the 12th century. The earliest is the Parasuramesvara, quite small, only 48-ft (15-m) long with the tower 44-ft (13-m) high, but remarkable for its extensive, small-scale sculpture which negates the potential heaviness of the slab-like construction. Somewhat later, but quite different in form from the Parasuramesvara and all other Bhubaneswar temples, is the even smaller Vaital Deul, which clearly derives from the Buddhist *chaitya* hall. Possibly the architect came from the south, though equally he may have been following local Buddhist traditions. The temple has Tantric connections, suggested by a frightening image of Durga in her aspect of an eight-armed Chamunda, sitting on a corpse and garlanded with human skulls.

The full blossoming of the Orissan style appears in the esteemed 10th-century Muktesvara Temple, again a relatively small structure, about 45-ft (14-m) long, but with its own sacred pool and a unique *torgana* (gateway), apparently the work of some individual and unknown genius. The porch, hitherto a rather squat, flat-roofed building, has now acquired a pyramidal roof and is unusual in having sculptural decoration inside as well as out. The whole temple is so encrusted with fine sculpture that is more jewel than building.

In the Lingaraja Temple (c. 1000), contrarily, sculpture is subordinated to architecture in this the largest temple in Bhubaneswar. Its sanctuary tower, the Sri Mandir, is 177-ft (54-m) high and dominates the town; in the sanctuary Shiva himself is to be found in the form of his symbol, a giant stone *lingam*. The temple consists of what became the standard four units, Tower, Porch, Dancing Hall and Hall of Offerings, the last two added a century or more later. The temple stands in an enclosure measuring 242,000sq ft (22,500sq m), which contains a number of freestanding shrines built by pious worshippers, their form often reflecting that of the temple itself, and is surrounded by a defensive wall.

European sailors called the Surya Deul the Black Pagoda to distinguish it from another coastal landmark, the White Pagoda, at Puri.

Temple of the Sun, Konarak

The huge Surya Deul, or Temple of the Sun, which stands on its platform among sand dunes on the Bay of Bengal at Konarak, represents the culmination of the Orissan style and is one of the greatest art treasures of India. Its popular name, the Black Pagoda, derives not, as some suppose, from its frankly erotic sculpture, but from Calcutta-bound sailors who used its dark bulk as a landmark. It represents the chariot of the Sun God, and has 12 pairs of giant wheels along each side of the platform and seven realistically straining horses to pull it.

Rescued from the sands in the early 20th century, the temple is largely ruined, though still hugely impressive. The great sanctuary tower (*deul*) is no more, and was possibly never completed, though legend insists it was. The best preserved element is the porch (*jagamohana*), which still has its distinctive pyramidal roof topped by the characteristically Orissan flattened sphere. A third element, either a Hall of Offerings or, as the sculpture of female dancers suggests, a Dancing Hall, stands separately and is also now roofless.

Built in the 13th century, the temple is said to have occupied 1,200 masons and sculptors for 16 years at a cost of 12 times the annual revenue of the kingdom. Most of it is in a pale softish stone, though doorways and major sculptures are of hard greenish chlorite, suggesting bronze. Mortar was not used, and the stones were hauled into place up earth ramps; as further reinforcement the builders added iron girders, which are unknown outside Orissa.

Practically every inch of this monumental building is covered with sculpture of extraordinary variety and of a universally high standard. The imagination of the sculptors was unlimited; for example, a continuous plinth running around the base of the temple is carved with elephants. There are over 1,700 of them, and no two are alike!

Khajarao, Madyha Pradesh

The temples of Khajarao were built by the dynamic Chandela Rajputs at the peak of their power in the 10th–11th centuries. The remoteness of the site, no doubt chosen for safety, resulted in its passing from general awareness until 'discovered' by a British officer in 1838. Having been built all within about 100 years, there is little stylistic variety in the temples which, interestingly, are dedicated to both Vishnu and Shiva and some to Jain saints, suggesting a marked degree of religious tolerance.

There were originally 85 temples, of which 25 remain in reasonably good order. Generally, they represent a refined and fully developed version of the style that evolved at Bhubaneswar, and this is the near-perfect culmination of a magnificent tradition. Building techniques may still be relatively simple, but these are highly sophisticated buildings by any standard.

Among innovations are the high platforms on which the temples stand, and the integration of the four basic units – which are separate structures at Bhubaneswar – into a single building, often on a cruciform plan. Each temple has a number of towers rising to the *sikhara* over the sanctuary, like mountains rising to a peak. The finest example is the magnificent Kandariya Mahadeva, the largest temple, with a tower nearly 115-ft (35-m) high and 84 smaller towers and turrets. The towers are more rounded than at Bhubaneswar, and windows are set back from projecting balconies, creating dramatic contrasts of light and shade.

The sculpture, largely of human or divine figures, is in high-relief, occasionally in the round, and is of extremely high quality. Again in contrast to Bhubaneswar, the temple interiors are also highly decorated, and the utmost skill is deployed on areas that, in normal light, are invisible. The sculpture engenders an atmosphere of contentment and good feeling, as if the sculptors fully shared the success and prosperity of the art-loving Chandela Rajputs. The effect is in striking contrast to the imagery of, for instance, a medieval Christian church with its demons, gargoyles and scenes of hell. There is a good deal of energetic sexual activity, but the sensuousness of the female musicians and entertainers is accompanied by a calm serenity which reminds us that, however sexy, these are heavenly beings. Michael Edwardes remarked that 'the men who carved these statues had very little to learn from anybody'.

One of the many magnificent temples at Khajarao.

Jama Masjid, Fatehpur Sikri

Concerned by the absence of an heir, the Emperor Akbar took the advice of a sage, Salem Chisti, that a son would be conceived at Sikri, the sage's village about 25 miles (40km) south-west of Agra. When this advice proved correct, in 1569, Akbar in gratitude declared he would make Sikri his capital, adding the name Fatehpur ('Victory') after his conquest of Gujarat. In about a decade a spectacular palace complex (hardly a town, there were no streets) was constructed. A vast army of workers was required, and although the style is generally uniform, it is sometimes possible to detect from particular details whereabouts the craftsmen came from.

The main buildings are the royal palace assembly and the Great Mosque, or Jama Masjid. In the palace, the most interesting room historically is the Diwan-i-Khas, or Hall of Private Audience, where Akbar would listen to the debates of representatives of various religions, including Portuguese Jesuits who hoped to convert him. There is ample decorative evidence of Akbar's open-mindedness in motifs of the lotus (Buddhist or Hindu), *chhatris* (Hindu), and Tree of Life (Muslim).

Chhatris also adorn the Buland Darwarza, the magnificent triumphal arch or gateway to the Jama Masjid complex. Approached by the broad flight of steps, the Buland Darwarza, which is 176-ft (54-m) high excluding the steps, looks like an octagon, the gate itself flanked by narrower elements receding at an angle. This is misleading: on the other side it tumbles away from the mighty façade in disappointing steps. The main entrance to the sanctuary, the King's

Gate, is less assertive, though high, and possibly served in place of a minaret. It is flanked by cloisters with domes rising behind. The mosque itself may be intended as a copy of the Great Mosque at Mecca, but here too there are Hindu motifs, as well as elaborate and colourful though faded floral decoration, carved, painted and inlaid. Beautiful vistas extend on all sides. Among the buildings within the enclosure is the

Tomb of Salem Chisti, a low building in white marble of such light-hearted charm that one might almost expect to buy exquisite ice cream there. Altogether, Fatehpur Sikri is a splendid monument of the mixture of Persian and Indian elements that formed the Mughal style. But a monument it remained. Akbar left in 1585, and Fatehpur Sikri was abandoned.

The characteristics of the Mughal style are already established in the magnificent Tomb of Humayun, seen from the ceremonial gardens.

Humayun's Tomb, Delhi

Humayun was the second Mughal emperor, who inherited a shaky empire on the death of Babur in 1530 and was swiftly forced out by rivals. He took refuge with the Safavids of Persia, and was understandably impressed by the splendour of Persian art and culture. He restored his authority with Persian help and a predominantly Persian court, but only regained Delhi in 1555, a year before his death.

Although the first mosques in India were built before 1200, the artistic and architectural traditions of Islam and India could hardly have been more different. For instance, the pointed arch and the dome were alien to Indian architecture, and so was the use of concrete. Hindu craftsmen adopted Islamic traditions successfully, but also introduced Hindu traditions of ornamentation. The Tomb of Humayun is a splendid, early example of that mixture of Persian and Hindu traditions that formed the so-called Mughal style, which would reach its peak with the Emperor Shah Jahan and the Taj Mahal.

Like most tombs, the building is set in lovely water gardens, representing Paradise, here divided into quadrants with the tomb, one of the finest funerary monuments ever built, in the centre. The plan is octagonal, with two tall and powerful gateways. In red sandstone outlined with white marble, the complex occupies a podium 156-ft (48-m) square. The dome, which rises to 125ft (38m), is the first double-skinned dome in India. There are fine inlays, and marble lattices (*jalis*) in the recessed windows, but in general the decoration of the complex is restrained, and the tomb itself, in glistening marble, is unadorned, without even an inscription. There is much evidence of Hindu architectural traditions, for instance in the kiosks, or *chhattris*, above the central gateway, as well as decorative details such as the twin stars above the arch of the central gateway. The tomb was built between 1564 and 1573 by Humayun's chief wife, Hamida Begum, mother of the great Akbar, who camped on the site to keep a closer eye on the workmen and is herself buried here.

The City Palace, from the landward side. Its many pavilions and balconies, some of later date, were for the use of the women of the royal harem.

Udaipur, Rajasthan

The walled city of Udaipur on the shores of Lake Pichola was the capital of the princely state of Mewar in Rajasthan, founded in 1567. Continuing conflict with the Mughals destroyed most of the original city, but when peace came in the 17th century the capital was rebuilt in a style that reflected it, though the vast blank walls of the City Palace fronting the lake, parts of which date from earlier times, are clearly defensive. The architecture of Udaipur reflects the blending of Indian and Islamic styles that, in Rajasthan particularly, long predates the Mughal era; the early work largely resists the influence of the Mughal court style current elsewhere.

The tradition of wall painting in Rajasthan is prominent in the courts of the massive City Palace, actually several palaces combined. The style varies from the bold and colourful Rajput style to a later, more sophisticated, courtly style which has an almost Rococo charm, extending over architectural boundaries. Elsewhere the decoration is jewel-like, sometimes actually employing semiprecious stones; a famous feature is the remarkable use of glass, mirrored, coloured or plain, which in some rooms covers walls, ceilings and even floors. One 19th-century ruler was so impressed with the material that he ordered a suite of glass furniture, made in France, and topped the pinnacles of the palace with diamond-cut glass globes.

In general, 17th-century Udaipur was up to 50 years behind the current fashion until after its occupation by the last effective Mughal emperor, Aurangzeb, in 1679. In the 18th century a new, distinctly Mewar style developed, fully employing the techniques and conventions of Mughal art but in a restrained, ordered style, with exquisite use of white marble. The pavilion erected on top of the City Palace, from gigantic blocks somehow hauled up the walls, is the outstanding example.

The famous Lake Palace, on an island overlooked by the City Palace, offers one of the most romantic vistas in India. It is often likened to a great white ship floating on the lake. Most of it is now a hotel and comprises a mixture of styles from Mughal to modern.

Gul Gunbad, Bijapur

Bijapur, a town in northern Karnataka, formerly Mysore, southern India, was the capital of a substantial medieval kingdom or sultanate, which was ruled from 1489 until 1686 by the distinguished Adil Shahi dynasty, whose domain briefly included Goa.

The dynasty had an admirable reputation for religious toleration, cosmopolitan culture and support of the arts, and their legacy is Bijapur's outstanding collection of Islamic buildings – tombs, mosques and palaces – perhaps the finest in the Deccan and more typical of a northern city. Among them are the Jama Masjid, with its shallow, onion dome and graceful, arcaded court, built by Ali Ardil Shah I (1557–79), and several large mausoleums, of which the 17th-century Tomb of Ibrahim Rawza is the most elegant.

The largest and most remarkable building is the Tomb of Muhammad Adil Shah, known as the Gul Gunbad (Gol Gumbaz), meaning 'Round Dome', built in 1625–56. Muhammad is buried here along with members of his family and his favourite court dancer. The dome is said to be the second largest in the world and to span the largest floor area unsupported by pillars, 59,795sq ft (5555sq m). Its form is a huge cube, with a hexagonal porch or gate and octagonal turrets eight-storeys-high on all four corners. The turrets are crowned with their own galleried cupolas.

If not a particularly beautiful building, Gul Gunbad is certainly an engineering marvel. The immense weight of the dome is skilfully transferred to the square building by a system of arches, but the springing of the dome is invisible from below because the arches also support a projecting and concealing platform, 10-ft (3-m) wide. This is said to be an effective whispering gallery which will carry a whispered message 11 times across the span of 125ft (38m). Unfortunately, conditions are seldom quiet enough to test it. The decoration is incomplete due to the early death of the builder, though it includes characteristic Bijapur motifs, such as leafy points to arches. The grave itself, besides the usual screen, has a canopy of mother-of-pearl.

The massive foursquare tomb of Muhammad Adil Shah is topped by one of the world's largest domes.

Golden Temple, Amritsar

The Golden Temple, or Harimandir, is the central shrine of the Sikhs, first built in the late 16th century on land given by the Emperor Akbar, whose eclectic attitude to religion the Sikhs shared. It was built on an artificial island in the Pool of Nectar (Amrit-sar), by the fifth guru, Arjan, who also compiled the original version of the Granth Sahib, the Sikh 'bible', now kept in the Temple under a golden canopy studded with emeralds and diamonds. In the 1760s the temple was destroyed by the Afghans but swiftly rebuilt. This building survives, though is largely obscured by alterations and additions made after Ranjit Singh, the 'Lion of the Punjab', united the Sikhs under his rule in 1802.

A white marble causeway leads to the temple, the lower parts of which are also of white marble. The upper parts, including kiosks and cupolas, are covered with gilded copper plates, Ranjit Singh having contributed 220lb (100kg) of gold for the purpose in 1830, and are inscribed with words from the Granth Sahib. The building has four entrances, one in each side, representing the four Hindu castes, all equally accepted by Sikhs, the doors of which are silver-plated, enhancing the brilliance and luxury of the temple. On top of the temple is a domed pavilion, the Shish Mahal or Mirror Room, topped by the royal umbrella symbol, such as appears on the Great Stupa at Sanchi.

The interior is richly decorated with painting, inlays and gilding. It is generally Mughal in spirit, but the largely floral and abstract designs contain occasional images of animals and human beings, which is rare in Mughal decoration. In the past, Sikh art and architecture was often disregarded, seen as the work of untutored folk aping courtly styles, if it was not literally stolen (some of the marble for the Temple was supposed to have been taken from the Tomb of Jahangir near Lahore). The marble floors and the immense pavement

around the pool were created by workmen from Jaipur, where the Mughal style had been adopted comparatively early. In any case, the status of the Harimandir as a work of art is irrelevant, since it is a shrine, and a hugely important one, rather than a museum.

294

Red Fort, Delhi

The Red Fort (Lal Qila), is the great citadel built by Shah Jahan within his projected new capital, Shahjahanabad (Old Delhi). Though requiring restoration, it is an immense achievement, a statement of imperial power and wealth that, by its combination of grandeur and delicacy, avoids vulgar pomp and equals, perhaps exceeds, that of any civilization.

A feature of the late Mughal style of Shah Jahan was the replacement of traditional sandstone by marble, previously used mainly for ornamental effect, as in Humayun's tomb, so the name, deriving from the walls and the massive Lahore gate, is slightly ironic. The palaces within, backing on to the river front and open on the inward-looking side, are marble, though some buildings, such as the Diwan-i-Am (Hall of Public Audience) are also of red sandstone. This hall, over 13,000sq ft (1200sq m) in area, is fronted by an arcade of double pillars with cusped or engrailed arches, and decorated with designs in *pietra dura* (marble inlaid with semiprecious stones), both characteristic features of the Red Fort. A panel of birds and flowers behind the raised throne is Florentine, which was once taken as evidence of European craftsmen in India but was more probably imported.

The Diwan-i-Khas (Hall of Private Audience) is, by contrast, of marble. It has the same arches, though here on square piers rather than faceted pillars. The silver plates that covered the ceiling were torn off by the Marathas in the 18th century, and the fabled Peacock throne was carried off to Teheran by Nadir Shah in 1732, later destroyed and now known only from written descriptions. Another

treasure in the Diwan-i-Khas illustrative of a Mughal speciality has survived, the Scales of Justice, a fretted screen of marble 4-in (10-cm) thick. The painted or inlaid decoration is mainly of flowers, and in spite of the losses this is still an impressively luxurious chamber. Who would quarrel with the verse, written in gold on the arches at the end, that proclaims, 'If there is a

Paradise on Earth, then this is it'. Some of the palaces, notably the Rang Mahal (Painted Palace), are, though restored, no less luxurious.

Of many other superb buildings, one of the most attractive is the Moti Masjid, or Pearl Mosque, built in white marble with less decoration as a private chapel by Shah Jahan's son, the more austere and devout Aurangzeb.

OPPOSITE
The buildings of the Red Fort mix the transitional sandstone of the early Mughal emperors with the glittering marble introduced by Shah Jahan.

LEFT
The Pearl Mosque, built by Aurangzeb as his private chapel.

The Taj Mahal has come to represent the peak of a mongrel style that produced some of the most beautiful buildings in the world.

Taj Mahal

The Taj Mahal at Agra, which marks the acme of the Mughal style under Shah Jahan, has often been called the world's most beautiful building, and few who have seen it by dawn light would contradict. It was also one of the world's most expensive buildings, and contributed to Aurangzeb's decision to overthrow its extravagant builder, his father Shah Jahan, who spent the last eight years of his life a prisoner in his palace at Agra.

The Taj, which Rabindranath Tagore described as 'a tear on the face of eternity', was built to demonstrate the Emperor's love for his wife, Mumtaz Mahal, who died giving birth to their fourteenth child in 1631. The mausoleum, in a luminescent white marble that was carried from quarries 186-miles (300-km) distant by 1,000 elephants, took nearly 20 years to complete. It employed thousands of workmen from all over Islam, and precious materials from a similarly wide area. A miracle of symmetry, it stands on a platform nearly 22-ft (7-m) high and 312-ft (95-m) square, with tall minarets at each corner, an arrangement introduced in the Tomb of Akbar. The minarets were set at an indiscernible outward slant so that, in the event of an earthquake, they would fall away, not onto, the tomb. The central, pearl-shaped dome, actually a double dome, rises to 187ft (57m) at its brass finial. Exterior decoration is of calligraphic reliefs and *pietra dura*.

In the centre are the tombs of Mumtaz Mahal and Shah Jahan himself, placed here by Aurangzeb and the one asymmetrical element in the entire complex. They are guarded by an octagonal screen of fretted marble, each section carved from a single piece, inlaid with precious stones. Some flowers contain 60 or more pieces. This masterpiece of craftsmanship was also installed by Aurangzeb, who feared the original solid silver screen would be looted, as was the case with some other furnishings.

The building is set in water gardens, such an important feature of the Mughal style, which though well maintained, can only suggest their former symbolic glory. The Taj was neglected after Mughal authority collapsed; it was nearly dismantled and auctioned off by an early British governor, but was restored by Lord Curzon in about 1900.

The Badashi Mosque presents a striking contrast to Aurangzeb's other creation, the Pearl Mosque in the Red Fort.

Badashi Mosque, Lahore

An important feature of Islamic architecture is the enclosed space, with the result that houses were generally built around a courtyard with few or no windows on the outside. The courtyard mosque, though less inward-looking, derives ultimately from the house of the Prophet in Medina. Its primary purpose is, of course, to accommodate a large number of worshippers.

The Badashi Mosque is attached to the royal fort in Lahore. One of the most splendid examples of Mughal architecture in today's Pakistan, as well as the biggest, it was built by Aurangzeb in 16733–74 and presents a striking contrast with the Pearl Mosque in the Red Fort at Delhi. It is by far the largest building of the reign of Aurangzeb, the last of the great Mughals, and in area it is the largest mosque in the Indian subcontinent, the enclosure measuring approximately 492ft (150m) on each side. The pool in the centre confirms the effectiveness of a fountain in a rectangle of open water as a visual experience, aside from its purpose of providing facilities for washing.

Raised on a high platform and approached by steps, it broadly resembles the Friday Mosque built by Shah Jahan in his new capital, adjoining the Red Fort, in Delhi, though the Badashi Mosque is altogether a grander structure. The Prayer Hall has a bold central portal with three domes, tucked into low cylindrical drums, in white marble, contrasting with the red sandstone of the façade and the four minarets at the corners, themselves topped by white marble cupolas, which here are octagonal in plan. Together with the large arcaded courtyard, it is in general characteristic of the plan of Friday mosques in South Asia.

The relief decoration employs semi-abstract floral mouldings in painted plaster and inlays worthy of comparison with the Taj Mahal. The sense of harmony is enhanced by the delicacy of the cusped arches.

Victoria Terminus, Bombay

The Chhatrapati Sivaji Terminus, formerly Victoria Terminus and still known popularly as 'VT', is the main railway station of Bombay (Mumbai), used in the 1990s by over half a million passengers per day. Perhaps India's most remarkable piece of Gothic-Revival architecture, it was completed in 1887 in the year of Queen Victoria's Golden Jubilee, hence its name.

Under British rule, public buildings in India generally reflected the fashions of Victorian Britain – racial architecture, some would say. Bombay, where a building boom followed the opening of the Suez Canal in 1870, contains the greatest number and variety of Victorian eclecticism, with examples of everything from Neo-Gothic (French and Venetian as well as English) to Renaissance Classical. However, a vocal minority of architects in the late 19th century held that the most appropriate style should at least draw on Indian architectural tradition, giving rise to the curious style

sometimes called Indo-Saracenic. The architect of the Victoria Terminus, Frederick Stevens, while influenced by St Pancras station in London, was sympathetic to this argument, as he also demonstrated in his vaguely Byzantine Churchgate Station and in several other Bombay buildings.

These 'Anglo-Indian' buildings, as Michael Edwardes observed, 'with their demented Mughal motifs [convey] a pleasant zaniness which was not in the minds of their designers'. Stevens' plum pudding of a building looks almost as if it might have been built for some eccentric maharaja impressed by medieval Venice. It commands affection rather than respect. The large central block is flanked by matching wings, and the central dome is topped by a large statue of Progress by Thomas Earp, who also designed the two great cats, an Imperial lion and an Indian tiger, on the gateway pillars. Inside, the influence of Scott's St Pancras is evident in the arcades and stained glass of the booking hall.

Purists may blanch, but Bombay's Victoria Terminus, suggestive of Venetian Gothic as well as mixed Eastern styles, has, at least, a certain presence.

301

Prospect of Rashtrapati Bhavan and the Jaipur Column.

Viceroy's House, now the presidential residence (Rashtrapati Bhavan), is the centrepiece of the new capital that the British embarked upon, south of the old city, in 1912. Like the Romans, they built for durability, assuming that their empire would last longer than it did. The architect was Edwin Lutyens, the ablest and most original English architect of the day. As a symbol of imperial might, solemn monumentality was required, and Lutyens planned a Classical palace with a faint flavour of India.

Monumental, it was at 630-ft (192-m) wide and 530-ft (162-m) deep, of local brick faced with sandstone from the Mughal quarries. The floors were concrete, covered with stone slabs or marble, and underfloor heating was included. The main approach is up a rise, peaking at the Jaipur Column, so that the building rises slowly into view, first the dome, then its drum, the wide colonnade, and finally the steps before the portico. The plan cunningly obscures the presence of windows of disparate shapes in the façade behind the columns, and thus achieves an impressive unity and symmetry. Closer to, the building has a slightly stark and menacing air, not alleviated by the shining copper dome with recessed apertures in the drum that according to common gossip concealed machine-guns. The garden façade is less formal. The overhanging eaves suggest the Mughal style, and the buttress on the drum, topped by cupolas, recalls the familiar form of Mughal *chhatri*.

The chief and most splendid state apartment is the Durbar Hall, which derives ultimately from the Pantheon and gains natural light only from the *oculus*. It is grand but plain, since

Lutyens counted on the colourful uniforms of British officers and Indian princes to provide colour and ornament on ceremonial occasions. Indeed, all the public rooms, even the ballroom, show cool restraint, but for all the imperial solemnity, Lutyens included touches of humour. A fireback has an Indian elephant above a row

of Tudor roses, but one of the roses is only a stalk, as the flower has been plucked by the elephant.

This splendid structure was officially inaugurated in 1931, when the Raj was 16 years short of extinction.

Chandigarh, Punjab

When India and Pakistan became independent in 1947, the Indian government decided to build a new capital for the Indian state of the Punjab, since Lahore, the former Punjabi capital, was now within Pakistan. After the death of one of the original US architects in 1950, Le Corbusier took over the project, together with the British partnership of Maxwell Fry, Jane Drew and a team of Indian architects. Le Corbusier's role was to supervise the general layout and design the government buildings of the Capitol, though he completed only the Law Courts, Assembly and Governor's Residence, with assistance from his brother, Pierre Jeanneret.

Prime Minister Nehru called for 'a new town symbolic of the freedom of India, unfettered by the traditions of the past'. Neither the general plan, which was influenced by Le Corbusier's urban master plan of 1935, called the Ville Radieuse, nor his individual, modernist buildings, truly reflect Indian traditions, although they do not contradict them. They are well adapted to the climate and landscape, and Le Corbusier, who admired Lutyens's Viceroy's House at Delhi, included certain acknowledgements such as the symbol of the umbrella, which appears in various guises. The most admired buildings, lapped by a large artificial pool, are the Law Court (1952–56), with its solid, concrete sun screens, and the Assembly Building, with its great, boat-shaped concrete roof that recalls the contemporaneous chapel at Ronchamp.

Religious and linguistic differences have complicated the political background: Chandigarh is currently the combined capital of Punjab and the new Hindu state of Haryana, but this may change. It is administered by the central government. There are other problems typical of utopian new capitals, including a severe disparity between the sexes (10 men to 1 woman) and increasing scarcity of land. Regardless of the merits of Le Corbusier's Capitol, Chandigarh is more concrete desert than garden city. And a city depending on the car in a country where most people cannot afford a bicycle adds weight to the accusation that the messianic genius Le Corbusier 'never understood other people' (Russell Walden).

Chandigarh: garden city or concrete jungle?

National Assembly Building, Dhaka

Louis Kahn was born in Estonia in 1901 but emigrated to the USA as a child. He taught for some years at the University of Pennsylvania and elsewhere, only achieving international fame comparatively late in life. His major commissions all came within a period of about 15 years. Formidably intelligent (his writings are not always easy to follow) and imaginative, he opened up new directions for modern architecture. Although some regarded him as a reactionary because of his affinity with the tradition of the French École des Beaux-Arts, the great *bête noire* of the avant-garde, and his desire to restore a certain historical grandeur to architecture, he was seen by others as not only the most creative pioneer of Postmodernism and of 'Rational Architecture' but also perhaps the most influential US architect of the 20th century after Frank Lloyd Wright.

Few would dispute that the formidably powerful, almost fortress-like and highly complex National Assembly Building in Dhaka (Dacca), in what was then East Pakistan (now Bangladesh), is his masterpiece. He began work on it in 1962 but actual building did not begin until shortly before his death in 1974. A truly monumental complex, it is really several buildings, secular and religious (it includes a mosque) that are both connected and separate, and illustrates Kahn's principle of the 'house within a house' and dividing 'service' from 'served'.

Kahn explained that what guided his work was 'not belief, not design, not pattern, but the essence from which an institution could emerge...' The complex is built of concrete, which Kahn, in spite of his association with the 'New Brutalism', had already demonstrated, with his attention to detail and finishing, was a less 'brutal' material than it had seemed, combined with marble, and red-brick exterior walls. It is based on simple geometric forms, but they are deployed in an endless variety of ways; there is much to remind us of another of Kahn's axioms: 'silence and light'. For all the aesthetic, even mystical qualities that informed Kahn's work, of course he did not ignore such practicalities as the need to withstand the extreme heat of the region.

Borobudur, Java

The Buddhist temple-stupa of Borobudur in central Java is one of the world's most impressive man-made structures. It was built in about 800, conceived as a whole and completed in a comparatively short time; but the circumstances of its construction are a mystery. Although there is emphasis on the legend of the royal *bodhisattva* (Buddhist saint), it does not appear to be associated with any great ruler or local cult. Though it must have been directed by some individual or group with considerable resources, it seems to have been a popular shrine.

It occupies the top of a mountain and can be thought of as a kind of ziggurat, rising through terraces that diminish in area as they ascend. The lowest terrace was built later, and is in effect a giant rampart no doubt constructed to prevent the structure slipping away down the slope under its own weight. Above it are five terraces basically square in plan, though each side is stepped out twice between corner and centre. The comparatively narrow path is lined by a sculptured wall high enough to conceal the terraces above and below. Above these are three more terraces that are circular, not square (in the Buddhist *mandala*, the Earth is a square contained within the circle of Heaven). They are occupied by 72 stupas in stone latticework through which it is sometimes just possible to make out a Buddha figure within. At the upper levels the slope becomes less steep, space opens out, and the summit is crowned by a single large, bell-shaped stupa 103ft (30m) above the lowest terrace.

The whole structure represents progress from primitive, everyday reality to a state of enlightenment, *nirvana*, illustrated in the relief sculpture along the walls. Thus, a pilgrim circling the building in a clockwise direction, as custom dictated, would complete nine circles to reach the summit. He first sees scenes from the earthly life, mostly carrying a warning message, such as the dire results in the next life for one who kills and eats fellow animals, then scenes from the life of the Buddha, ascending to more philosophical themes from the Buddhist scriptures. The lowest stage of reliefs was obscured when the retaining wall was added.

By 1000, the site was overgrown, having apparently been neglected for nine centuries until it was 'rescued' by the Dutch colonial authorities. It has recently been more thoroughly restored.

Detail of one corner of the temple-mountain of Borobudur. The hefty wall and terrace prevents the whole structure toppling down the hillside.

Angkor Wat, Cambodia

The spread of Indian culture to other lands produced two religious structures of mind-boggling size, Borobudur in Java and Angkor Wat in Cambodia, which is equal to any of the great temple complexes of India both in size – it is usually described as the largest religious structure in the world – and beauty. It was built by the greatest of the Hindu rulers of the Khmer empire, Suryavarman II (reigned 1113–c.1150). It was dedicated to Vishnu and was probably also intended to be the tomb of Suryavarman, who appears frequently among the sculpture as Vishnu himself. As in India, the pyramidal temple symbolizes the sacred mountain, home of the gods.

A broad stone causeway, with monumental balustrades in the form of the universal serpent, leads to the great cruciform gateway to the temple complex, itself nearly 650-ft (200-m) long. The courtyard beyond is divided into four by beautifully decorated galleries. Staggeringly steep steps lead to the second level, lined by galleries, with towers at each corner. Another breathless ascent leads to the central court, again divided into four, with corner towers and, at the centre where the galleries intersect, the central tower containing the shrine. It rises 215ft (66m) from the stone platform on which the vast pyramidal temple stands.

Although the Khmer style ultimately derives from India, it is far from identical, and the inventiveness and imagination of the Khmer builders, not to mention their technical skill, amounts to something much more than a variant. The curved form of the towers, of which only five of the original nine survive, may derive ultimately from Bhubaneswar, but it is quite different, and so is their overall effect – like growths from a common stem. The main structural principle is based on the corbel, pillars having broad capitals to support weighty architraves, and though iron dowels are used, there is no mortar. The sculpture, originally painted and gilded, which even extends to roofs, is mainly in low-relief, yet it portrays scenes of vigorous action, mostly deriving from Hindu mythology, with rare accomplishment. Significantly, figures in the round show less assurance.

Angkor was sacked soon after Suryavarman's death, and though his successor restored the Khmer empire, the Hindu gods were discredited and the Wat became a Buddhist temple. Angkor was abandoned by the 16th century and largely overgrown. It was unknown to the world for centuries, and the first European visitors felt much like the aliens in the science-fiction story who stumble on the long-ruined towers of Manhattan.

LEFT
One of the four gateways of Angkor Wat, reached via a steep flight of steps.

OPPOSITE TOP
A corner tower and gateway beyond the first courtyard.

OPPOSITE BELOW
The central towers silhouetted against the night sky.

ISLAM

—◆—

Chapter Eight

The Great Mosque, Mecca

Dome of the Rock, Jerusalem

The Great Mosque, Cordoba

The Great Mosque, Samarra

Mosque of Qairouan, Tunisia

Masjid-i Jami, Isfahan

Citadel, Cairo

Caravanserai, Aksaray

Citadel, Aleppo

Alhambra, Granada

Tomb of Timur, Samarqand

Selimiye, Edirne

The Great Mosque, Djenné

Süleymaniye, Istanbul

Topkapi Palace, Istanbul

Masjid-i Shah, Isfahan

Khwaju Bridge, Isfahan

Khan of Azad Pasha, Damascus

Madrasa of Mir-i-Arab, Bukhara

Islamic architecture here is intended to include all structures built by Muslims, whether religious or non-religious, throughout the many lands that make up Islam. An exception is South Asia, where the cultural circumstances are different because other religions, notably Hinduism, existed alongside Islam and the interaction of the two resulted in a distinctive architecture of mixed heritage.

The qualities that distinguish Islamic architecture are quite different from those of European, or Christian, architecture. In general, Islamic buildings are inward-looking, typically surrounded by walls, with no interest shown in outward appearances; however, there are many exceptions, such as tomb towers and other 'monumental' buildings. It is often difficult to tell what kind of building lies behind them; while, for example, a great gateway or a dome may be visible, it could belong to either mosque or palace, or to some other type of building. It is the interior space that matters, and to experience a building, you have to get inside it.

Islamic buildings are surprisingly adaptable: a Gothic cathedral can scarcely be anything else, but in Islam, the plan of the courtyard mosque could be, and was, employed for many other types of building at one time or another.

Islamic buildings often appear to have no specific axis or direction, or they have two contrary ones, and there is generally no particular central point or focus. Patterns repeat themselves, with no clear start or finish. Nor were Islamic architects interested in large-scale planning; new buildings were added without regard for the scale or situation of older ones so that, where growth is ongoing for a long time, the result can be something of a jumble, as in the Topkapi Palace in Istanbul.

Another, perhaps the major disparity between Islamic and other architectural traditions, is the attitude to structure. Instead of emphasizing the form and structure – the actual mechanics – of a building, Islamic architects are intent to disguise it. They wish to make it light and insubstantial: domes float, vaults and walls disappear, thanks to the panoply of decorative techniques – mosaic, painting, cut stone, modelled plaster and, above all, glazed tiles – available to obscure their mundane solidity. Decoration is not only astonishingly rich but, at least in religious buildings, predominantly abstract or floral-based, with striking use of calligraphy and geometrical patterns although, of course, this kind of effect has other motives than the purely decorative. The symbolism may be less easy for non-Muslims to comprehend, and without that knowledge a full understanding of the buildings is impossible, because, apart from the many traditions, Arab, Turkish, Iranian, involved, what makes Islamic architecture so distinctive, so different from other traditions, is that it is an expression of Islamic culture, deeply rooted in religion and society.

Umayyad caliphs and decorated with mosaic. An Abbasid caliph built the colonnades. It was rebuilt again by the Ottomans, on a grander scale, and most recently by the Saudis.

The Ka'aba is a stone building which stands in the centre of the courtyard. It is almost a cube, 42 x 36ft (13 x 11m) in plan and about 52-ft (16-m) high, and is oriented so that its corners face the points of the compass. It is believed to date from the days of the Prophet Abraham (Ibrahim), whose grave is also in the courtyard. It has been rebuilt many times, in the same form, and is normally hung with black silk, renewed annually. In one corner is the Black Stone, an object of veneration for the pilgrims who walk around the Ka'aba seven times, which is probably of astronomical origin. There is a door in the Ka'aba high up on one side, its frame sent by the Ottoman sultan when it was rebuilt in 1627.

Views of the Mosque of the Haram at Mecca, Islam's holiest site.

The Great Mosque, Mecca

The Great Mosque at Mecca, or Masjid al-Haram, is the most sacred place in Islam. It contains the very centre of the Muslim religion, to which the *mihrab* of every mosque in Islam is oriented, and every Muslim is expected to make a pilgrimage there, at least once during their lifetime.

The origin of the mosque, the most familiar of Islamic buildings, was the house of the Prophet Muhammad in Medina, a square courtyard with rooms around two sides for his wives. When some of the Companions complained of the heat, an arcade was made with palm trees to provide shade. Many other features of the mosque originated there. The *minbar*, or pulpit, derived originally from the pillar that Muhammad leaned on when preaching, like teachers in a *madrasa* to this day, though later he had one made of cedar, with three steps (he stood on the top step; all imams since put their feet on the second step).

The mosque at Mecca was already a religious building, with the Ka'aba already present, long before Muhammad cleared out the idols in 630. It was much enlarged by the

Dome of the Rock, Jerusalem

The Dome of the Rock is the third most sacred shrine of Islam (after the Ka'aba at Mecca and the Mosque of the Prophet in Medina). Its site could hardly be more holy, for it was here that Abraham nearly sacrificed his son, Isaac. Later the site was occupied by the Temple of Solomon and later still by a Roman Temple of Jupiter. This had disappeared along with the Hebrew Temple when the Caliph 'Abd al-Malik ordered the construction of the shrine (690–692) on the the rock that represents Mount Moriah, whence the Prophet is said to have taken flight to heaven.

One of the world's best known and most beautiful buildings, it is a highly unusual, indeed unique, building in Islamic terms since, apart from its plan, it is as decorative on the outside as it is on the inside. It owes something to the Byzantine tradition and something also to the tradition of Near Eastern builders.

The ground plan is almost a perfect octagon, slightly narrower on two sides. It produces the double octagonal ambulatory beyond which, at the centre, a circle is formed around the rock and below the drum by four piers with three pillars between each pier. Above the round drum of masonry is the semicircular dome, in fact a double dome of wood, which is said to have been covered, when built, with gold plates. Inside it demonstrates a fine sense of proportion, the height from the floor to the springing of the dome being approximately the same as the diameter of the central space, and the octagonal ambulatories about half that height. The diameter of the octagon is about 164ft (50m). The upper part of the octagon and the drum are

decorated with mosaics, the dominant colours being gold and greenish-blue. The dome is now covered by gold-anodized aluminium. The original decoration was replaced under the Ottomans in the 16th century, and the present version is recent. Inside, however, the original decoration has survived more or less intact, though the columns of the octagon have been faced with marble.

*OPPOSITE and ABOVE
This exquisite building
has survived many
centuries despite its
contentious site.*

The Great Mosque of Cordoba, one of the most magnificent buildings in the whole of Islam, was founded by 'Abd ar-Rahman I in 784, having escaped to Spain where Muslims were already established and where he founded a dynasty with Cordoba as its capital.

The Great Mosque, Cordoba

When the Umayyads were supplanted by the Abbasids in 750 and the centre of Islam moved from Damascus to Baghdad, one Umayyad prince, 'Abd ar-Rahman I, escaped to Spain, where Muslims were already established. He founded a dynasty with Cordoba as its capital, and the kingdom flourished, lasting for nearly 300 years (756–1031). In 929 a restored Umayyad caliphate was set up in Cordoba, in rivalry with the Abbasids in Baghdad: by any standard, Cordoba, where Christians and Jews were at least tolerated, was the richest, most sophisticated city in Europe.

The Great Mosque of Cordoba, one of the most magnificent buildings in the whole of Islam, was founded by 'Abd ar-Rahman I in 784. It followed the customary Arab plan, a large courtyard with a prayer hall on the south side. It was substantially enlarged on three subsequent occasions, making it today the largest mosque in Islam outside Samarra. The *qibla* wall (nearest Mecca) and the minaret date from the 10th century. The extensive arcades, which eventually quadrupled in number, amounting to 19, or 18 rows of arches, follow an unusual pattern which was faithfully followed in each successive extension. Roman columns were used but, as they were not tall enough, rectangular piers were placed on top, supporting a semicircular arch that in turn supports the roof. The *voussoirs* of each arch are alternately red brick and white stone, creating, as one looks along the aisles, a striking striped effect. This is repeated in the complex cusped arches before the central *mihrab*, a space sometimes called the sanctuary or the *capella del mihrab*, where stone of two

contrasting colours is employed. This elaborate and intricate chamber dates from 965 and is almost a separate artwork, unusually large and deep, with introductory trios of three-tiered arches. The decoration here is at its richest, basically floral with inscriptions from the Qur'an in carved plaster, marble and glass and gold mosaic. The vaults whose intersecting ribbed arches support the domes are so complicated they challenge eye and brain.

The famous 'winding tower' or minaret at Samarra.

The Great Mosque, Samarra

The architectural heritage of the Abbasids (750–1258) has been sadly depleted. Nothing survives of their great capital city in modern Baghdad, and Samarra, which extended 19 miles (30km) along the River Tigris and, as suggested by Ernst Grube, was 'probably the most magnificent city the Muslims ever built', was deserted by the 13th century and fell into ruins. One of the few surviving, though largely ruined, buildings is the Great Mosque of al-Mutawakkil, the caliph who founded it in 847. It is said to be the largest mosque in the world and probably the largest ever built. Al-Mutawakkil later built another mosque, that of Abu Dulaf, in Samarra which was almost as large.

All that survives of the Great Mosque is the vast fortified rectangle of brick wall, with half-round bastions at intervals, which surrounds the whole enclosure, and the minaret, a famous landmark, to the north of the enclosure. The wall measured about 784 x 512ft (239 x 156m)

and is still about 30-ft (9-m) high. The mosque followed the established pattern of the Umayyad period, but the material here is brick. The prayer hall, in the south, had no less than 25 aisles, and was covered by a flat wooden roof. The *mihrab* was rectangular and decorated with mosaic.

The minaret, for obvious reasons, is known as *al-malawiya*, 'the winding tower'. Over 90-ft (27-m) high, it is set on a solid, square base but the tower itself is round and tapers towards the top. It is ascended by an exterior spiral ramp, circling the tower anticlockwise five times in decreasing circles, giving it a suggestion of a scroll uncoiling. Since symmetry is preserved by keeping the same distance between each circle, the climb grows steadily steeper towards the top. The purpose of a minaret is, of course, to facilitate the muezzin's call to prayer, but clearly a tower of these proportions is not necessary. It is also a symbol of the authority of Islam; al-Mutawakkil's minaret was imitated elsewhere, notably in the Mosque of ibn Tulun in Cairo.

Mosque of Qairouan, Tunisia

The mosque at Qairouan in Tunisia was founded soon after the Arab Conquest of 670, on a site that had formerly been occupied by a Roman building. It was completely rebuilt in 836 and although it has been partly rebuilt or restored several times since, its form has not changed greatly since the 9th century, unlike the Great Mosque of Sfax, which was originally modelled on it. The 9th-century builders were a local dynasty, the Aghlabids, the first native North African dynasty. They had cultural ties both to Umayyad Spain in the west and to the Abbasid caliphate in the east, as well as to Roman predecessors.

The simple clarity of this impressive building, the first 'monumental' mosque in North Africa, was to prove influential throughout the Maghreb, although it is not particularly distinguished architecturally and is comparatively lacking in decoration (the 9th-century painted wooden ceiling has not survived). It follows the established plan for a large, courtyard mosque, consisting of a huge rectangular prayer hall divided into 13 aisles by columns, which were appropriated from Roman remains, a common practice in Muslim North Africa. A double arcade, added later, lines the other sides of the courtyard. The central aisle of the prayer hall, leading from the entrance to the *mihrab* and thus bisecting the hall, is wider and higher than the others – an Umayyad feature. It is surmounted by a fluted dome on a drum on a square base, these elements being plastered white; there is a second dome over the marble *mihrab*, which is decorated with plant-based carving and lustreware tiles imported from the East. The minaret, on the same axis, is built within the outer wall. It is a strikingly large, square tower in three sections, the upper ones again white, and is closer in form to a Christian church tower than to the slender minarets of Ottoman Constantinople. The top storey is crowned with a cupola and is probably of 11th- or 12th-century date. The porches at the eight entrances also belong to that period.

FAR LEFT
The massive minaret is the most impressive feature of the mosque at Qairouan.

ABOVE
The courtyard.

LEFT
A small tower over a gateway.

Masjid-i Jami, Isfahan

The Seljuk Turks, named after the founder of their fortunes, were one of the semi-nomadic groups of Turkic people in Central Asia who converted to Islam in about the 10th century. They moved into Iran, the cultural heartland of a much wider region and, by the mid-11th century, they controlled it. They upheld the caliph in Baghdad, officially at least, and took the title of sultan. In the next century they conquered virtually all of Asia Minor, defeating the Byzantines in the process.

In spite of the cultural unity of Islam, a slight division between east and west had been evident since the Umayyad-Abbasid rivalry, and the Seljuks, great builders with powerful ideas on architectural form, introduced new ideas which had great influence not only in the Iranian cultural sphere but in most of Islam. Their innovations included the round minaret; the plan of four *iwans*, vaulted halls open on one side and placed on each side of the courtyard, associated especially with *madrasas* (religious teaching colleges similar to mosques);

greater emphasis on the exterior of the building; and the creation of complex patterns in brick.

The Masjid-i Jami or Friday Mosque, i.e. a mosque designed for the main weekly services, was originally founded in the 8th century; the present mosque contains some remnants of the 10th-century rebuilding. The Seljuk mosque consisted of a courtyard with arcades, a prayer hall and four *iwans* attached to the arcades. The main dome, erected in 1080 above the prayer hall forward of the *mihrab*, is of classic form, entirely undecorated, with a polygonal base, all in magnificent brickwork. The inside of the dome bears a Kufic inscription commemorating Malik Shah (1072—92, also in brick). There is another splendid domed chamber directly opposite on the far side of the courtyard.

Later rulers added new elements, most of the glazed tiles and the twin minarets on the principal *iwan* dating from Safavid times, so that the final form is complicated and less well integrated, but it offers a practical encyclopaedia of Iranian style over many centuries.

The Seljuk Friday Mosque at Isfahan is almost a textbook of Iranian architectural styles.

Citadel, Cairo

The Fatimids, whose name derived from their
claimed descent from Fatima, daughter of the
Prophet, were Shi'ite Muslims who gained
control of most of north-west Africa in the 10th
century. Already Egypt, in effect Cairo, was rich
and vigorous, and its comparative security from
invasion made it a pre-eminent centre of Islamic
architecture throughout the late Middle Ages.
The Fatimids aimed to supplant the Abbasid
caliphs, who had already surrendered all
meaningful power. They extended their rule to
Syria and founded the district called al-Qahira
(Cairo), which became the nucleus of the
Egyptian capital. They also introduced an
architecture of stone, rather than of brick.

Between 1087 and 1092, the Fatimid vizier
replaced the existing mud-brick fortifications of
the city with stone. The works included several
powerful, monumental gates of similar design
but with different-shaped towers, the Gate of
Victory, Gate of God's Help, etc, which,
according to tradition, were designed by
architects from Anatolia. This seems to be
confirmed by marked similarities with Seljuk
structures. However, by that time, Fatimid
power was also fading under the impact of the
Seljuks and the Christian Crusaders, and Egypt
came under the remote control of a Damascene
dynasty. In 1171 the Damascus-appointed
governor Salah ad-Din (Saladin) overthrew the
last Fatimid caliph and seized power himself,
establishing the Ayyubid dynasty.

Salah ad-Din built the Citadel as the centre
of government, while simultaneously extending
and restoring the city fortifications, with the aim
of enclosing all the disparate parts of Cairo.
This huge project was incomplete at his death,
and much work continued in later times. Cairo
is the best preserved of all Islamic cities, and
substantial parts of Salah ad-Din's structures
remain today. In spite of the impregnability of
the defensive towers, the Cairo Citadel is, from
a military point of view, slightly less substantial
than the Citadel of Aleppo, but it remains one
of the most notable existing examples of Muslim
military architecture. The skilful masonry work,
and the impressive vaulting in particular have
no precedent in Egypt.

Caravanserai, Aksaray

People in Muslim society tended to be comparatively mobile. The relative cultural unity of Islam allowed an educated traveller like Ibn Battuta, inspired largely by curiosity, to spend years travelling all over Islam, and beyond, in the 14th century and, as son of a *cadi*, meeting like-minded people, and gaining employment, almost wherever he went. Apart from the movements of merchants and armies, all Muslims, given the means, were supposed to undertake the *hajj* once in their life, and there was considerable movement of scholars and of pilgrims to other places besides Mecca. Since these long journeys often passed through inhospitable country, the need for stopping places providing food and shelter was obvious. Resthouses, called caravanserais (long-distance travellers usually travelled in caravans), were therefore built along the main routes. They were commonly 'prestige projects', built and endowed by a ruler or some rich dignitary and, if so, sometimes no charge was made for a limited stay. Although they existed much earlier, the development of the caravanserai as an architectural type is chiefly associated with the Seljuks in Anatolia; nowadays, unfortunately, they are often in a ruined state, though some have been restored and a few converted into modern hotels.

The usual plan was a walled rectangle with a single gateway wide enough to admit a heavily laden camel. Rooms, stalls and workshops of various kinds, often on two storeys, were ranged along the inside walls and provided accommodation for travellers and their servants, livestock and their fodder, and merchants' goods. Resident staff were housed in the gatehouse. Water was available for drinking and ritual ablutions, and usually there was a prayer hall. Larger buildings had pillared halls and acquired many extensions and annexes, eventually becoming almost self-contained villages.

One of the largest and grandest Seljuk caravanserais is on the road between Aksaray and Konya, built in 1229 by the Sultan Kayqubad I. It covers an area of 48,000sq ft (4500sq m). The impressive stone-faced gatehouse is over 40-ft (12-m) high, and intricately decorated, with *muqarnas* (corbelled brackets) in the vault of the entrance. The hall, entered through the central courtyard which contains a central prayer room, has five aisles and a dome. The general air of luxury proclaims that it is a *Sultan Han*, or Royal Caravanserai.

Although much has been recently restored, parts of the Caravanserai of Aksaray are in ruins. However, they do give some idea of the scale of the building.

The formidable main gate is the best-preserved survival of the Citadel at Aleppo.

Citadel, Aleppo

A feature of major cities throughout most of Islam was the citadel (*qal'a or qasaba*), a fortified, largely self-contained centre of power, a city within a city, like the kremlins of Russia. They varied considerably in size and importance, some being largely military in character, others, like Cairo, mainly political and containing comfortable buildings for gracious living. Militarily, much the most impressive survivor is the spectacularly sited citadel of Aleppo, in Syria, which withstood a siege by the Christian Crusaders in 1124–25.

It is built on top of a steep, exposed hill, which is partly the work of nature and partly of man, and is surrounded by a moat. What remains today is the citadel of the Ayyubid governors built over a long period, but mainly in the early 13th century, together with alterations and additions made under the Mamluks (1260–1517). Inside the rough oval of the walls were a palace, mosque, baths and various other buildings, forming something of a jumble, probably the result of problems posed by the terrain and the different periods of construction. Though the walls and the minaret of the mosque still stand, most of the other buildings are now in ruins.

What does survive in good order is the most impressive structure of all, the entrance gate; few buildings make a more forthright statement of power. On the town side of the moat is a barbican, which leads via a handsome, upward-sloping stone bridge to the main gateway, a substantial fortress in itself. It presents a squarish face of limestone with battlements, machicolations, arrow slits, and a plain, narrow entrance to a vaulted passage. Beyond this façade, the building is more relaxed, with a large hall for receiving visitors built over the entrance. Sculpture and decoration in inlaid stone dates from the end of the 13th century.

Alhambra, Granada

The Nasrid dynasty was established in Granada in the 13th century, after Muslim Spain had broken into separate states. The founder of the dynasty, Muhammad I, also founded the citadel of the Alhambra, probably the best-known Muslim building after the Taj Mahal. Construction continued under his successors, and the palace itself was largely built in the reigns of Yusuf I (1333–54) and Muhammad V (1354–91). The contrast between exterior, with the mighty stone walls and square towers innocent of decoration, and interior, with the richly decorative refinement and delicacy of courts and chambers, is nowhere more startling.

The general layout is rather confused, no doubt partly the result of different periods of building; the hilltop site does not explain the arrangement. The palace is divided into separate units, each with a central courtyard, though the units bear no obvious relationship to each other and the axis changes from west-east to north-south (the Hall of the Ambassadors and Court of Myrtles), then back to west-east, around the well-known Court of Lions. With its elegant arcades, palm-shaded pools and fountains, its fine-cut stucco, tiles, and geometric, calligraphic and floral designs, the Alhambra has often been likened to an oasis, or a dream world emerging from dour reality. Like a dream world, it is easy to get lost in, being both highly intricate and in total area very large. The compulsion of Muslim architects to make solid buildings dissolve before the eyes is seldom more successfully realized. Standing in the Chamber of the Two Sisters, probably the most magnificent single room, the view up into the cupola, the amazing vault with its myriads of *muqarnas*, is like some optical illusion, achieved by the skilful manipulation of light.

This is a highly sophisticated building but, unfortunately, little is known of its builders. There are evident connections with North Africa, but the serene spaces and subtle decoration of the Alhambra surpass any building in the Maghreb. Once, it would have looked even finer. The Lion Court, with its central fountain supported by sculpted lions, a rare example of freestanding sculpture in Islamic art, was once a mass of blossom and foliage, and the roof, which is modern, would probably have avoided seeming rather too heavy for the slender arches and columns below.

Muhammad I established his Nasrid dynasty in Granada and established the Alhambra as his seat of power, construction of it continuing during the reigns of his successors.

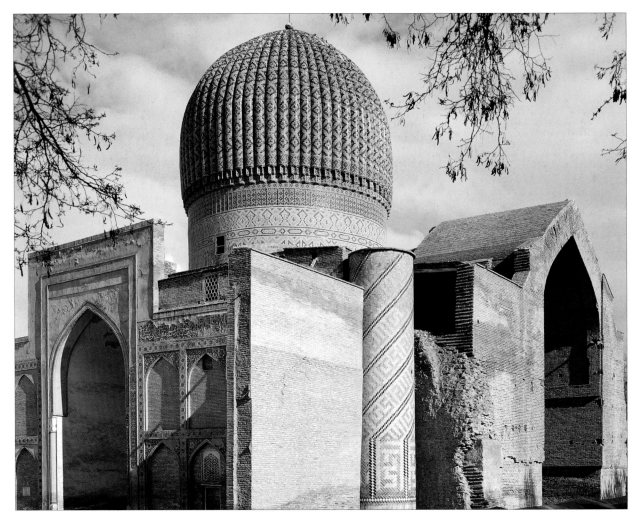

Tomb of Timur, Samarqand

The invasion of Timur (Tamerlane) put an end to Mongol culture in eastern Islam in the late 14th century, but did not immediately introduce any dramatic new directions in art and architecture. Timur made his capital at Samarqand, now in Uzbekistan, and although his successors preferred Herat, Samarqand remained an important centre of art until the 16th century.

The family mausoleum of Timur is part of a complex of buildings, the Gur Emir, that includes a mosque, a *madrasa* and other buildings ranged around a courtyard. The tomb that Timur ordered to be built here was originally intended for his heir, Muhammad Sultan, who was killed fighting the Ottoman Turks in 1402. However, the building was completed just in time to accept the body of Timur himself, who died in 1405. Unlike most Timurid buildings, including the gigantic palaces known only from contemporary descriptions, it is well preserved.

It follows a well-established plan for the tomb tower, an octagonal chamber, though square on the inside, with a dome; it is similar to tombs of the mid-14th century in the nearby necropolis of Shah-i Zinda, where the tall drums and fluted domes are clearly related to Timur's tomb. The double-shelled dome, about 110-ft (34-m) high is, at its base, the same diameter as the drum and swells outward slightly before curving inward towards the finial. The outstanding feature, however, is the decoration, which consists of glazed bricks and tiles and of carved marble. Around the tall drum is an inscription in huge Kufic script, while the octagon walls are covered with irregular panels in a diagonal pattern, that are filled with a different, highly stylized, type of calligraphy. A monumental gateway to the courtyard was erected by Timur's grandson, Ulugh Beg, in 1434. Inside, the square tomb chamber, covered by the rising curve of the inner shell, is decorated in gold leaf and onyx. The dark-green sarcophagus of Timur, and others of marble, are surrounded by a carved marble barrier, though the bodies are actually under gravestones in the crypt below.

The Gur Emir at Samarqand. It has a double dome, the outer one being raised on a very high drum.

327

Selimiye, Edirne

Edirne (Adrianople), near the point where the modern boundaries of Turkey, Greece and Bulgaria meet, was the Ottoman capital for nearly a century before the capture of Istanbul (Constantinople) in 1453. The complex of the Selimiye, begun in 1569, was built, almost 20 years after the similar Süleymaniye, in the reign of Süleyman I's son and successor, Selim II (1566–74), although here the mosque itself is even more dominant.

Most experts, including, it is said, the architect himself, regard the Edirne mosque as Sinan's masterpiece. It is the final result of years of development in making the most of the central space of the mosque, which here conveys a perfect sense of order and calm. The dome is 104ft (32m) in diameter, approximately the same size as Hagia Sophia, and 137-ft (42-m) high. It is buttressed by a circle of walls and half-domes, and the main thrust is skilfully distributed via arches to eight columns, but they are positioned so close to the walls that they appear to be part of them. The result is that, seen from the floor, the dome seems to float effortlessly without obvious support, and the sense of weightlessness is amplified by the numerous, relatively large windows. The minarets, which at over 230-ft (70-m) in height are even taller than those of the Süleymaniye, are shifted from the usual position at the corners of the courtyard to the corners of the mosque itself, and thus help to emphasize its compactness and upward movement. They each have three balconies, with separate staircases. The decoration is of the highest standard, with outstandingly fine Iznik tiles in the apse of the *mihrab*.

Sinan died within a few years of the completion of the Selimiye, and Ottoman art and architecture would lose its originality and dynamism in the 17th century, but his heritage lived on in the early 17th-century mosque of Sultan Ahmet I, in Istanbul, by a possible student of his, Sedefkar Mehmet Agha.

The Selimiye is widely regarded as Sinan's masterpiece. He died within a few years of its completion.

The Great Mosque, Djenné

Islam, 'the religion of trade', percolated through to West Africa via the Sahara trade routes around the 10th century but made little progress until the rise of Mali under a black Muslim dynasty in the 13th–14th centuries, when it spread swiftly through a large region of the Sahel, especially around the towns of the upper Niger, Djenné (Jenne), Timbuktu and Gao. Both Timbuktu and Djenné later acquired a considerable reputation in western Islam for Muslim scholarship, and inaccurate legends concerning the riches of Timbuktu circulated in Europe.

It was in that area that the characteristic type of mosque, built of clay reinforced with timber, evolved as a mixture of Islamic influences of Arab origin and pre-Islamic West African architectural traditions. Buildings of clay lasted a considerable time in the arid climate, but were nevertheless often restored or rebuilt, usually, it is assumed, in the same form. On his journey to Mali in the 14th century Ibn Battuta mentioned many mosques, although he said nothing about their structure. The mosques at Djenné and Timbuktu were seen by the French explorer, René Caillié, in 1827, though he is little more enlightening and his picture of Timbuktu, in which the mosque appears in the distance as a long, buttressed building with the typical square, tapering minaret deriving from indigenous conical shrines or pillars, was criticized as inaccurate by the next European visitor, Heinrich Barth. The mosque seen by Caillié was demolished soon after his visit.

The large and impressive mosque of today, one of the most striking monuments in the whole region, dates from 1909, and received considerable input from the French, conscious of establishing an official ethnic architectural tradition. Archaeological and other evidence suggests that the previous building may have been rather different. The original building was probably built in the 14th century, possibly the 13th. It was rebuilt in the 15th century, and restored at many later dates.

In the West African architectural tradition, timber horizontals provide support for the relatively frail adobe. During actual construction, they act as scaffolding.

Süleymaniye, Istanbul

After the decline of the Seljuks in Anatolia, a brief interlude followed before another dynasty, the Ottomans, began to subjugate their neighbours in the 14th century. Overcoming the setback of Timur's invasions, within the next two centuries they came to dominate western Islam as well as conquering south-east Europe, including the old Byzantine capital of Constantinople, which became the centre of western Islamic civilization.

The Ottomans introduced new developments in architecture. Their great achievement was the monumental domed mosque plan, in which a central dome spans a uniform space, the perfect circle on the perfect square, with a uniform system of vaulting. An early step was taken at Bursa, the old Ottoman capital, in the late 14th century, where the rectangular Great Mosque has 20 domes in four rows of five. Following the capture of Constantinople in 1453 the great dome and spacious interior of Hagia Sophia exerted some influence. After two centuries of development, the scheme was fully realized in the Ottoman 'golden age' of Süleyman I (Suleiman the Magnificent, 1520–66), in the hands of the great architect Sinan, who finally, in the Selimiye in Edirne, achieved the final resolution of the problem of supporting the domes while maximizing the spatial concept.

The earlier Süleymaniye complex covers an area of about 650,000sq ft (60,000sq m) and includes colleges, hospitals, hostels, tombs and many other features as well as the great mosque. It was founded in 1550 and built by Sinan; it is his largest building and many consider it his greatest, and it has been the chief mosque of Istanbul ever since. Süleyman had already reigned for 30 years when he commissioned the building and he clearly intended it to be a monument of unparalleled magnificence. The overall proportions, observing strict ratios, indicate unusually careful planning. The main dome is 174-ft (53-m) high and it is surrounded by a cluster of cupolas, arches, and semi-domes: there are more than 500 subsidiary domes in the whole complex. The workmanship is peerless and the decoration, though that is secondary in Sinan's geometrical masterpieces, is of a similarly high order, and includes tiles from the famous Iznik potteries.

In Ottoman buildings such as the Süleymaniye, the priority of structure and space over decoration and detail was derived from Seljuk tradition.

Topkapi Palace, Istanbul

The Topkapi Palace of the Ottoman sultans, now a museum, was begun in 1462 and remained the residence of the sultans into the 19th century. Originally it was two palaces, a summer palace by the water and a winter residence on the hill above, overlooking the city, where it occupies the northern tip of the peninsula south of the Golden Horn. The buildings date from the 15th century onwards and some have disappeared in recent times, for instance to make room for a railway. Islamic buildings, especially palaces, were seldom designed as a single coherent unit and the original plan has been obscured by later changes; this is a site in which the parts amount to more than the whole. There is certainly no statement of imperial power and glory such as one would expect in the West.

The palace consists rather of a series of comparatively small buildings, not arranged in any particular pattern but mostly ranged around two large courtyards, actually Second and Third Courts, the Throne Room being situated in Third Court, opposite the handsome and well-named Gate of Felicity. Some of the quite small buildings are of exquisite appearance and many contain furnishings and decorations of the richest kind imaginable. A notable example is the domed bedroom of Murad III (1574–95) in gold, white and blue, with a beautiful Kufic inscription on a deep blue background running in a band around the walls. Next door is the handsome building known as 'the Cage', with a central courtyard and iron grilles. It was the residence of the Sultan's brothers, a dangerous class to belong to.

One of the most attractive pavilions is the Chinili kiosk which, although dating from 1473, is actually outside the palace walls. It is square in plan, with a dome and an elegant and refined arcaded portico. Its form was influential on later Ottoman architecture, but it is chiefly famous for the glazed earthenware tiles from Iznik with which it is covered. The open-sided Baghdad kiosk, built by Murad IV to celebrate his capture of that city in 1638, has its own pool and stone fountain, surrounded by a marble terrace. The women's quarters (*harem*), a warren of small buildings and chambers with small domes and pinnacles, form a palace within a palace on the north-east.

LEFT
The main gateway to the Topkapi Palace.

OPPOSITE RIGHT and LEFT
In the astonishing maze of the Topkapi, the eye is constantly caught by fascinating sights and structures. It contains about 100 individual buildings.

OPPOSITE
The turquoise dome of the Masjid-i Shah from the east, a madrasa *in left foreground.*

BELOW
Night-time view from across the courtyard.

BELOW RIGHT
The interior of the prayer hall.

Masjid-i Shah, Isfahan

The Safavids, a native dynasty, reunited Iran in the early 16th century and reached a peak in the reign of Shah Abbas I, called the Great (1587–1629). He moved the capital to Isfahan and, in a rare example of Iranian town planning, reorganized the whole city in a series of interlinked squares according to the grandest plans conceivable. The largest square, in the north, is the Maidan-i Shah, a vast open space big enough for polo, with a major building complex on three sides. One of these is the Masjid-i Shah, or Royal Mosque, the greatest building in a magnificent city. Its monumental gateway, with minarets 110-ft (34-m) high,

occupies a substantial part of the southern side of the *maidan*. In order to align with Mecca while maintaining the integrity of the square, the mosque is set at an angle of about 45 degrees to the gateway, yet this is hardly apparent on the ground. The same plan was followed in the slightly earlier Mosque of Shaykh Lutfallah on the east side of the square.

The building largely follows Seljuk tradition, conforming to the four-*iwan* plan, each leading to a domed hall and flanked by double-storey arcades with pointed niches of the Seljuk type. The largest *iwan* is on the *qibla* (i.e. nearest Mecca) side and has a truly massive portal and dome, itself set on a large drum. Beyond the

iwans east and west of the courtyard are *madrasas* or religious colleges. The whole complex was completed in only four years, 1612–16, though the decoration took longer.

The visible exteriors of the mosque are largely covered with ceramic tiles, in colour predominantly blue or turquoise, cool colours contrasting agreeably with the warm tones of brickwork and landscape round about. The interior tiling is mainly polychrome; up to seven colours were fired at the same time. Designs are varied and fluid, mostly based on stylized floral devices. The concentration on decorative façades is a departure from Seljuk tradition which was less determined to conceal structure.

The Khwaju Bridge represents the culmination of the Seljuk tradition. Not only is it a means of crossing the river, it is a delightful place to pause and enjoy the beauty of the situation.

Khwaju Bridge, Isfahan

Muslims are historically great travellers, partly because of the popularity of the pilgrimage, partly because of the importance of trade in Islam. Good rulers were almost invariably builders of roads, bridges and caravanserais, although, for the most part, the roads of Islam followed the ways trodden out by earlier people, such as the Sassanids in Iran, while in the Near East and North Africa there was the example of the Romans. Former structures, or parts of them, were often incorporated. Bridges are also unusual in Islamic architecture because, being totally functional, no attempt is usually made to disguise their structure.

In Anatolia a number of Seljuk bridges not only survive today but, though heavily restored, are also still in use. These brick or stone arch bridges represent an advance on their Roman predecessors because the Seljuks were able to span a greater width by widening (and raising) the central arch, which is slightly pointed. (The famous single-arch Ottoman bridge at Mostar, destroyed in the recent Yugoslav wars but rebuilt, is similar.) There was often a caravanserai built close to the bridge, as at the particularly fine, five-arched bridge east of Antalya in ancient Pamphylia, southern Turkey.

Probably the most famous bridge in Islam is the Khwaju Bridge over the Zayandeh river in Isfahan, built by Shah Abbas II in the mid-17th century, which is exceptional in that aesthetic as well as practical ideas plainly governed its design. The river here is too shallow to be navigable, and the bridge, about 443-ft (135-m) long, is really a weir, the water deeper on the upstream side, with a road and superstructure. The latter is in essence a two-storey arcade, similar to those flanking the courtyard of a mosque, and is suitable for social gatherings as well as for crossing the river, with arched niches lining the roadway and larger structures in the centre and at each end. The passer-by may also descend steps down to the water.

Khan of Azad Pasha, Damascus

A *khan*, or *han* in Turkish, was the name given to a caravanserai in a city or town. They differed in several respects from caravanserais, which were usually situated in comparatively remote spots. They did not need a high, fortified wall, and had greater capacity for storing merchants' goods while not requiring to stock so much food and fodder. They often functioned as an exchange or market, and even a manufacturing centre, no doubt as a convenient social centre too. Comparatively few have survived to the present, being vulnerable to urban renewal as well as to the variety of disasters, natural and man-made, that have demolished most of the caravanserais; they sometimes seem to have been almost indistinguishable from markets (*suqs*). The famous market at Fustat on the Nile, destroyed in the 12th century, had tall houses lining the streets, reported to be up to 14-storeys-high, no doubt an exaggeration, which combined the functions of living accommodation and warehouses. A later successor was the 16th-century Khan al-Khalili, which was the primary market for luxury goods in Cairo. Later still, the important port of Suakin on the Red Sea had an immense *khan* equipped to handle caravans of 100 camels or more. The buildings around the courtyard were three- or four-storeys-high, with two sides of the square occupied by stores and warehouses.

Damascus was another great centre of trade and contained many *khans*, of which the largest was the Ottoman Khan of Azad Pasha, built around the mid-18th century. The courtyard was roofed and covered by nine domes, and the surrounding buildings were organized on the common system, with living quarters above storerooms and stables. The columns and arches that supported the domes, and that are still standing, were built in alternate bands of light and dark marble, as in the Great Mosque of Cordoba and elsewhere. The main stone gateway into the *khan* from the *suq* (*souk*) next door is decorated with colourful *muqarnas*.

The mightiest khan in this great trading city of Damascus, the coutyard was once roofed and covered by nine domes; the surrounding buildings were organized on the common system with living quarters above storerooms and stables.

Madrasa of Mir-i Arab, Bukhara

Education is closely linked with worship in Islam and distinguishing between a mosque and a *madrasa* (literally school) is often difficult because early mosques, beginning with the Prophet's house in Medina, were used for either purpose. When the *madrasa* became established as an institution – it is believed to have originated in Seljuk Khorasan – it closely resembled the four-*iwan* mosque in plan. Minor differences included the absence of a minaret. Teaching, which was often conducted in an informal way with the students forming a circle on the ground and the teacher leaning on a pillar, took place in the *iwans*, and accommodation for students was ranged along the intervening walls. Rooms might be rather spartan, though some *madrasas*, such as the Madrasa-i Shah in Isfahan, are extremely elegant.

The ancient city of Bukhara, already flourishing when the Arabs conquered it in 709, is famous as a seat of learning. Its *madrasas* include the Mir-i Arab, built about 1535, when Bukhara was entering its most glorious period as capital of an extensive Uzbek state. It was one of only two *madrasas* allowed to function in the Soviet Union (the other was in Tashkent). Founded by a Yemeni sheikh, for whom it is named, it was built (possibly under the Sheikh's direction since he is described as an architect) on the four-*iwan* plan, with 100 cells for students studying Islamic literature, law and Arabic. It is not open to non-Muslims, who can admire from a distance the calligraphy and mosaic around the drums supporting its two blue domes but are said to be missing some of the finest ceramic decoration in Bukhara.

Among other *madrasas* of Bukhara are the 15th-century Madrasa of Ulugh Beg and, standing opposite it, the later Madrasa of Abdal-Aziz Khan, begun in 1645, which resembles it in plan though it is much larger. Apart from its great size, its most notable feature is the great *pishtaq* (gateway), which is beautifully decorated with mosaic, plaster relief work and painting. Immediately south of the Mir-i Arab Madrasa is the 19th-century Madrasa of Amir Alim Khan, which breaks with architectural tradition and seems to have been primarily used as a library.

The Madrasa of Mir-i Arab was built according to a four-iwan plan, with 100 cells to accommodate students.

THE 20TH CENTURY

CHAPTER NINE

Auditorium Building, Chicago

Guaranty Building, Buffalo

The Exchange, Amsterdam

Flatiron Building, New York

AEG Turbine Factory, Berlin

Grand Central Station, New York

Helsinki Railway
Station

Einstein Tower, Potsdam

Chilehaus, Hamburg

Selfridge's Department Store

Bauhaus, Dessau

Sydney Harbour Bridge

Golden Gate Bridge, San Francisco

Church of the Sacred Heart, Prague

Fallingwater, Pennsylvania

Johnson Wax Building, Racine

Chrysler Building, New York

Empire State Building, New York

Rockefeller Center, New York

Seagram Building, New York

Eames House, Santa Monica

Ford House, Illinois

Unité d'Habitation, Marseilles

Chapel of Notre Dame du Haut,
Ronchamp

The Atomium, Brussels

Coventry Cathedral

Guggenheim Museum, New York

Maracaibo Lake Bridge, Venezuela

Gateway Arch, St Louis

TWA Terminal, New York

Palace of Labour, Turin

Brasilia Cathedral

Marina City, Chicago

Lake Point Tower, Chicago

Habitat, Montreal

University of East Anglia, Norwich

Sydney Opera House

Neue Staatsgalerie, Stuttgart

Pompidou Centre, Paris

Lloyd's Building, London

High Museum of Art, Atlanta

Commerzbank, Frankfurt

Reichstag, Berlin

Petronas Towers, Kuala Lumpur

Guggenheim Museum, Bilbao

The 20th century was dominated by what is called the Modern Movement, a name that will grow increasingly inappropriate as time goes on. Influenced by such figures as Gropius and Mies van der Rohe, patriarchs of the Bauhaus, the cradle of Modernism, and less obviously but no less importantly by the prodigious genius of Le Corbusier, a new international style which, though it cannot be pinned down in a sentence or two, developed from several basic ideas. They sprang first from technological advance and new materials, iron, glass and reinforced concrete, which created such possibilities as the skyscraper, and a fairly rigid devotion to the idea that the function of a building should define its form; 'form follows function', in the words of the doyen of the Chicago School, Louis Sullivan. In other words, buildings should be 'honest'.

Architects looked to the future, not the past. They rejected historical styles and sought a new kind of architecture adapted to a new age, an architecture that was useful, democratic and universal, which led to what came to be called the International Modern style. Its spread was facilitated by the great advances in communications and mobility, comparable to the effect of the invention of printing in movable type on the spread of knowledge in Renaissance Europe. Architects all over the world knew exactly what their colleagues were up to. Paradoxically, the effect of the Nazis' closing down of the Bauhaus was actually to increase its international influence, notably in the USA, where many of its leading figures took refuge. However, within the general criteria of Modernism, great variations existed, national differences did not altogether disappear under the impact of the International Modern style, and it is increasingly obvious in retrospect that many of the best 20th-century architects were 'modern' without being 'Modernist'. Hence, perhaps, the rigid dogmatism of Modernists, manifested at its most extreme in such statements as that of Adolf Loos, back in 1908, that 'Ornament is crime', and more subtly by Mies, 'Less is more'.

While classic buildings such as Mies van der Rohe's Seagram Building are likely to command respect indefinitely, the proliferation of inferior glass and concrete blocks after the Second World War, many of them highly non-functional in that they were loathed by the people who lived or worked in them, caused increasing restlessness. But what next? By about 1970, architects in general were rejecting the strict tenets of Modernism, but no clear idea had emerged of what should replace it. Post-Modernism is something of a bran tub: one ingredient is the High Tech style of, for instance, the Centre Pompidou, a transparent building that emphasizes the engineering. Concrete, previously admired for strength and honesty, is often used in freer, more sculptural forms, often precast. There is more colour, sometimes in startling tones, and some masquerade, forms pretending to be something other than they are; there is deliberate provocation, such as hefty columns combined with fragile walls, and calculated bad taste, like Disneyland. There is more symbolism, not always easy to interpret. There is often humour too, a well-known example being the AT & T building (1978) of the American veteran Philip Johnson, which has a broken pediment like a Chippendale bureau; but the trouble with architectural jokes on that scale is that they quickly stale. And of course architects haven't all gone to California to get high. Most of them are serious and committed, and a firm like Norman Foster and Partners has produced a succession of innovative and effective buildings, making use of the unstoppable advance of technology, including computers. One thing is certain. Although architecture inevitably remains international, it is far more varied. Style has returned.

Adler & Sullivan's Auditorium Building, a product of the Chicago School, was one among other buildings seminal to the development of 20th-century architecture. Its construction saw the beginning of the career of Frank Lloyd Wright, who managed to impress Adler & Sullivan with his talent and was subsequently employed by them.

Auditorium Building, Chicago

In the last quarter of the 19th century, Modernism arrived, though not at once and not everywhere. New man-made materials and new engineering techniques on the one hand, and the failing of the dynamic of architectural style on the other, gave rise to a growing awareness that the future belonged to the new methods and new materials, and that the primary consideration in designing a building should be, not its appearance, but its purpose. Or, in the words of Louis Sullivan, the leading figure of the Chicago School, 'form follows function'.

Iron had been used to strengthen buildings, and the idea of using iron as the frame of a building was current as early as the 1850s though not until later were such buildings regarded as 'architecture'. This technique resulted in a completely new type of building, the skyscraper. But that only became a practical proposition after other developments in the 1850s: the spread of Bessemer's convertor, which sharply reduced the cost of steel-making, and the invention of a successful elevator, or lift, by Elisha Otis.

This was also the era of architectural partnerships, with architects often working in teams such as (in Chicago) Adler & Sullivan, who were responsible for the Auditorium Building (1886–89), Burnham & Root, and Holabird & Roche, architects of the Tacoma Building (1886–88).

The Auditorium Building was a revolutionary concept, one of the first multi-use structures, and included a hotel, offices and a large performance hall.

Although Buffalo's Guaranty Building obeys Sullivan's dictum that form follows function, he was equally interested in ornament, which at least one contemporary scholar regards as the area of his greatest genius. The feathery foliage (right) is characteristic.

Guaranty Building, Buffalo

The leading figure of the Chicago School was Louis Sullivan (1856–1924), by birth and upbringing a New Englander of part-Irish descent, who moved to Chicago in 1873. He worked first for William Jenney, whose Home Insurance Building of 1883, with iron beams and girders, was one step away from the metal skeleton, and spent a year in Paris at the École des Beaux-Arts before joining Dankmar Adler in the firm that became known as Adler and Sullivan.

Sullivan's first metal-skeleton building was the ten-floor Wainwright Building in St Louis (1890); it was followed by the the Guaranty Building in Buffalo (1894), 14-storeys-high, both notable landmarks among the first large office blocks. As in the Wainwright Building, the structure is quite evident in the exterior appearance, a grid-like arrangement of identical cells, and uncompromisingly vertical. The

ground floor is more spacious and is suggestive of the future fashion for raising buildings on *pilotis* or pillars. But in spite of his emphasis on function, Sullivan was not at all averse to decoration, in fact he was hardly less interested in decoration than he was in the expression of structure. It is most evident in the brick cladding of the Guaranty Building, especially on the topmost floor below the overreaching cornice. Sullivan's delicate, abstract, decorative patterns, which tend to vanish at any distance, place him unexpectedly close to Art Nouveau, though he later came to feel that current ornamentation of buildings was retrograde. But then the notion that 'form follows function', while it may look forward to the Bauhaus, also looks back to the 'truth to materials' principles of William Morris and John Ruskin and the Gothic Revival.

The work of the Chicago School effectively rejected dependence on historical styles. That did not mean that the past ceased to have any influence on the present, far from it; but the heavyweight revivalism of the mid-19th century which Sullivan so deplored was finally and no doubt permanently abandoned.

Berlage's massive Exchange Building, a very personal structure displaying its architect's profound knowledge of historical forms, was of seminal influence in the development of Modernism.

*OPPOSITE
Detail of the clock face on the tower, showing Berlage's close attention to detail.*

The Exchange, Amsterdam

This massive brick building has three large trading halls, of which the Commodities Exchange is the largest, with a glass roof supported by parabolic iron beams and broad but unobtrusive arcades on the lower levels. Around the halls are grouped offices and other smaller rooms; the Amsterdam chamber of commerce met in the large room above the entrance.

The original design won an open competition in 1884, though the building when finished (1903) was somewhat different. It is the masterpiece of the influential Dutch architect, Hendrik Berlage (1856–1934), and is one of the icons of what is sometimes called the 'proto-modern' movement that includes Art Nouveau, where Berlage is sometimes placed. His influence depended largely on his writing and lecturing, and he was the first great European champion of Frank Lloyd Wright, even before he had seen any of Wright's buildings. Yet he was essentially a traditionalist, sympathetic to the Romanesque especially, and influenced by Viollet-le-Duc's insistence that even the Gothic style was essentially practical and logical rather than spiritual in motivation. Berlage's liking for historical materials and his emphasis on 'honesty' in architecture went so far as refusing to apply plaster to a brick wall, even in a domestic interior. He was not against historicism, but only against that aspect of it called eclecticism, the selective exploitation of historical styles that marked the 1880s and 1890s. 'What is modern?' he asked, 'Usually something ... without a distinct character ... modern Gothic, modern Renaissance, and even modern Norse, Indian, Japanese ... If

it weren't so sad one could laugh at it.'

Berlage's Amsterdam Exchange is a testament to his mastery of past styles, especially the Romanesque, evident in the use of round arches as well as the massive scale, and to his love of brick (there are some details in stone); but he also openly embraces contemporary technique, for instance in the iron trusses supporting the roof of the main hall, which are left exposed.

351

Flatiron Building, New York

The proper name for this heroic survivor of the first age of the skyscraper, whose place in popular affection should safeguard it from demolition, is the Fuller Building; but it was called the Flatiron Building from the time it was built, in 1901–03, and is a comment on its unusual shape. It occupies an awkward triangular site on 23rd Street where it is crossed by Broadway and Fifth Avenue. It was built by the firm of Daniel H. Burnham (formerly Burnham and Root, pioneers of the steel-frame building in Chicago); but at this time Burnham was occupied with his town-planning schemes and the architect credited with the design of the Flatiron Building is Charles B. Atwood.

A certain amount of myth has accrued to the Flatiron Building. City guides sometimes maintain that it was the first steel-frame building, which of course it was not, and that it was New York's first real skyscraper, which people feared would fall over. In fact it was not the tallest building in New York in 1902, and any fears that it would tumble probably arose from its shape. It is essentially a three-sided building but unlike, say, the Chilehaus in Hamburg, the 'sharp' end is rounded off and is about 6.5-ft (2-m) wide at the narrowest point.

The building is 285-ft (87-m) tall and 21-storeys-high and, when built, loomed mightily above its neighbours. Described by one critic as 'an energetic mix of Gothic and Renaissance styles', it obeys the Classical three-tier division of base, tall middle section and top, it is clad in rusticated stone, with dirt-collecting terracotta reliefs of flowers and busts, and is altogether unashamedly decorative. The central section is also divided into three by vertical lines of slightly bowed pairs of windows. With its great height and dramatic shape, it impressed even New Yorkers.

New York City has always displayed a sometimes breathtaking readiness to pull down the old, however honourable, in order to build something bigger, if not necessarily better; but the Flatiron building has survived.

AEG Turbine Factory, Berlin

Peter Behrens (1868–1940) was originally a painter and designer sympathetic to the Arts and Crafts movement and Art Nouveau. His career took a new direction when in 1900 he was invited to the artists' colony at Darmstadt where, like Josef Olbrich, he designed his own very original (despite debts to Charles Rennie Mackintosh) Art Nouveau house. In 1907 he and Olbrich were among the founding members of the Deutscher Werkbund, which embraced industrial design as well as craftsmanship, and in the same year he was appointed architectural adviser to the progressively minded AEG company, for whom he designed everything from office blocks and manufacturing plants to office stationery and electric toasters. But what,

above all, makes him one of the most admired of the immediate precursors of Modernism, was his industrial buildings.

Behrens's massive, monumental Turbine Factory (1909) was part of a vast industrial complex. It was his first and most important industrial building, the first basically steel-and-glass structure in Germany and one of the first anywhere to proclaim that a factory is or can be 'architecture'. A highly functional building, which employed the most sophisticated engineering methods, it was built on a light steel frame, and its powerful-looking (in fact thin) concrete corner elements, a common Behrens characteristic, are clearly not load-bearing. Although there is no obvious connection with any historical style, the Turbine

Factory has a certain timeless monumentality that suggests a Classical heritage; the front has the general form of a Classical temple, while columns march along the sides. (Some of Behrens's later, non-industrial buildings, such as the German Embassy in St Petersburg, had more obvious Neoclassical attributes.) It is also, in spite of the architect's arts-and-crafts sympathies (others see a greater resemblance to a barn than a temple), an anthem to industry on a massive scale, as Behrens, reluctantly or not intended, for in an article published in 1908 he defined 'monumental art' as an expression of whatever is the dominant force of the time. He became an extremely influential teacher, with no less a trio than Le Corbusier, Gropius and Mies van der Rohe among his students.

RIGHT
Disgust at the destruction of Penn Station, generally regarded as the finer structure, saved Grand Central from a similar fate, though not from the looming presence of the 1960s Pan-Am Building.

OPPOSITE
The concourse of Grand Central, before its recent restoration.

Grand Central Station, New York

In the early 20th century, before the challenge of motor vehicles had made itself felt, railways were still very big business, especially in the USA, for whose booming prosperity they were largely responsible. The railway companies not only had the resources to build grand new stations but, relatively progressive in spirit, they were one of the few patrons for adventurous architectural schemes on a large scale. The two outstanding products of these circumstances were both in New York City, where Pennsylvania Station (1902–11) and Grand Central (1903–13) were built at roughly the same time.

Both were inspired by the monumental structures of ancient Rome: the Baths of Caracalla are frequently mentioned as a source for Penn Station. Equally, they were a total success from a functional point of view, and made use of the latest engineering techniques. Penn Station was the work of the outstanding firm of McKim, Mead and White, which was also responsible in New York for the Washington Triumphal Arch and Columbia University. Sadly, and to the irritation of thousands, the station was needlessly demolished in 1963. Grand Central only escaped a similar fate after a defensive campaign that ended victoriously in the US Supreme Court.

In 1900 trains ran by steam, and it was an accident caused by a build-up of steam underground that led to the reconstruction of the station, with electric engines replacing steam. This allowed more freedom in placing about 100 platforms, on two levels, below the streets of Manhattan. The original architects

were a Mid-Western firm that concentrated on railways, but in 1911 Warren and Whitmore, former students, like McKim, at the École des Beaux-Arts in Paris, took over the project; they were responsible for the famous concourse,

perhaps the world's most famous rendezvous, a gigantic and astonishingly quiet space over 27,000sq ft (2,500sq m) in area and 125-ft (38-m) high. If the traveller is delayed, there is no more attractive place to wait for a train.

Helsinki Railway Station

Nationalism is often a spur to architectural innovation, not necessarily in the best of taste. Finland, a country that has produced a disproportionate number of brilliant architects in the past century, was looking towards emancipation from Russian control in the early years of the 20th century, and this encouraged a return to traditional, solid and simple methods and materials of building, based on the abundance of timber and rugged granite. The National Romantic style also bore an affinity with the masculine style of the great American architect, Henry H. Richardson (1838–86), with his shingled houses and solid Romanesque masonry, whose buildings, incidentally, included a number of small railway stations.

In partnership with others, Eliel Saarinen (1873–1950) built the Finnish Pavilion for the Paris Exposition Universelle in 1900, and by himself, the National Museum in Helsinki in 1905, a fairly typical product of the Finnish national style. His railway station, which won a competition in 1904 and was built, after a series of revisions, in 1906–14, also belongs basically to the Finnish National Romantic school, with a flavour of Art Nouveau, but advances a large step forward. This self-assured and monumental building made a considerable impact far beyond Finland, establishing Saarinen on the international scene and easing his future move to the USA in 1923, when he had become more of a Modernist.

The Helsinki Station is both massive and sleek. Its powerful, greyish granite is elegantly sculpted, and the tall clock tower, soon to spawn progeny in both Europe and North America, is almost slick. The massive round

arch of the main hall, delicately scalloped in outline, is famously flanked by pairs of vast, decorative *atlantes*, each holding a large lamp. Saarinen, who had studied painting as well as architecture, was married to a sculptress, Louise

Gesellius, and collaborated with her and other sculptors in later buildings. This interest was to be inherited by his son, and for a time his partner, Eero.

Façade of the elder Saarinen's most famous building (opposite), with (below) a detail of the light-bearing figures flanking the entrance.

Einstein Tower, Potsdam

Erich Mendelsohn (1887–1953), starved of commissions for a considerable period of his life, was one of the major European architects of the 20th century, though the quality of his imitators was not always impressive. The Einstein Tower is one of his most famous buildings, though one of his least influential. He was fascinated by buildings whose form is not dictated by function, which are more like Expressionist sculptures, moulded rather than built; he designed, or at least sketched, many of them while he was stationed on the Russian Front during the First World War. The drawings made a stir at an exhibition in Berlin after the war, but the Einstein Tower is the only one that was ever built, mainly in 1917–21. It originated in a project encouraged by an assistant of Einstein, then a professor in Berlin, to test the theory of relativity. It had an observatory on top and a laboratory in the basement. The government presented the land at Potsdam, and the official inauguration took place in 1924.

One acknowledged influence was the theatre (1914) for the Deutscher Werkbund, the design-oriented group founded in 1907 by Behrens and Olbrich among others, by the Belgian Henry van der Velde, which Mendelsohn admired for its 'concrete used in the Art Nouveau style, but strong in conception and expression'. Unfortunately, German industry was in ruins after the destruction of the First World War; as Mendelsohn was unable to obtain the flexible material he needed – reinforced concrete – he was forced to use brick, steel and concrete, disguising this amalgam by covering the whole building with plaster to suggest uniformity of material. Nevertheless, the result, which faintly resembles some futuristic form of transport, is highly dramatic and uniquely original. One curious effect remarked on by many is that the building appears to be larger than it actually is.

The form of the Einstein Tower was to some extent affected by the exigencies of the German post-war economy, but it is one of the most interesting structures of an immensely fertile architect.

Awkward sites often generate interesting solutions, as in Höger's Expressionist masterpiece in Hamburg, with its spear-like leading edge.

Chilehaus, Hamburg

The influential Deutscher Werkbund, an association of craftsmen, designers and others founded in 1907, had obvious affinities with the earlier English Arts and Crafts movement, although it was more sympathetic to machines and mass-production, which, by 1907, had clearly come to stay. One of the founders of the Werkbund, Hermann Muthesius, had spent some years in England and was an expert on the Arts and Crafts movement. He in turn influenced younger German architects like Fritz Höger (1877–1949). As a result, the revivalist English domestic architecture represented by Philip Webb, Charles Voysey and others makes itself felt in the building that is generally considered to be one of the architectural masterpieces of German Expressionism, the Chile House in Hamburg, which was built in 1922–23 and somehow survived the carnage of 1943.

In fact, Höger's earlier private houses exhibit that connection more closely. He was the best known of a group of architects who revived the North German tradition of dark red brick in the years after the First World War. The Chilehaus, built for a shipping company engaged in the nitrates trade with Chile is, like the Flatiron Building in New York, a fine demonstration of how to turn an awkward, roughly triangular site to advantage. At the sharp angle, one might almost say the prow, the roof line sweeps up to a sharp point. The ocean-liner impression is furthered by the exaggeration of perspective resulting from the shape, and confirmed by the audacious, asymmetrical 'wave' in the long south façade. The base is a round-arched arcade, occupied by shops, with odd but effective twin porches

flanking the angle; the walls of the top three (of eight) storeys are recessed in an unusual and highly effective way, both vertically and horizontally, the breaks marked by a change

from rectangular to rounded windows below projecting balconies. Altogether, the Chilehaus is a triumph and a startlingly original design, perfectly suited to its place and function.

Selfridge's Department Store

Oxford Street, London, is one of the world's great shopping centres, full of 'shops as big as towns'. In recent years, the numbers of the big stores have been depleted as less costly means of retail selling have been developed, but Selfridge's, the first, the biggest and the mostest, still flourishes.

H. Gordon Selfridge, though British-born, was a junior partner in Marshall Field of Chicago, the first great American department store, who in 1906 decided to try something similar in England. He had backing from the furniture firm of Waring and Gillow on condition that Selfridge's did not sell furniture, and some mind-blowing schemes for this vast temple of consumerism were put forward; the end result, though more sane than some, was exotic enough, though subtlety was not on the brief. The original scheme was apparently by Daniel Burnham, the famous pioneer of the Chicago School, but the architect on the spot was Frank Swales, together with others. Although the store opened in 1909, when the western part of Oxford Street was largely neglected and unvisited, the building was not entirely finished until 1928; the huge central tower that was part of the original plan remained unbuilt.

The store looks like an oversized Roman palace, in an approximation of the Ionic Order and on a steel frame. The base contains the all-important shop windows, between piers, with the hefty columns rising from the second storey. The *pièce de résistance* is the clock above the entrance, with a robed, winged, female figure in bronze, by Gilbert Bayes, standing on a stone ship's prow and attended by tritons. The open-plan interior was a novelty in Edwardian Britain. Customers could stroll about, freely inspecting the wares without being pressured by salesmen or stared at by security guards; there were other amenities such as restaurants and wash rooms, as well as 'events' and exhibitions, like the first demonstration of television.

Detail of the clock and sculpture group above the main entrance of Selfridge's.

Bauhaus, Dessau

In 1919 Henry van der Velde resigned as director of an arts-and-crafts school in Weimar and recommended Walter Gropius (1883–1969) as his successor. Gropius was a former student of Peter Behrens, an advocate of mass-production in housing, and one of the originators of the International Modern style exemplified in cubic blocks, glass walls, no extraneous decoration, asymmetrical composition and little colour other than white. The Bauhaus ('Building House'), as Gropius renamed it, aimed to encourage all kinds of artists to work together to 'build the future'. Perhaps his greatest achievement was to make a potentially difficult group of the finest contemporary artists and designers co-operate so successfully.

The Bauhaus was originally dominated by Expressionism and the arts-and-crafts tradition, but soon became oriented more towards technology and industry. It became the heart of the International Modern Movement, and when it moved to Dessau in 1925–26, after its left-leanings had prompted the Weimar government to withhold funds, Gropius designed new buildings that were intended to represent the 'new unity' of art and technology, as proclaimed by Gropius in a 1924 memorandum. The complex comprised the impressive main building with its huge glass walls, several other buildings including a two-storey structure that bridged a street and housed Gropius's office and homes for teachers. The students' (originally called 'apprentices') block included a gymnasium as well as classrooms, dining hall and living accommodation. There was also a theatre. Function is the guide to form, and the

buildings, which have recently been restored, are no less visually impressive for being well-adapted to practical purposes.

Gropius resigned in 1928 and was eventually succeeded by Ludwig Mies van der Rohe. As at Weimar earlier, the school fell from political favour and was shut down in 1932.

Mies restarted it on a private basis in Berlin, but when the Nazis gained power in 1933, they closed it for good. In a way this was the making of the Bauhaus, because its staff and ideas were scattered abroad, to the USA in particular, and its influence thus greatly expanded.

Sydney Harbour Bridge

The desirability of a north-south crossing (some favoured a tunnel) of Sydney Harbour became increasingly pressing as the city underwent rapid expansion in the late 19th century. The project was first put out to local tender in 1900, but all 24 designs were considered wanting and over 20 years passed before work began.

The presiding genius of the bridge was the chief engineer John Bradfield, the builders the British firm of Dorman and Long. As an arch bridge carrying a heavy load, including a railway, careful planning was needed to avoid making costly changes later; Ralph Freeman of London, the consulting engineer, filled 28 books with calculations. As it was, the bridge would be expensive to maintain, needing constant repainting. A suspension bridge would have been less expensive both to build and maintain, but it would not have been the grand monument that Sydney was expecting.

About 800 houses had to be demolished before construction began in 1924. About 1,400 workers were employed and 16 were killed in accidents. The span of the main arch between the pylons is 1,650ft (503m) and clearance above the water is 170ft (52m), allowing free passage to the largest ships. The total length is 3,770ft (1149m). The arch was built out from the sides, held by steel cables, and with hinges at each end to spread the load and the permitted substantial sway in high winds. When the two sides of the arch were finished, the cables were slackened off over 12 days to bring them together. The deck was then built from the centre outwards.

The bridge opened in 1932. The opening ceremony did not go quite according to plan, because the Labour prime minister's cutting of the ribbon was pre-empted by a royalist militia officer who rode up and slashed through it with his sword, 'for King and Empire' (he was charged with damaging government property). Today, although assisted by the Gladesville Bridge (opened 1964, the world's longest concrete span) and the Sydney Harbour Tunnel (1992), the bridge can barely cope with the unanticipated increase in traffic, more than ten times what it was in 1932.

Golden Gate Bridge, San Francisco

Although in recent years its span has been many times exceeded, the Golden Gate Bridge was for years the longest suspension bridge in the world. It is one of the engineering marvels of the 20th century and, due largely to its superb situation, is a magnificent and evocative spectacle.

The Golden Gate is the strait between San Francisco Bay and the Pacific Ocean, about 3-miles (5-km) long and up to 2-miles (3-km) wide. Though the bridge was first proposed in 1872 as a great maritime asset, it presented a serious obstacle to overland communications in a fast-developing area. The idea was revived in 1916 and the city polled leading engineers. Many considered a bridge impossible, others put the cost at over $100 million; but one veteran, Joseph B. Strauss (1870–1938), believed not only that it was possible but that it could be done for only $30 million (the actual cost was £35 million). Strauss was an experienced bridge builder and specialized in long spans; his earlier bridges included the George Washington Bridge over the Hudson at New York City.

Lacking state or federal funding, capital was raised by a bond issue secured against tolls. The statistics were daunting. The main span was 4,200ft (1280m), a world record and, as this was a major shipping lane, the roadway had to be 220ft (67m) above the water at high tide. The towers for the suspension cables were 500ft (152m) above the bridge deck, and the load of the main cables on each tower was 61,500 tons.

In spite of strong opposition from the ferry companies, the project was approved in

1923–24 and Strauss's scheme accepted in 1930. Construction began in 1933. Safety precautions were elaborate, and included a net suspended under the deck, which saved the lives of 19 men, though not of 12 on a section of

scaffolding that fell and broke the net. The bridge was formally opened in 1937, just six months after the San Francisco–Oakland Bay Bridge, which was built with government funding at almost double the cost.

The romantic Golden Gate Bridge by night and by day.

Plecnik was a little-known figure until quite recently, but his remarkable, uniquely personal style and his inexhaustible fund of ideas are now seen as indications of a true genius.

Church of the Sacred Heart, Prague

Josip Plecnik (1872–1957) is something of an odd man out among 20th-century architects. A few years ago, few people had heard of him; now, he is increasingly seen as a remarkable genius, with an apparently inexhaustible fund of ideas, but with little sympathy for his own time. He belonged to no school and left no followers. His architecture seems to be an attempt to express the whole process of civilization, which led him to use the styles and ideas of the past, but in a thoroughly imaginative way.

Born in Ljubljana, Plecnik was a devout Catholic and a committed Slav who worked mainly in the Slav lands. He trained in Vienna under Otto Wagner and arrived in Prague in 1911 as head of the School of Decorative Arts, remaining in the Czech capital for over 30 years. He was employed at the castle under President Masaryk, though arguments over his alterations led to his departure in 1935. His most notable building is the Church of the Sacred Heart (1928–32) in Zizkov, a district somewhat removed from the tourist-packed historical area. Elements of Plecnik's romantic nationalism, religious devotion, historicism, rationality and not least of all his bravura gift for design are all displayed in this extraordinary church, which, if it had been built 40 or 50 years later might be described as Postmodernist.

It is most remarkable from the outside. The first, immediate shock is the slab-like tower, almost as wide as the basilica it adorns, and whose restrained pediment it repeats. In the centre of the tower, in a touch of Surrealism, is a huge circular opening which contains a see-through clock. The lower part of the basilica

and of the tower is brick, the upper parts, together with doorways, plastered white. The building is simple yet decorative, with Classical

swags above the rows of small, almost-square windows, and vertical lines of projecting stones on the brick walls.

Fallingwater, Pennsylvania

Frank Lloyd Wright (1867–1959), the most famous American architect of the 20th century, lived the best part of a century himself and remained extraordinarily prolific for most of that time, designing a great variety of different types of building, finding his own solution to the problems posed by each one, never repeating himself, and never losing his creativity. He was very much his own man, subscribing to no school or style but relying on his own inspiration. As a young man he worked with Louis Sullivan, one of comparatively few architects he respected; he remained thoroughly American, negating his affinities with the Modern style, which in origin at least, was a European invention.

He first gained a reputation as a designer of houses for the rich in the Chicago area, the type he called 'Prairie Houses', low and spread out, with rooms opening into each other and with cantilevered roofs and terraces that merge with the landscape. Although larger projects began to come his way after about 1905, he continued to design private houses for the rest of his career, including his own, Taliesin in Wisconsin, which had three incarnations, a community of disciples over which he presided like a rather demanding guru. The most famous of his houses is Fallingwater (1936–39), at Bear Run in Pennsylvania.

Here Wright carried out the integration of house and landscape most successfully. The house is set among woods on a steep hillside; the ground floor is set on piers, with projecting terraces over a waterfall immediately below. There is a high vertical core in stone, while the remainder is in concrete and glass, which makes up most of the walls. Horizontal elements interpenetrate in a complex and inventive way. Thoroughly modern, this is also a romantic house (Wright's claim that it was partly based on a Mayan temple does not seem very significant), built as a country retreat for a city entrepreneur and retailer. Today it has become such an icon that, in summer at least, it is rather well frequented.

Fallingwater, probably the 20th century's most famous private house, combines Modernism and Romanticism.

Johnson Wax Building, Racine

The late 1930s was possibly Frank Lloyd Wright's most fertile period. The Johnson Wax Administration Building (1936–39) was built at about the same time as Fallingwater, and showed that he could bring a new vision to the design of offices as well as houses. This building is almost square in plan and basically a single-storey, with an executives' penthouse on top. It has rounded corners and the attractive brick walls are uninterrupted on all sides, except for the entrance. The lack of windows is the only obvious outward sign of a highly unconventional interior.

The office is open-plan, then still a novelty, and is lit by a continuous glass band round the top of the walls. The glass is in the form, not of panes, but of layers of Pyrex tubes, which are translucent but not transparent, though too high to look out of anyway. The other striking feature is the manner in which the roof, also a light source, is supported – by concrete columns with a reverse taper (thinner at the base) which, at the top, expand into flat mushroom forms. This system worried the building inspectors, and before he could get a permit Wright had to demonstrate that the columns could actually support six times as much weight as was required. The lofty 30-ft (9-m) office is too spacious to induce claustrophobia; Wright insisted that 'you catch no sense of enclosure whatever at any angle, top or sides... Interior space comes free, you are not aware of any boxing in at all'. He also designed the movable furniture, which included three-legged chairs for the typists that tipped up if they deviated from their correct posture.

At a time when some of the finest architects in Europe were arriving in the USA as refugees from Germany, there is something faintly uncomfortable about this building, brilliant though it is. The main later addition was a 15-storey tower (1944–50), which matched the brick and glass arrangement of its horizontal companion, even to the rounded corners. Inside, alternate floors are mezzanines cantilevered from the tower's concrete core, which contain elevator and services. Additional offices were also built adjoining the 1936 Administration Building.

RIGHT
The suggestion of a space rocket from early science fiction is even stronger when the Chrysler building is lit up at night.

OPPOSITE
Though increasingly challenged, the Chrysler Building remains a distinctive landmark among the towers of Manhattan.

Chrysler Building, New York

In the early years of the 20th century, there was a vogue for skyscrapers in the Gothic style, headed by New York's Woolworth Building (1913). Curious as this may seem to us, for historicists it had some logic, since a skyscraper is by definition a vertical building and verticality was the essence of Gothic. William van Alen in his building for the Chrysler Corporation also featured a spire, but a spire of an altogether different style and spirit. The gleaming, stainless-steel spire, with its arcs of sunbursts, is an Art Deco creation which, for no obvious reason, appears absolutely right. It also makes the building quite unmistakable (this is the one skyscraper that everyone recognizes, even though some may still regard it as frivolous). Art Deco, which has been described as a sort of pop-Modernism, had limited applications in architecture. Although there was a brief vogue for Art Deco skyscrapers, they lack the appeal of the Chrysler Building. The style did, however, prove ideal for the new pleasure palaces, the movie theatres.

The 77-storey Chrysler Building (1928–30) was originally commissioned by a construction company, but was taken over by motor magnate Walter P. Chrysler, who wanted a building to make people stop and stare. It was planned to be the highest in the world, exceeding the Eiffel Tower, and in the process tested the current technology to the limit. It included several decorative motifs referring to automobiles, such as the gargoyle-like radiator tops, although it was never occupied by the car company. It achieved its aim at a height of 1,046ft (319m), but held the record only for a matter of months before the Empire State Building outclimbed it. The architect, William van Alen (1883–1954), finds little coverage in textbooks and seems to have faded from view after his one great success. Among his other gifts, however, he was a showman: the steel-faced spire, seven-storeys-high, was put together inside the tower, so that no one except the workers saw it until, on the appointed day, it was raised through a hole in the top and fixed in position – all in 90 minutes.

Though outreached, since the 1970s, by the twin towers of Minoru Yamasaki's unappealing World Trade Center (1,350ft/411m), the Empire State Building is still the king of Manhattan's skyscrapers.

Empire State Building, New York

The USA, as we all know, is a country of wide open spaces, where small towns tend to spread themselves across the landscape in a way that seems profligate to visitors from the Old World. In the big cities, however, the opposite occurs. Office and apartment blocks shoot upwards, claiming the maximum possible space from a given site. The obvious explanation is that in cities like Chicago and New York, prime metropolitan building land is scarce and expensive. But is that the whole story? Perhaps the impulse to create ever more spectacular skyscrapers may have been rooted in a desire to pit human technology against the abundance of Nature. And there was a more mundane reason: a spectacular building carried more prestige and therefore higher rents.

No sooner had the spire of the Chrysler Building appeared to dominate the Manhattan skyline than the Empire State Building, a few blocks south, rose to challenge it. Whereas Chicago skyscrapers could go straight up from the street, New York's building restrictions demanded that very tall buildings be stepped back, to prevent streets and neighbouring buildings from being cast into permanent darkness. This was a rare example of planning regulations acting, on the whole, to enhance appearances.

The Empire State Building of 1929–31 was built at the beginning of the Great Depression. The architects were the firm of Richmond H. Shreeve, William Lamb and Arthur L. Harmon. It is a handsome, even elegant tower but, because it is set back, it is only visible from a distance; when Le Corbusier said he could lie down on the pavement and stare at it all day, he would have been disappointed by the view. In any case, the building acquired its immediate and lasting fame by its sheer size. At 1,250ft (381m), not including the mast, intended, apparently seriously, to provide mooring for airships, it was easily the tallest building in the world and held the record for over 40 years. Its steel frame is clad in stone and its Art Deco decoration is less assertive than that of the Chrysler Building. Well over 1 million people have been up to look at the view since 1931.

Views of the Rockefeller Center.

RIGHT
Hercules brandishing a skeletal globe.

OPPOSITE LEFT
A pedestrian area.

OPPOSITE RIGHT
The former RCA Building, whose extreme verticality makes it seem even taller than it is.

Rockefeller Center, New York

The Rockefeller Center was built between 1931 and 1940 in a consistent style, with strong verticals, belonging really to the Art Deco period. Although it could be said to be slightly out of date by the time the last building was completed, it represents the peak of high-rise construction in the interwar period and, although its heights mean nothing to the man and woman on the street, it has become an attractive area. One of the first great high-rise urban ensembles, it consists of ten major units (14 buildings altogether) occupying three city blocks between Fifth and Sixth Avenues in midtown Manhattan. A variety of architects, including Raymond Hood (1881–1934), architect of the Modernist McGraw-Hill Building not far away, worked on the buildings.

The Art Deco style is best displayed in the six-storey foyer of Radio City Music Hall, by Donald Deskey and others, which opened in 1932, the first building to be completed. The world's largest (6,000 seats) and technologically most advanced theatre, it soon became an international attraction. Predominantly, however, the Rockefeller Center was a commercial venture, sponsored by John D. Rockefeller Jnr, and the chief ingredients of the ensemble are office blocks. The largest is the former RCA building, with 70 storeys, which, being very thin, was found to require special bracing. It governs the axis of the other buildings, parallel or at right-angles, resulting in an interesting handling of space. There were also shops, restaurants, a second theatre (since demolished) and, most famously, a skating rink in an outdoor plaza, overlooked by a slightly comical golden Hercules. This is one of the most attractive public places in New York City on a winter evening, but it was something of an afterthought. The plaza was originally intended to be an area for small shops, but it attracted insufficient tenants. Recent advances in refrigeration techniques led someone to suggest, as a rather forlorn hope, a skating rink. Serendipity!

Seagram Building, New York

Ludwig Mies van der Rohe (1886–1969) was, with Le Corbusier, among the greatest exponents of the Modern style, and cannot be held responsible for the sometimes unfortunate influence he had on later, less talented builders of high-rise offices and apartments. Mies was director of the Bauhaus for the last three years before it was shut down by the Nazis. Soon afterwards he went to the USA and became a professor at the Illinois Institute of Technology in Chicago, for which he designed a new campus. Although his reputation was extremely high, at least among fellow-architects and designers as early as the 1920s, his buildings are comparatively few until after 1945, when he was nearly 60 years old.

By that time, Mies's austere style ('Less is more') was fully matured, and had already been displayed in his buildings for the Illinois Institute. His buildings are basically cubic or box-like in form, on a revealed steel frame, predominantly glass-walled, clean-lined and marked only by vertical and horizontal lines, with very precise detailing and virtually no decoration. (His first glass skyscraper was designed in 1921, though technology was not then up to building it.) In practical terms, they are very adaptable: the interior has no effect on the exterior, and Mies soon demonstrated that they were equally suitable as apartments or offices. In outline, it sounds a simple recipe, but the fact that his numerous imitators were responsible for so many awful buildings suggests that it was not. One of their more obvious failings was a lack of the acute awareness of proportion that is what Mies signally possessed.

The Seagram Building (1954–58), built by Mies with Philip Johnson for the big Canadian distillers, is by general consent the prime example of the Miesian office tower, and one of the finest buildings of the past half-century. The building, the largest of its kind when built, occupies only one-third of the site, rising from a broad plaza that introduces welcome space in a congested area east of Park Avenue. It rises in smooth lines, cliff-like, for 38 storeys, its seductive colour deriving from the fact that it is clad in bronze (one advantage that Mies enjoyed over inferior imitators was that he could usually spend more): the Seagram Building was notoriously expensive. Even the slightly earlier Lever Building (Skidmore, Owings and Merrill, 1951–52), a near neighbour and another superior example of the International Modern style, looks outclassed.

A dramatic street sculpture outside the Seagram Building.

The rectangular office tower, based on simple principles (grid construction, mass-production of units, central service core, etc.) was an all-too-popular format. But the Seagram Building was not a signpost to the future, it was more of a ne plus ultra.

OPPOSITE
*General view of the
house, which is slotted
into a wooded hillside.
The studio is off camera
to the right.*

RIGHT
*The terrace of the Eames
House, constructed
entirely of units from
catalogues.*

Eames House, Santa Monica

The husband-and-wife team of Charles (1907–78) and Ray (1916–88) Eames was among the best design collaborations of the 1950s, from which came the famous moulded-plywood chair. California-based, they had Californian attitudes, a laid-back approach, no great high-art aspirations, and an amiable, sometimes inspired, eclecticism. Their house, No. 8, Pacific Palisades, tucked into woods on a hillside, was their only building. Though they lived in it, it was commissioned by *Arts and Architecture* magazine in 1947 as part of an effort to convince the house-buying public that modern designers had as much to offer as conventional builders.

The house (1945–50), its long and narrow plan dictated by the site, includes living quarters and a studio divided by a courtyard. The light and airy main living room ascends through two storeys and opens on to a roofed terrace. This means that the upper floor is only about half the area. But its most important characteristic is that it is a DIY house, made up of machine-made, mass-produced components selected from catalogues, and put together on what might be called the Meccano principle. It was no more expensive, and far more attractive, than a mass-produced, lowest-common-denominator developer's house, and far less expensive than a one-off, architect's house. Despite its steel frame, the house looks, and indeed is, extremely light and insubstantial, with a pronounced Japanese flavour; yet it has proved solid enough. The Eames House was designed to grow, or rather change, along with the tastes and requirements of the occupants. It is a negation of Classical order: there is no symmetry; parts were meant to be added or taken away without damaging the whole, something you cannot do with a Greek temple!

Though ideal for its place, time and purpose, the house has obvious limitations. The sunny climate is essential, and it is not suitable for young children as there is no rail on the spiral staircase. After completing it, the Eames turned to films and never built another house, thought they did design one. They had great influence internationally, not for the architecture of the house itself, but in the approach to building that it represented.

Goff designed and built a large number of remarkably disparate houses. The Ford House is one of his most successful.

Ford House, Illinois

Bruce Goff (1904–82) began his career in Chicago in the 1930s but moved to the south, teaching for some years at the University of Oklahoma. His buildings, almost exclusively private houses, make a strange and varied collection. It is difficult to imagine him finding so many clients in any country other than the USA, for Goff was an eccentric. His early work may show the influence of Frank Lloyd Wright, with whom he had studied, and he also shared Wright's tendency towards the bizarre in later years. He has been called an Organic Expressionist Modern, all relevant terms, but rather too inclusive to be helpful. For all that, his houses are technically very well planned, and many, like the Wilson House (1950) at Pensacola – wholly timber-built, while employing avant-garde devices – now look almost traditional.

An early building, Colmorgan House (1937) in Glenview, near Chicago, is in fact fairly conventional, in that it is a wood-frame house with projecting roofs and the massive masonry central block of the chimney, redolent of Wright. Nevertheless, it hints at the more audacious, open-ended approach of Goff's later houses.

Of these, the Samuel Ford Residence (1949) is perhaps the most successful. It is a low, round, domed building, 166-ft (51-m) across, with a red-painted steel frame. The steel dome is covered with dark shingles and admits light through a central lantern with spectacular effect inside, where the upper floor takes the form of a gallery. Construction is simple, much is prefabricated, and the house illustrates Goff's liking both for simple materials and complex forms. It also looks forward 20 years or so to the types of house devised by and for the ecologically-minded.

Designed a year or two later, the spiral Bavinger House at Norman (1950–55) is probably the most famous or controversial. The length of time building it was the result of construction being largely DIY. It looks very odd, and the upper rooms are supported by tension cables from a central mast; but it is in fact an exposition of sophisticated theories, and was described by Goff as 'a continuous study in contemporary architecture'.

Unité d'Habitation, Marseilles

This is probably the most famous work of the 20th century's most famous architect, Le Corbusier (Charles-Édouard Jeanneret, 1887–1965). Regarded as the great hero of the Modern movement (or great villain, according to taste), Corbusier, like most geniuses, is hard to categorize because of his sheer fertility, the great cornucopia of his creativity.

Soon after the end of the Second World War he was invited by the French government to build housing for 1,600 people in Marseilles. He accepted, on the characteristic condition that he could ignore building regulations. Since urban planning and large housing schemes had exercised him for many years, he welcomed the commission, but in the post-war circumstances skilled workers were few and many materials were hard to come by: a steel frame had to be abandoned on grounds of cost.

The Unité d'Habitation (1946–52) is a single concrete block 540-ft (165-m) long and 184-ft (56-m), or 17 storeys, high, raised on mighty stilts, for Corbusier believed that traditional architecture wasted land; a raised building offered more space, if only for car parking. It contained 337 apartments and much besides, including shops, a hotel, school, gymnasium, swimming pool, etc., and was virtually a self-contained settlement. It represented Corbusier's belief in community as opposed to the concept of family that characterized contemporary 'garden cities'. The flats were slotted into the skeleton grid like small drawers in a cabinet, which makes them blessedly soundproof. Living rooms rise through two storeys, with the outside wall glazed and a balcony beyond; but the effect is to make the main 'bedroom' a gallery

over the living room, an unsuitable arrangement for families. The flats, comparatively long and thin and partly two-storey, slot in alternately, one facing east, the next west. Since two flats occupy three storeys, space is left for a rather dark, because windowless, 'interior street'.

Concrete was by this time a familiar material, but it was normally smartly finished, plastered and painted. Corbusier left the concrete rough, with the marks of the wooden shuttering into which it had been poured still

evident. However, the decision, which reduced costs significantly, was largely forced on him. It did produce a pleasingly rugged effect, and had a powerful impact, not always favourable, on the numerous architects who visited the construction site; but it was to become tiresome when overused by imitators. But nobody dared imitate the extraordinarily inventive array of features, again in rough concrete, that turned the roof into a kind of playground for adults.

This famous block is another example of a seminal building whose influence on later architecture was sometimes unfortunate.

THIS PAGE AND
OVERLEAF
Le Corbusier's pilgrimage
chapel at Ronchamp is
one of his most original,
least controversial, and
widely admired
buildings.

Chapel of Notre Dame du Haut, Ronchamp

Two predecessors of the pilgrimage chapel at Ronchamp (1951–55), high in the Vosges, were successively destroyed in the two world wars. Their replacement is unlike any other significant modern building, and unlike any other building by Le Corbusier, yet for many people it is his finest work. It is, at least, a relief from the severity and logic of the International Modern style, although it does apparently conform with the system of proportional dimensions that Le Corbusier called the modulor, and its architectural significance lay not in inspiring imitations (there were some) but in demonstrating that even the most 'rational' of architects could design a building that is essentially personal and poetic, a work of sculpture in concrete which springs from faith, not reason. As the architect wrote to the bishop when it was finished, 'I sought to create a place of silence, of prayer, of peace and inner joy.' It

is hard to see how his achievement of those aims could be improved.

The design was clearly influenced by the landscape; Le Corbusier visited the site several times, making drawings of the ruins of the earlier chapel, though he also asserted, very plausibly, that the design was inspired by a seashell he had picked up on the beach: he is known to have made small-scale models before he drew up the plans.

Within the great, curving concrete walls that reflect the line of the hills, the interior is lit by small windows, seemingly placed at random, some of them with coloured glass, some clear. The extraordinary, boat-like roof, which would be echoed later at Chandigarh, is in fact a hollow shell and quite light: it rests not on the massive concrete walls but on thin steel columns rising from them, which leaves a narrow band of glass between roof and wall. The roof also extends over an outdoor altar, where mass for hundreds is celebrated. Inside, the cult figure of the Virgin, the object of the pilgrims' devotion that was rescued from the ruins, is set before a clear window, against the heavenly blue of the sky.

LEFT
The Atomium may be kitsch, but it is kitsch on a very grand scale.

RIGHT
Detail of the interconnected spheres.

The Atomium, Brussels

The Atomium (1954–58) in north Brussels, bestriding the Boulevard de Centenaire and not far from an earlier scientific architectural marvel, the Laeken Glass Houses, was built as the symbol of the 1958 World Exposition. It is a model, on a vast scale, of an atom of iron, and sprang originally from a notion put forward by a representative of Belgium's metal industries. Many Belgian designers and engineers worked on the project.

The somewhat banal theme of the Exhibition was Progress and Mankind; the motif of the atom seemed suitable in spite of the fact that to most people it stood for massive destruction or possibly a future menace to the planet, nuclear power. Still, the 'atom', in approximately this rather misleading form, was a fashionable motif in the 1950s, and in fact an earlier, smaller version had been seen at the Festival of Britain (1951).

The total height of the structure is 335ft (102m). It consists of nine giant steel spheres, each about 60ft (18m) in diameter and weighing about 200 tons, and with two floors. The topmost sphere contains a restaurant; the others, each with seating capacity for about 200 people, stages special events and exhibitions. The spheres are linked by tubes, representing the bonding power of the atom, which contain elevators and provide passage from one sphere to another. The central shaft contains an 'express' elevator.

The Brussels Atomium, as it loomed above the city, was considered an almost miraculous structure. It could be imagined as a cube balanced on one corner; but unfortunately fire regulations demanded the steps which appear to prop up two of the flanking spheres, rather spoiling the effect and, at a certain angle, giving it the disconcerting appearance of a science-fiction machine about to advance menacingly on the spectator. The Atomium was cleaned and restored for the millennium and some spheres are still open to the public. The view at least repays a visit.

Coventry Cathedral

The city of Coventry lies at the geographical centre of England. Unlike its neighbour, Birmingham, offspring of the Industrial Revolution, it is an ancient city (Lady Godiva's famous protest ride through the streets took place before 1066). In November 1940, Coventry was the target of an 11-hour German bombing raid which destroyed much of the old city, including the Perpendicular Cathedral of St Michael. A competition in 1950 to design a replacement was won by Basil Spence (1907–76), who later became a very successful 'establishment' architect, though he has never found great favour among architectural critics and scholars.

It was, perhaps, a relief that the Church of England authorities did not insist on the Gothic style. But Spence's Coventry Cathedral (1954–62) is not exactly modern, although proclaimed in a slightly defensive pamphlet at the time of its consecration as being 'definitely and sincerely of the present day'. It is built largely in an attractive pinkish-grey sandstone. The cliff-like walls of the large and blocky nave perform a kind of zig-zag, with the thinner edge forming an uninterrupted vertical series of window lights. The roof, of copper-covered concrete, is invisible from the ground. Inside, slim columns rise to form a kind of ribbed vault, as if Gothic leanings were not entirely dead.

A pleasant feature of the construction was the opportunity for contemporary artists and craftsmen to contribute works of a kind for which there were few other opportunities. Best known are the enormous tapestry of Christ behind the altar designed by the painter Graham Sutherland, and the 25-ft (8-m) bronze of St Michael and the Devil by Jacob Epstein next to the porch. The curious, detached Chapel of Unity has a pleasing mosaic floor by a Swedish artist, Einar Forseth.

One aspect of this building that finds more general approval is the way in which the architect combined it with the ruins of the old, whose fine Gothic spire still stands.

The windows in the zig-zag walls (opposite) direct light towards the altar and the enormous tapestry of Christ by Graham Sutherland (below).

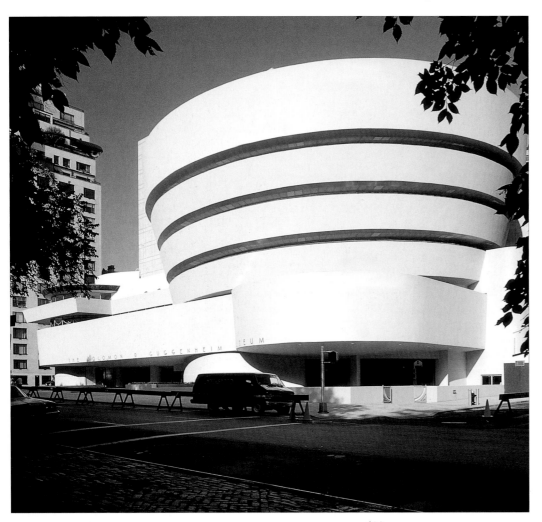

Guggenheim Museum, New York

Although it has not quite succeeded in dethroning the Statue of Liberty as the symbol of New York City, the Solomon R. Guggenheim Museum (1956–59) on 89th Street and Central Park is probably the city's most easily recognized building.

Its patron, who had inherited a vast industrial fortune, originally founded the museum to house the collection under another name, in 1937. When considering a new building, Guggenheim and his agents favoured something appropriately avant-garde; why, otherwise, should they have hired Frank Lloyd Wright? But in 1943, when he was commissioned, Wright was 76, not an age associated with radicalism; but once again, he surprised them all. In a letter to Guggenheim's agent advising that he was bringing the plans for inspection, he wrote: 'The whole thing will either throw you off your guard entirely or be just about what you have been dreaming about.'

Though startling, the building is simple in form. It is essentially a giant concrete drum which grows steadily larger in diameter as it rises, looming out over Fifth Avenue. Inside, a spiral ramp against the wall ascends from the ground to the top, which is covered by a flattish glass dome unseen from the outside at ground level. The pictures are ranged along the wall, the spectator viewing them while descending the ramp, having gone up in an elevator. Only Wright, who had first experimented with spirals in a planetarium designed in 1925, would demand that visitors contemplate paintings in a museum where you are forced to stand with feet on different levels!

Construction was delayed for over a decade, and some contractors were wary of getting involved, doubting, like other Wright contractors before them, whether the structure would be viable. By the time it was officially opened, both Wright and Guggenheim were dead; its reception was mixed, though predominantly favourable. Like most architectural landmarks, it attracted good-natured epithets that signified popular acceptance, but it did not inspire any significant successors. A ten-storey annexe, forming a kind of backdrop, was added in 1992.

The bold Guggenheim Museum in New York introduced a completely new way of arranging pictures in a gallery.

This dramatic but foreshortened view of the Maracaibo Lake Bridge shows the main (300-ft/92-m) high, V-shaped supports of the cantilevered main spans and (foreground) the H-shaped trestle piers.

Maracaibo Lake Bridge, Venezuela

Maracaibo, Venezuela's second city and seaport, lies close to some of the richest oil reserves in the world. By the 1950s the ferries could not cope with the volume of traffic across Lake Maracaibo, which, though the largest lake in South America, draws to a bottleneck only about 5-miles (8-km) wide approaching the sea. The Venezuelan government resolved to cross it, either by a bridge or tunnel or a combination of the two, as in the Chesapeake Bay Bridge Tunnel under construction at the same time. Twelve tenders were submitted, of which 11 proposed a bridge with a superstructure of steel. The government commission recommended acceptance of the twelfth, for a concrete bridge. It was based on a design by Riccardo Morandi (1902–89), second only to Pier Luigi Nervi among 20th-century Italian engineer-architects; but its construction (1959–62) became a large international enterprise involving Portuguese geologists, Swiss technicians, German contractors, and others.

The commission gave several reasons for choosing this design, among them cheaper maintenance (steel needs frequent painting) and visual appeal: it was aesthetically the most satisfying. Another reason was that it would give the Venezuelan construction industry experience of prestressed concrete, a development of reinforced concrete with the steel rods replaced by wires, running in ducts, which can be tensioned after casting. This material permitted much more slender, and therefore economical structures, as had been demonstrated in the lightweight bridges and airship hangars of Eugène Freyssinet (1879–1962).

The bridge, over 70 per cent of which was prefabricated, is made up of three sections, two landward sections of prestressed concrete beams on plain, V- or H-shaped piers, and a central section, to accommodate shipping, of five main spans of 780-ft (238-m) each. These consist of a pair of cantilevers which, to reduce the depth of the box-section beam carrying the road, are supported by inclined ropes from 300-ft (90-m) towers. These six simple and economical structures are reminiscent of the Forth Railway Bridge near Edinburgh, which Morandi acknowledged as an influence.

The sleek and shining, stainless steel parabolic arch on the riverfront of St Louis, the Gateway Arch, as it came to be called, justifies its claim to be the tallest memorial in the USA.

Gateway Arch, St Louis

St Louis, Missouri, is proud of its heritage as the 'Gateway to the West', when it was not only the biggest centre of trade on the Mississippi but also the main crossroads for westward expansion in the half century or so following President Thomas Jefferson's Louisiana Purchase (1803). It retained its dominance in the railway age. A competition for the design of the Jefferson National Expansion Memorial was instigated in 1947, and the winning design was by Eero Saarinen, who was virtually unknown and whose work up to that time had all been done in association with his then more famous father, Eliel. The design drew on a ten-year-old project by Adalberto Libera (1903–63) for the gateway to an Italian international exhibition that was planned for 1942 but which was submerged by greater events.

A sleek and shining, stainless steel, parabolic arch on the riverfront of St Louis, the Gateway Arch, as it came to be called, was built between 1963 and 1965; all survey work was done at night to avoid distortion caused by the rays of the sun. It is 630-ft (192-m) high, which justifies its claim to be the tallest memorial in the USA, and is gently tapered towards the crown. The height is the same as the distance across the base, and takes the structurally sound form of a catenary curve – the shape formed by a chain when held at both ends. It weighs 17,246 tons and sways about half an inch in normal weather; it is calculated that it could sway safely up to a maximum of 18in (46cm), and that a 150-mph (240-km/h) wind would be required to make it do so.

The city authorities have shown some enterprise in making the Gateway Arch, which cost $13 million to build, a major tourist attraction. According to the Arch's web site, it is 'the fourth most visited tourist attraction in the world', a claim which, sadly, induces a certain amount of scepticism.

From some angles, Saarinen's airport terminal has a shark-like appearance. Like railway stations before them, airports called forth some innovative designs from architects in the late 20th century.

TWA Terminal, New York

Eero Saarinen's unashamedly symbolic terminal for Trans World Airlines (1956–62), at New York's Kennedy (then Idlewild) Airport, has been described alternatively as a late Expressionist and an early Postmodern building. Equally, it could be said to signify Saarinen's emergence as a Mannerist, or to reflect his early interest in sculpture. The design, of which there had been a foretaste in Saarinen's skating rink for Yale University (1956–58), represented a more flexible attitude to space and form that became increasingly evident in the 1950s, encouraged by Le Corbusier's chapel at Ronchamp.

The building created a sensation at the time. It was criticized by purists of the Modern movement (a declining breed) but greeted enthusiastically by others and, unusually for a controversial building, by the general public. Saarinen said he was aiming to capture the 'excitement of flight', and passengers might have been forgiven for thinking, on seeing the terminal, that it could transport them through the air all by itself, though they would have revised their opinion on entering the vastness of the interior space.

From the air, the four concrete shells of the roof look like a pair of gigantic and slightly distorted butterflies in close conference – distorted because the shells are not identical. They are supported by large, athletic, Y-shaped buttresses that almost strike a pose, with a line of skylights running between them. Free, curving forms are repeated throughout the interior: the Arrivals and Departures screens are housed in an 'organic' structure with a hint both of Art Nouveau and the science-fiction hero ET.

An enclosed concrete walkway conveys passengers direct to the aircraft and makes Saarinen's building the most passenger-friendly as well as the most exciting terminal in the airport. There were reports that its introduction resulted in a rise in TWA's ticket sales.

Saarinen designed another, even more audacious terminal building for Dulles Airport in Washington, DC, almost his last, completed in 1963. Even for such a technological virtuoso it proved slightly too audacious, however, and part had to be rebuilt in the 1980s.

Nervi was a sensitive artist who largely operated in a tough commercial world with outstanding success. However, the space and openness of his plan for the Turin pavilion was, in execution, somewhat modified by practical considerations.

Palace of Labour, Turin

Pier Luigi Nervi (1891–1979) was one of the most influential architects of the mid-20th century. He was an engineer first, and on many of his most notable buildings he co-operated with other architects. A master of structure, he was a genius in reinforced concrete with a powerful aesthetic sense, qualities first demonstrated in his stadium at Florence (1928).

He ascribed to the undoubtedly correct if logically unjustifiable dictum that a building which looks good aesthetically is good structurally, and vice-versa.

The commission for the Palazzo del Lavoro, like most of Nervi's work, resulted from his submitting a tender that was less expensive and potentially easier to build quickly than other competitors'. It was for a hall honouring the

contribution of labour for an exhibition marking the centenary of Italian independence (1961) in Turin. The terms were challenging. Maximum construction time was 17 months – for a building of over 275,000sq ft (25550sq m) – and the building had to be capable of subsequent conversion into a technical school.

The building is a huge square hall with walls of glass, protected by louvres on the sunny sides, and a roof of steel, which was preferred to concrete because its design promised speedier construction. To avoid the common delays resulting from one operation having to wait for another, the main parts of the structure were made as 16 independent units. They consist of a steel roof section 125-ft (38-m) square, supported by concrete columns 65-ft (20-m) high. A space 6.5-ft (2-m) wide between the squares is glazed to admit light to the centre of the building. Each column is circular at the top of a diameter of 8ft (2.5m), where it meets the tapering steel girders that resemble umbrella spokes. At the bottom it is cross-shaped, 18-ft (5.5-m) across. The shape is dictated by structural considerations, but a dramatic profile results from straight lines drawn between the angles of the cross and the circle. Yet the straight lines are themselves structurally desirable because such members are easier to cast. Around the walls runs a cantilevered mezzanine gallery. The result is – or was, as the building was later altered – not only structurally unique, but visually magnificent.

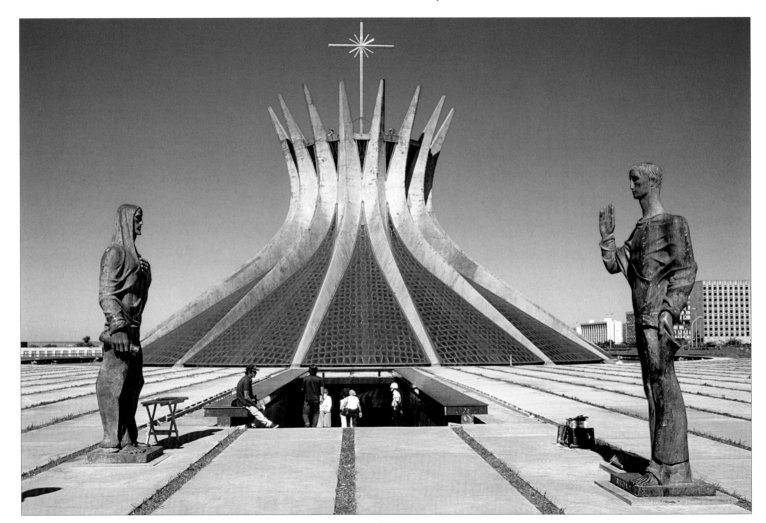

Brasilia Cathedral

The idea of moving the capital of Brazil into the interior was first canvassed as early as 1808 and was enshrined in the constitution of 1889, but it was not until 1956 that a site was chosen and construction begun. Cost apparently was not a problem. The general plan of the new capital was by Lúcio (Luis) Costa, but the presiding genius was the architect Oscar Niemeyer (b. 1907), 'the Brazilian Le Corbusier', with a vigorous creativity to match the master and a similarly cavalier attitude to the strict tenets of Modernism; nearly all the main public buildings in Brasilia were designed by him. At the heart is the monumental Plaza of the Three Powers (1953–60), i.e. buildings of the legislature, judiciary and administration, headed by a giant double slab of offices with, in front, the long low parliament buildings surmounted by two large, shallow domes of which one is turned upside down.

Although the the city's inaugural mass had been held there ten years earlier, the cathedral was not completed until 1970. It is the most interesting building. Niemeyer had often shown himself interested in curving shapes formed with reinforced concrete, which some have traced to an affinity for Brazilian Baroque. The cathedral, which employs sophisticated engineering techniques, is more sculpture than architecture. It takes the form of a crown of thorns, fashioned from 16 hollow concrete ribs, about 100-ft (30-m) high. They slope inwards from the base while expanding in section until they meet near the crown, where they turn outward again and taper off. Some have seen them as hands raised in prayer, others as a flower opening. The spaces between the ribs

are entirely glazed, the leading forming a honeycomb pattern.

The building is entered via a dark Passage of Reflection, from which one emerges into the light and airy space of the circular nave. Being below ground level, it is larger than it appears from the outside and holds 4,000 people. The interior is rather austere. Glass panels in the roof reflect the water in a surrounding pool, which in turn magically reflects shimmering images of nearby buildings.

Like most planned urban utopias, Brasilia failed to realize the hopes of its builders, and tended to develop into two units, the impressive public citadel and the inhuman, fast-deteriorating, geometric slabs of the residential city. It has contributed to the growing dissatisfaction with Modernism.

OPPOSITE
The subterranean entrance to Brasilia Cathedral.

BELOW
Inside, the eye is drawn towards the marble altar and the figures of angels and St Peter suspended from the roof.

Marina City, Chicago

The twin towers, popularly known as corn cobs, of Marina City (1964–67) are the best-known work of Bertrand Goldberg (1913–97) at the culmination of his long career. They were the final manifestation of his belief in the advantages of circular forms: superior aerodynamic qualities, potential offered by a central core, equal distance of units from the centre, etc. It was even possible to find advantages in the fact that internal walls are not parallel. However, the towers of Marina City aroused some derision, especially among high-minded Modernists, when they first appeared and, although they certainly belong to a very different ethos from Mies van de Rohe's classic East Shore Drive Apartments, a close neighbour, it is increasingly difficult to see why. Now that familiarity has made them less startling, however, their structural integrity can be better appreciated.

Built at a time when land prices were rising even faster than buildings, Marina City optimizes a remarkably small riverside site on Chicago's Loop, making the most of the view by placing the lowest apartments, whose semicircular balconies create the corn-cob appearance, on the 21st floor (out of a total of 60 storeys) and by placing the cars of their occupants underneath. There are 450 apartments in each tower, the car park, with its continuous, spiral ramp, accommodating the same number of cars. Theoretically, residents might seldom have to leave the complex, as it also contains offices, shops, restaurants, a theatre between the towers, a gym, even a bowling alley among other amenities, not forgetting the marina. The apartments are grouped around a central core, 35ft (11m) in diameter, containing the services. This powerful core was built first and provided a rising platform for the erection crane, which contributed to the relatively economic construction, matching the economy of space.

When built, Goldberg's towers were said to be the tallest residential buildings in the world and, indeed, the tallest concrete structures. They offer one solution, though perhaps not the most flexible one possible, to the problem of devising the economical, multi-purpose complexes that contemporary cities seem increasingly to demand.

LEFT
The towers of Goldberg's Marina City, which originally failed to attract tenants as easily as was hoped, possibly due to astronomical rents.

OPPOSITE
Chicago with Marina City in the foreground.

Lake Point Tower, Chicago

Although this block was built in 1967–68, its history really begins nearly 50 years earlier, when Mies van der Rohe, stimulated by the burgeoning artistic movements in Europe after the First World War, was going through a particularly creative phase of his development and producing some remarkably varied ideas. Among them were two skyscrapers, the first based on the triangle, the second (1920–21) a glass-clad tower of free, curving forms which was never built, chiefly because finance was not forthcoming, although it was also doubtful if contemporary technology could have coped. All the architects associated with Lake Point (Schipporeit-Heinrich Associates) were former pupils of Mies at the Illinois Institute of Technology, and some of them had also worked in his practice.

Lake Point Tower is an apartment block with various extra amenities, whereas Mies's 1921 design was for an office block. It stands in comparative isolation in Navy Pier Park, then a rather neglected area, at some distance from Chicago's high-rise clusters, which it appears to regard with calm disdain. More recently the pier itself, beyond the park, has been transformed with a $200-million investment of public funds, and in 1996 topped the list of popular attractions in Chicago; but Lake Point has nothing whatever to do with the throngs heading for the amusements on the pier.

The tower is a dizzying 645-ft (197-m) high and contains 900 extremely expensive apartments. It has, strictly speaking, one wall only, a dead-smooth curtain of glass that flows silkily around a three-lobed, clover-leaf plan with a central, triangular core. The view, whether of Lake Michigan or the Chicago skyline, is splendid.

OPPOSITE
The sleek, sophisticated sentinel of Lake Point Tower, the work of former students of Mies van der Rohe who started from a then-practical plan of the master made many years earlier.

RIGHT
Among other amenities, the Tower offers marvellous views.

The Habitat housing complex was the sensation of the Montreal World Fair in 1967. The ingredients are simple but the design is unbelievably complicated.

Habitat, Montreal

The Habitat housing complex on the St Lawrence River was the first major work of the Israeli-Canadian architect Moshe Safdie (b. 1938). Although intended to be permanent, it was designed for 'Expo 67', the Montreal World Fair, and caused a minor sensation. The use of prefabricated reinforced-concrete units was not new, and the Habitat community in many ways reflected the ideas of Gropius and the Bauhaus school in the 1920s. What was new about Safdie's extraordinary block was that 'it lifted the concept of the prefabricated concrete-box unit from a utilitarian technique to the level of emotive architecture' (Gilbert Herbert).

It consists of 554 prefabricated units which are put together to form a single complex. Its form is intricate, a geometric puzzle requiring computer assistance, and superficially looks a jumble, as if someone had thrown a lot of containers together into a pile. The units are put together in different combinations to form,

altogether, 15 different layouts. They are held together with steel cables and connected by internal walkways to make 158 homes with from one to four bedrooms each. The ingenious deployment of projections and recesses provides privacy and a view for each unit, and gives each its own roof garden. As the architect said, the idea was to offer 'privacy, fresh air, sunlight and suburban amenities in an urban setting'.

Originally, 900 apartments had been planned, but no more were ever built; although they had proved more popular than might have been expected, one snag that emerged was the relatively high costs of construction. That may be, partly at any rate, why the Habitat project did not have any obvious successors, although Safdie developed these ideas further in Israel, a region where there is, of course, a tradition of cube-shaped houses; other architects, such as Kisho Kurokawa in Japan, produced similar concepts.

Though many find its weather-streaked concrete unattractive, the late Sir Denys Lasdun's design for the University of East Anglia is successful both overall and in detail.

University of East Anglia, Norwich

The British architect Denys Lasdun (1914–2001) was a leading figure of the so-called 'New Brutalist' school of the 1950s–60s, whose commitment was to the 'honest' architecture of Mies van der Rohe and Le Corbusier, where structure and materials are expressed without disguise. In fact the New Brutalists were originally more thoroughly committed to this principle than even Mies, though with time the movement merged with other, sympathetic international influences and acquired other priorities. Lasdun, whose most famous work was the National Theatre in London (1967–76), described his work as 'the combination of the vertical and the horizontal'.

The University of East Anglia was one of the new provincial universities built in something of a rush in England after the Second World War. A popular generic term for them is 'red-brick' (i.e. not ivy-covered stone) but UEA is uncompromising concrete. Locally it is widely dismissed as ugly, the dinginess of rough concrete, stained by the weather, overcoming its 'honesty'. Nevertheless, the campus was in many ways both innovative and successful. Instead of the prevailing dispersed style for a university campus, with the buildings spread out in groups, UEA is highly centralized, with living, teaching and administration accommodation comprising a single mass that is convenient yet not congested. At the same time, the plan made far-sighted allowance for future growth.

Lasdun's greatest success is the terraced accommodation blocks that take the form of ziggurats, with predominantly glass façades on each recessed floor. They exploit a sloping site to provide a fine view for practically every student over the grass and down to what is called, this being Norfolk, a 'broad' (lake). Both individually and as a group, they make a splendid composition, and although the interior has inevitably become shabby and the staircases are very steep, like those in a cross-Channel ferry, the individual rooms are not unreasonably small.

UEA also boasts a notable arts building, the Sainsbury Centre (1977), a typically innovative structure by Norman Foster and Partners.

Sydney Opera House

The Sydney Opera House (1957–73) was one of those controversial projects whose endless teething troubles seemed to threaten failure; but it has proved a success beyond the city fathers' dreams, and beyond what some of them deserved, since the saga of problems were largely the result of political interference which drove the Danish architect, Jørn Utzon (b. 1918), to pull out before the building was completed. There was also some initial genuine doubt over whether the ambitious design could actually be built. However, the firm of Ove Arup, the outstanding civil engineers, accomplished it in co-operation with Utzon after several contractors had funked the project.

It stands on a small peninsula in Sydney Harbour within nodding distance of the famous bridge. Utzon's design was chosen in an international competition in 1956, allegedly on the basis of a handful of sketches. Utzon, an undoubted genius but not the easiest man to pin down, tended to design, or redesign, as he went along, and no one knows if the building would have taken exactly its present form if he had remained in charge until the end; the interior would probably have been rather more exciting. It contains four theatres altogether, but the building, it is said, is 'all roof'. The structures beneath are substantial enough (the concert hall holds nearly 3,000 people), but the soaring shells, rising to peaks over 200-ft (60-m) high, make them if not invisible, unnoticed. What do these thrilling forms symbolize? They are more suggestive of canvas than concrete, and are often compared with the sails of the boats in Sydney harbour, or with the fins of sharks in the ocean beyond; the Australian gift for a colourful phrase has dubbed them the 'Nuns' scrum'. They have, of course, no practical function and sad to say, while the Opera House is a wonderful place for staging most kinds of entertainment, critics say that classical opera is not among them. The building has not worn well either, though it was revamped for the Olympics in 2000.

Australia's famous Postmodern Opera House sails boldly out into Sydney Harbour in total defiance of the doctrine that function dictates form.

Sir James Stirling's Stuttgart gallery overflows with invention, wit and excitement.

Neue Staatsgalerie, Stuttgart

This addition to the State Gallery in Stuttgart (1977–84) by James Stirling (1926–94) in association with Michael Wilford, ended a decade in which Britain's perhaps most gifted and original architect had been starved of major commissions. Though a thoroughly modern architect, Stirling was far removed from the dogma of the International Modern style, and his later buildings, from about 1971, in which his unconstrained, expressive eclecticism is more evident and geometric abstraction mingles with Neoclassical motifs, are usually classed as Postmodernist. They often manifest a Postmodern jokiness, like the Staatsgalerie's wall lights in the form of a 'fallen' section of cornice, suggesting that architecture should not be treated too solemnly.

Stirling's Staatsgalerie won a competition held in 1977, beating nine German designs. It is skilfully organized as a succession of spaces created by angled surfaces and changing levels. On one hand a display of imaginative invention, it also seemed to provide a kind of collage of contemporary ideas on design. The central unit is a stone-faced drum or rotunda, open to the sky, its wall pierced by openings offering intriguing glimpses of other parts. There is no façade as such. The entrance lobby on one side of the rotunda gives on to the temporary-exhibition hall, with its undulating, green-mullioned glass wall. The masonry walls consist of alternate bands of travertine and sandstone and lend the building a more imposing aspect. That balances the relative frivolity of the poster-paint colours – the bright green floor of the entrance area or the bulky, red, cylindrical handrails of ramps and walkways. The galleries are on the top floor and are lit from the glazed roof. They are fairly conventional, a succession of plain rooms with a centrally aligned walk-through. Stirling considered the traditional arrangement 'more convincing' than 20th-century alternatives.

The building was a great success from the start, equally popular with ordinary people and, despite some initial dissent, with Stirling's architectural colleagues. In the year after it opened, the Staatsgalerie moved from 51 to first place in the popularity poll of German museums.

Pompidou Centre, Paris

The idea that a ruler should be commemorated by great works was enthusiastically embraced by Georges Pompidou, president of France (1969–74), no less than Louis XIV, leading him to conceive the idea of the Centre National d'Art et de Culture Georges Pompidou (1971–77), to give it its full title. It was the work of the British architect Richard Rogers (b. 1933), in partnership with the Italian Renzo Piano (b. 1937) and, like the Sydney Opera House, was built by the firm of Ove Arup, in particular, its most brilliant engineer, Peter Rice, also largely responsible for getting the Sydney Opera House up and running. Both architects, who entered the competition for design of the building on the spur of the moment and, being young, little known, and foreign, had little expectation of winning, were devoted to the idea of form defined by function in a Modernist context, as first defined by Louis Sullivan in Chicago in 1896, not of course to the total exclusion of aesthetic considerations, but by abandoning traditional concepts of, for instance, a façade by boldly placing service facilities on the exterior.

The structure, described as a six-storey culture machine, forms a huge transparent box 550-ft (168-m) long, 194-ft (59-m) wide and 138-ft (42-m) high, with a frame of exposed cylindrical steel columns and trusses spanning the entire length. Unsupported spanning beams 157-ft (48-m) long create a highly flexible interior, while steel cantilevers support various service systems outside the columns. They include escalators in transparent plastic tubes, elevators painted red, and further large tubes for air ducts (painted blue), water (green) and electricity (yellow).

The uncompromisingly 'industrial' nature of the design, for a building in an historic district of Paris, not surprisingly caused a good deal of controversy and provoked several blocking actions in the courts. However, if (as someone complained) the outside looks like a half-built factory, by banning service systems to the exterior, the Centre acquires a vast, calm and uncluttered space. The result is that it has proved almost too successful and has become a packed tourist attraction. Offices were moved out to make more room for culture and, only 20 years after it opened, it has had to be temporarily closed for intensive refurbishment.

Full advantage has been taken of the idea that industrial installations can be beautiful, with service elements, usually concealed, comprising the whole aesthetic of the building.

Lloyd's Building, London

Lloyd's of London is an ancient and often misunderstood institution. It is not an insurance company but an association of underwriters in hundreds of syndicates, who between them can insure almost anything anywhere. Its name derives from Lloyd's Coffee House in Lombard Street, where shipowners and marine insurers met from the 1690s. However, after many generations of comparative security and high profit, Lloyd's has experienced troubled times in the last quarter of the 20th century.

Underwriters are generally people of conservative tastes, and many of them were appalled by their dynamic new high-tech building (1978–86) by Richard Rogers, with the engineering firm of Ove Arup. The views of the occupants, however, are not definitive. As the architect has said, 'Though the client's program offers the architect a point of departure, it must be questioned, as the architectural solution lies in the complex and often contradictory interpretation of the needs of the individual, the institution, the place and history.' The design exploited many of the practical devices developed with such success for the Pompidou Centre in Paris; while the framework of the building is built to last, the numerous service systems are built with easy access and future obsolescence in mind. It is perhaps an aesthetically superior structure to the Pompidou Centre, and it is certainly one of the best modern buildings in London.

The structure is mainly concrete with stainless-steel cladding and a great deal of reflective glass. As in Paris, a spacious and flexible interior is achieved by placing the services outside the building: the fast-moving all-glazed lifts offer fine views of London once breath has returned to the body. The main building is rectangular in plan and surrounded by service towers. Its vast central atrium ascends through a series of concentric balconies for the whole height of the 12 storeys. This is 'the Room', where brokers do business, and it can hold about 1,000 of them. In the centre, between four cylindrical columns that also give support to the balconies, an escalator rises in dramatic diagonals within the rectangular space.

The grace of power is again evident in what is perhaps Richard Rogers most successful building to date.

Richard Meier's buildings remain faithful to clarity and order and reject ill-disciplined Postmodernism.

High Museum of Art, Atlanta

The New York architect Richard Meier (b. 1934) was a member of the 'New York Five' who gained prominence through an exhibition at the Museum of Modern Art in 1969, another member being the future Disney architect Michael Graves. All their designs were for family houses, commonly in wood and in the tradition of Le Corbusier and the pre-war International Modern style. All, but especially Meier, displayed a preference for white in their buildings, which helps to account for the unblemished purity of his style. The group of five soon dispersed, but the exhibition led to larger commissions, which for Meier culminated in a succession of prestigious museums, including the High Museum of Art in Atlanta, Georgia (1983), and the vast Getty Center in Los Angeles (1984–97) until, by the end of the 20th century, he was one of the most successful and sought-after international architects.

The Atlanta High Museum, which is part of the Woodrow Arts Center, is perhaps the most striking example of the cool assurance of Meier's buildings, all the more striking in view of his prolific output; the adjective 'high' might almost indicate a moral stance. Meier has emphasized 'the sense of spiritual activity expressed in architectonic forms'.

The design was the unanimous choice of the judges in the competition of 1981. The building is constructed of concrete slabs on a steel frame, with steel columns, and is clad in Meier's characteristic white, porcelain-enamelled steel panels, with a granite plinth. The grid of the panels is echoed by the plinth and the windows. Between cubic wings is the curved, glazed façade of the atrium, which has circling ramps prompting memories of the New York Guggenheim. The atrium is filled with natural light, like the rest of the building, entering, direct or filtered through skylights, glazed strips, or through small windows in the galleries. Besides displaying paintings, sculpture, furniture and other objects, the building includes an auditorium, café, shop, members' lounge, and offices.

Commerzbank, Frankfurt

Not many people, given an alternative, would choose to work in run-of-the-mill high-rise office blocks – 'elongated filing cabinets' – as Jonathan Glancey calls them. The design by Norman Foster and Partners for a bank headquarters in Frankfurt is a bold attempt to escape from the anonymous vastness, the monotony and the second-hand air supply of the typical office tower. Some of the devices by which Foster overcame these drawbacks depended on up-to-the-minute technology and the expertise of the near-legendary engineers of the Ove Arup engineering partnership.

Instead of being built around a central core containing lifts and services, the plan of the 57-storey Commerzbank tower (1997), the tallest building in Europe, is an equilateral triangle, with the services placed in the three corners. In the vacant centre, a vast atrium rises about 500ft (150m) from the lobby to a glass roof, with the sky beyond, which acts as a giant ventilation shaft, drawing in fresh air from outside. On the side of the building, but within the outer glass skin, are a series of nine

gardens, strictly speaking conservatories, which rise around the tower in a spiral. Each of the gardens, which individually represents the flora of different parts of the world, is four-storeys-high. There is a view of plants and shrubs from any desk in the office, and the wide windows also give a view of the city. Windows on the inner skin can be opened, tilting from the top, by pressing a button. The outer skin is of course closed, except for air intakes.

The perhaps romantic idea was to replace corporate vastness with a more villagey community. There are 240 people for each garden, working in offices where the view is unrestricted, as in open-plan but with sound sealed off by glass partitions. The absence of columns adds to the sense of space.

The building is less remarkable from the outside, partly due to planning restrictions and partly to economy. Foster's previous bank headquarters, in Hong Kong (1986), where the budget was less limited, had proved notoriously expensive, and the German bankers were understandably wary.

OPPOSITE
The Commerzbank is the tallest building in Europe, designed with many innovations by Norman Foster and Partners to escape the anonymous vastness of the typical office tower.

RIGHT
Interior view of one of the nine conservatories or winter gardens.

OPPOSITE
Built for the Second Reich, the Reichstag Building failed to survive the Third, but the restored version, so everyone hopes, may last much longer in a united, democratic state.

RIGHT
The new glass dome above the debating chamber.

Reichstag, Berlin

The Reichstag was built in rather heavy Neo-Renaissance style in 1884–1894 for the legislature of the new German Empire. The infamous Reichstag fire (1933) seriously damaged it and Hitler's subsequent suspension of the constitution made it redundant. In 1945 Soviet guns all but flattened it and the division of Germany in 1945 left it still without a role, though it was patched up. With the reunification of Germany in 1990, Berlin regained its status as capital, and the old Reichstag building, restored and expanded, became the home of the federal parliament (Bundestag) in 1999. Remarkably, the commission was won by an architect who, though of international stature with a staff of over 500 and possibly the most successful in the world, was British, Sir Norman Foster.

There is a well-known story of how Foster, interviewed about his plan in 1992, told the competition jury, who did not know, what the current running costs of the building were and how they could be vastly reduced. Ecologically, the building is very advanced, using solar power, rapeseed fuel oil and a regeneration system that reduces emission of carbon dioxide by 90 per cent.

The most striking feature is the new glass dome above the debating chamber, the old one having been destroyed. Inside the dome is a large inverted cone containing energy-producing photovoltaic cells and covered with 365 mirrors. It reflects light into the chamber and, from below, a myriad of refracted glimpses of the sky or the people on the spiral ramp that ascends inside the dome to a viewing platform. 'What you see [from the chamber]', Foster explained, 'is the people walking, climbing above the politicians paid to serve them. The people are the masters here, not the politicians.' Undeniably, the dome throws a lot of light on the conduct of the lawmakers.

Though little more than 100-years-old, the Reichstag building has had a momentous history, and Foster and Partners have endeavoured to preserve it. Some of the graffiti made by Soviet soldiers in 1945 are still present.

The Malaysian sky rockets pose several questions. Is there now any point in token acknowledgement of local traditions in architectural design? Has rivalry over claims for the world's largest building, once confined to North American cities, become even less edifying since becoming an international contest?

Petronas Towers, Kuala Lumpur

In the 1980s the Selangor Turf Club, with its race track, was ordered to move out of its site in Kuala Lumpur to reduce traffic congestion on race days. This opened up a vast site in the heart of the Malaysian capital. Originally, it was to be a park, but the government, weighing the advantages of a park that would be expensive to maintain against a commercial development that would bring large profits, opted for the latter. There would still be a small park, but there would also be mixed-purpose development. Petronas, an oil company, became the major investor and planned new headquarters in the Kuala Lumpur City Centre Company, formed to control the whole site. Urged by the forceful prime minister, Dr Mahathir Mohammed, a major monument was planned. This was the genesis of the Petronas Towers (1993–98).

The winning design was by the Argentinian-born US architect, Cesar Pelli (b. 1926), whose earlier buildings included the Canary Wharf Tower in London. It was for twin towers of 88 storeys each, joined midway by a 'sky bridge' and each with an attached cylindrical tower of 44 storeys. An identifiably 'Malaysian' building was called for, and the star-shaped plan of the main towers reflects an Islamic motif, while the profile vaguely suggests Buddhist models.

A great deal of preparation and planning was required before construction could start. Experts around the world gave advice, project managers were sent to study for a year in the USA, geological sampling was carried out down to 330ft (100m) below the surface, complete systems were ordered in advance of construction to prevent costly hold-ups, and with up to 7,000 workers on a site in the middle of a busy city, stringent safety precautions were required.

At a late stage, the height of the pinnacles was increased so that the towers could claim the title of the world's tallest building, at 1,483ft (452m). However, 240ft (73m) of that is taken up by the spire and both the Sears Tower in Chicago and the World Trade Center in New York have more storeys.

Guggenheim Museum, Bilbao

One thing that makes the Bilbao Guggenheim (1993–97) an appropriate building on which to end the 20th century is that it evidently would not have been possible without the aid of the computer. It looks more like a gigantic piece of abstract sculpture, with perhaps a nod towards early movements in modern art, particularly Picasso and Cubism. The assembly of disparate, interconnected forms obey no observable logic. They are mainly clad in titanium, with some glass and stone. The museum has been unhelpfully compared with an unfolding flower or a huge fish, but its design should not have been a total surprise since its Canadian-born, California-based architect, Frank Gehry (b. 1929), had displayed his free-form style ('no-rules architecture') in earlier buildings, including his own house in Santa Monica (1978), though on nothing like this scale.

It arose from a major programme to reinvigorate the run-down Basque city of Bilbao (including a metro system designed by Norman Foster), combined with the desire of the Guggenheim Foundation for a major new museum in Europe for its vast collection of modern art. It was built on a disused industrial site, at a cost of about $100 million (about one-tenth the cost of London's Millennium Dome), and opened in October 1997; an attempt by ETA terrorists to send it off with the wrong sort of bang was forestalled by vigilant security. During its first year, besides hordes of film crews looking for an original backdrop for a TV advertisement, it attracted more visitors than the Prado, Spain's premier museum of art. According to one study, 80 per cent of the visitors admitted they had come to see the museum rather than its contents.

The interior is well adapted to cater for the often very large dimensions of contemporary artworks. The main exhibition gallery is 450-ft (137-m) long and over 150-ft (50-m) high, and there are small spaces for more intimate works. The total exhibition space amounts to about 100,000sq ft (9000sq m), on three floors. Gehry is currently planning another Guggenheim, twice the size of Bilbao, for Manhattan's Lower East Side.

It is an interesting paradox of popular taste that, while almost any modern building provokes disapproval, the most extravagantly unconventional design often excites general enthusiasm, the Sydney Opera House and the Bilbao Guggenheim being cases in point.

adobe: sun-baked clay brick

aisle: one of the lateral divisions in a church

ambulatory: a walkway within or around a building or an apse

apsaras: sculpted female figures on Indian temples

apse: an addition to the east end of (usually) a church, semicircular, square-sided or polygonal

aqueduct: a bridge-like structure carrying a water channel overland

arcade: a row of arches on pillars

arch: a curved structure bridging a space

architrave: the lowest element of an entablature

Art Nouveau: late 19th-century decorative style, characterized by sinuous, plant-like forms and vivid colour

Art Deco: decorative style of the 1920s–1930s based on geometric forms and influenced by streamlining and plastics

Arts and Crafts: movement influenced by John Ruskin and William Morris in Victorian England, favouring the artist-craftsman and hostile to industrialization

ashlar: a hewn stone, blocks of squared stone cut to fit precisely

atlantes: similar to caryatids but with male rather than female figures

atrium: the central courtyard, roofed on the sides, of a Roman villa; hence a similar feature in modern buildings

axial: forming an axis, as in a building with units ranged along a straight line

azulejos: decorative tiles of glazed earthenware characteristic of Iberia and Latin America

bailey: the courtyard of a castle

baldacchino: an ornate canopy, on pillars or suspended, above throne, altar or tomb

baptistery: the part of a church where baptism takes place, often a separate building

barbican: an outlying fortification defending the entrance to a castle

Baroque: the style predominant in 17th–18th-century Europe, characterized by energy, movement and a sense of mass

barrel vault: a vault in the form of a continuous semicircle

basilica: a hall-like building with arcade, aisles and clerestory

bastion: a projecting element in a castle wall, typically at a corner, giving defenders a better view of the walls

battered: of a wall, often the lower wall of a castle, that slopes inward from the ground

battlement: an indented, or crenelated, parapet in a fortified building

bay: a division of a wall, space, or building created by two vertical architectural features, such as pillars

blind arch: a 'filled-in' arch, a decorative feature on a solid wall

boss: a carved, ball-like ornament typically covering the point in a vault where ribs intersect

bracket: a small, weight-bearing platform or shelf, often in the form of volutes

buttress: a solid, vertical feature built against a wall to support it

campanile: a bell tower

cantilever: a horizontal member, such as a beam, projecting beyond its point of support

capital: the top part of a column, above the shaft

caravanserai: a roadside rest house for caravans in the Near East

caryatid: a column in the form of a female figure

cella: the main room of a Classical temple, beyond the portico

centring: the wooden support for an arch during building

central plan: of a building that is more or less symmetrical in all directions

chaitya: A Buddhist sanctuary or shrine

chancel: the eastern arm of a church, containing the altar

château: originally a castle (French); later a grand country house

chhattri (chatri): open, pillared kiosks, often appearing on the roof of a larger building in India

choir: the part of the church occupied by the choir, often used synonymously with chancel

Churrigueresque: lavishly ornamental style in 18th-century Spain derived from the work of the architect José Benito de Churriguera (1665–1725)

Classical: the style of ancient Greece and Rome, often revived (Neoclassicism), the predominant historical influence in Western architecture

clerestory (clearstorey): the wall above the arcade in a basilica-type building, its windows being the main source of light

cloisters: open arcades surrounding a courtyard

coffering: decorative panels in a ceiling

collonnade: a row of columns supporting an entablature, arches or a roof

column: a vertical, cylindrical, supporting member made up of base, shaft and capital

concrete: a stone-like substance made by mixing cement with sand and aggregate, such as gravel

corbel: a projecting block, usually stone, in a wall, providing support for a beam or member

Corinthian: third of the Classical Greek Orders, distinguished by elaborate capitals carved with acanthus leaves

cornice: the topmost section of an entablature; hence, a projecting, ornamental moulding that crowns a wall or building

crenelation: see *battlement*

crockets: small knob-like ornaments in the form of a curling leaf, carved at regular intervals on the angles of Gothic spires, gables, etc.

crossing: in a cruciform church, the area where the arms intersect

cruciform: cross-shaped

cupola: a small dome

curtain wall: in a castle, the main, fortified wall; in modern architecture, the outside, non-load-bearing wall

cusp: the point created by the meeting of two arcs forming part of the inside of an arch or window

Decorated: a style of English Gothic architecture in the late 13th–14th centuries, marked by highly decorated surfaces and extensive use of ogee curves

dome: a curved roof, typically round at the

base and approximately semicircular in section, with infinite variations

donjon: the main building or tower of a castle, often called the keep

Doric: first of the three Classical Greek Orders, characterized by fluted columns with no base and simple capitals

drum: a circular wall supporting a dome; or one of the blocks making up a column

Early English: the earliest style of English Gothic architecture in the late 12th–13th centuries, less determinedly vertical than French

elevation: the plan of a building seen from the side

engaged column: a column attached to a wall

engrailed: decorated with concave arcs, forming cusps

entablature: in Classical architecture, the horizontal elements above the capital of a column, consisting of architrave, frieze and cornice

entasis: the slight outward swell in the shaft of a column

façade: the main front or face of a building

fan vaulting: a complex pattern of ribs fanning out from a single point above the shafts in the walls

finial: an ornamental feature at the top of a gable, pinnacle, etc.

Flamboyant: the final stage of French Gothic architecture, 15th–16th centuries, marked by luxuriant, sinuous tracery

fluting: vertical grooves in the shaft of a column

flying buttress: a buttress attached to the

wall by a half-arch, absorbing the thrust of the vault

foliate: in the form of leaves

frieze: the central band of a Classical entablature, or a continuous decorative band around the top of a room or building

gallery: an upper floor open on one side, on the outside of a building or overlooking a courtyard; also the storey above the arcade in a Gothic church

gargoyle: a water spout, throwing rainwater clear of the building, carved as a grotesque head

Gothic: the prevalent style in most of Europe from the late 12th century to the Renaissance, characterized by pointed arches, rib vaults, large windows and flying buttresses

Greek cross: a cross with four arms of equal length

groin vault: a vault formed by four barrel vaults meeting at right angles

gumbaz: a dome

hall church: having nave and aisles of equal length, with no clerestory

horseshoe arch: a rounded arch narrowing towards the bottom

hypostyle: a large interior space in which the roof is supported by many pillars

Ionic: second of the three Classical Greek Orders, characterized by column capitals in the form of volutes

iwan: a large vaulted hall open on one side occupying the centre of the wall on each side of the courtyard of a mosque in eastern Islam

keep: see *donjon*

khan: see *caravanserai*

kiosk: a small open building like a summerhouse, often on pillars, associated chiefly with Iran and Anatolia

lancet window: a narrow, pointed window, a feature of early Gothic

lantern: a small, glazed turret on a dome, tower, etc.

Latin cross: a cross in which the vertical part below the horizontal is longer than the other three parts

lattice: an openwork screen, or a window with glazing bars making a similar pattern

light: the glass between two mullions of a window

lintel: a horizontal slab above a door or window

loggia: an arcaded gallery open at the sides; sometimes an independent structure in a garden

louvre: an air vent, sometimes under a lantern, which can be closed by slats, similar to a venetian blind

machicolation: a projecting parapet on a castle, with holes in the floor for dropping missiles onto attackers

madrasa: a Muslim training college

mahal: a palace

Manueline: the ornamental, late Gothic style in Portugal denoting a style of architecture developed during the reign of Manuel I (1495–1521)

masjid: a mosque

mausoleum: a grand, monumental tomb

metopes: square spaces, often carved, that alternate with triglyphs in a Doric frieze

mezzanine: a low intermediate storey, usually above the ground floor

mihrab: the central prayer niche in the

qibla wall of a mosque

minaret: a tall, slim tower in a mosque from which worshippers are called to prayer

minbar: the high pulpit in a mosque

mosaic: decoration of a surface with small glass or stone cubes (*tesserae*) set in cement

moulding: projecting bands decoratively shaped or carved in one of many ways

mullions: the vertical bars dividing a window into lights

muqarnas: carved decoration resembling stalactites on an Islamic vault

nave: the area of a church west of the crossing

obelisk: a tapering, four-sided pillar with pyramid top

oculus: a round window, or circular opening in, for example, the top of a dome

ogee curve: a double curve, like the letter S, a common form of moulding

Order: one of the five Classical categories, three Greek plus two Roman, based mainly on the form of the columns

pagoda: a multi-storey Buddhist temple tower

Palladian: A popular style in early 18th-century Europe, based on the designs of the Renaissance Classical architect Andrea Palladio (1508–80)

pediment: the triangular gable above a Classical entablature

pendentive: a type of spandrel for supporting a dome on a square or polygonal drum, in the form of a concave triangle, with the point at the angle of the walls and the (curved) base at the dome

peristyle: a row of columns around a building or courtyard

Perpendicular: the English Gothic style in the mid-14th–16th centuries, marked by strong emphasis on verticals and huge windows

piazza: a large open space, or square, in a town

pier: a vertical masonry support, like a column but thicker, sometimes in the form of a cluster of engaged pillars

pietra dura: a type of inlaid mosaic incorporating semi-precious stones

pilaster: a rectangular column projecting slightly from a wall of which it forms a decorative part

pillar: a free-standing, vertical support that, unlike a column, need not be cylindrical nor related to the Classical Orders

pilotis: pillars that raise a building from the ground, like stilts

pinnacle: a terminating feature like a small turret, on gables, buttresses, corners, etc.

Plateresque: the lavishly decorative style, resmbling silversmiths' work, of 16th-century Spain

plinth: the projecting, squared-off base of a pedestal or building

podium: the base on which a building, especially a temple, is built

porch: a roofed entrance to a building

portcullis: the iron gate of a castle, raised to open, lowered to close

portico: a substantial entrance or porch, occupying the whole façade in a Classical temple

post-and-lintel: see *trabeate*

precast concrete: concrete elements cast, often in a factory, before being placed in position

presbytery: see *sanctuary*

prestressed concrete: concrete reinforced with tensioned wires which, by imparting tension, cause compression in the tension area of the concrete, thus cancelling out stresses caused when loaded

pylon: a flanking tower of a monumental gateway in ancient Egypt, like an extended, truncated pyramid; hence, similar structures elsewhere

qibla (wall): the wall of a mosque nearest Mecca

quadrangle: a rectangular courtyard surrounded by buildings

quadripartite vault: a vault with four units meeting in a point at the centre of a bay

quoins: cut stones forming the corner of a building, usually arranged to appear alternately long and short

Rayonnant: the classic style of French Gothic architecture in the 13th–14th centuries, marked by the integration of tracery with overall design, refinement of mass and willingness to experiment. The word means 'radiating' and describes the pattern of radiating lights in the rose windows characteristic of the time

reinforced concrete: steel rods intoduced to concrete to compensate for its relative weakness in tension

reredos: a wooden or stone carved screen behind the altar of a church

rib vault: a vault in which the divisions (groins) between the curved units are marked by a raised band or moulding

Rococo: the decorative style of the Late Baroque period, peaking about 1730–60, marked by asymmetrical, boldly curving shapes.

Romanesque: the prevailing style, deriving from ancient Rome, of European architecture up to the mid-12th century, characterized by round arches, hefty piers and thick walls

rondel: a circular form, usually ornamental, like a medallion

rose window: a large circular window, with mullions radiating like spokes of a wheel

rotunda: a circular building, typically with dome and colonnade

rustication: large stone blocks, typically on a lower wall, left rough or boldly textured and with deep joints between them

sanctuary: the holiest part of a church or temple, location of the altar or sacred image

scagliola: imitation marble, plaster- or cement-based, with marble fragments or other material and colouring added

scroll: a curling, ornamental form suggesting a paper scroll unwinding

section: a vertical representation of a building, as if sliced through the middle

sgraffito: 'scratched', a form of decoration of tiles or in plaster, with the design cut through to reveal a contrasting colour underneath

shell (roof): a curved roof or other structure in which the thickness of the material is very thin compared with the surface area

shingles: overlapping wooden tiles on the exterior of a building

sikhara: the main tower, usually over the sanctuary, of an Indian temple

spandrel: the roughly triangular surface between the curve of an arch and the right angle formed by a horizontal drawn from its apex and a vertical rising from its springing; hence also, for example, the space between two arches in an arcade

springing: the point at which an arch 'springs' from its vertical support

squinch arch: a series of expanding concentric arches, usually to cover the interior junction of a square tower and a round or polygonal spire or dome

strapwork: carved decoration in the form of interlacing bands or straps

stucco: plaster

stupa: a domed-shaped Buddhist monument containing sacred relics

stylobate: the top level of the base on which a Classical building stands

tatami: Japanese straw mats whose dimensions provided the unit of measurement for designing interiors

terracotta: baked, unglazed clay, most often used decoratively

torana: gateway to a Buddhist or Hindu temple

trabeate: the method of building with vertical posts and horizontal beams

tracery: intersecting stone framework of Gothic windows; also, similar patterns used on walls, vaults, etc.

transept: the projecting arms of a cruciform church, meeting at the crossing

triforium: the open passageway along the wall of a Gothic church above the level of the nave and below the clerestory; sometimes called the gallery

triglyphs: the fluted, squarish blocks

alternating with metopes in a Doric frieze

truss: a wooden, self-supporting framework bridging a space, as in a roof

tunnel vault: see *barrel vault*

turret: a small tower, usually built above another structure, attached to a corner, etc.

Tuscan: A Roman Order, one of the five Classical Orders, supposedly derived from Etruscan architecture, similar to Doric, but with a base and unfluted columns

tympanum: the semicircle between the lintel and the arch of a doorway; also, the triangular space within a Classical pediment

vault: an arched, masonry ceiling

villa: historically, a large country house

volute: the spiralling, scroll-like form as seen in an Ionic capital

voussoirs: wedge-shaped stones forming the inside curve of an arch

ward: see *bailey*

ziggurat: a monumental building of successively smaller concentric stages, a 'stepped' pyramid

INDEX

Acknowledgements

P.2 A A Photo Library: P.3 AA Photo Library: P 5 AA Photo Library: P.6 Edifice: P.7 AA Photo Library: P. 9 AA Photo Library: P. 12 AA Photo Library: P.13 (both) AA Photo Library: P. 14–15 (both) AA Photo Library: P. 16–17 (all) AA Photo Library: P. 18–19 (all) AA Photo Library: P. 20 NW004837 © Nik Wheeler/CORBIS: P. 21 (all) AA Photo Library: P. 22 Sonia Halliday Photographs; Photographer James Wellard: P. 23 Werner Forman Archive: P. 24 (left) AA Photo Library; Photo by Rick Strange: P. 25 (both) AA Photo Library: P. 26 and 27 (both) Werner Forman Archive: P. 30 AA Photo Library: P. 31 AA Photo Library: P. 32 AA Photo Library: P. 33 AA Photo Library: P. 34 AA Photo Library: P. 35 A.F. Kersting: P. 36–37 MN001255 © Michael Nicholson/CORBIS, MN001258 © Michael Nicholson/CORBIS, DB001144 © Dave Barlruffi/CORBIS: P. 38 AA Photo Library: P. 39 AA Photo Library: P. 40–41 (both) AA Photo Library: P. 42 (all) AA Photo Library: P. 43 (all) AA Photo Library: P. 44 and 45 (both) © TRIP/M. Barlow: P. 49 AA Photo Library: P. 50 and 51 (both) A.F. Kersting: P. 52 AH002075 © Angelo Hornak/CORBIS: P. 53 EG001415 © Carmen Redondo/CORBIS: P. 54 AA Photo Library; Photo by Rick Strange: P. 55 AL003030 © Paul Almasy/CORBIS: P.56 (both) AA Photo Library: P. 57 AA Photo Library: P. 58 DC001490 © Dean Conger/CORBIS: P. 59 AW003880 © Adam Woolfit/CORBIS: P. 60 (both) AA Photo Library: P. 61 (both) AA Photo Library: P. 62 and 63 AA Photo Library: P. 64 AA Photo Library: P. 65 VN003319 © Ruggero Vanni/CORBIS: P. 66 IH049930 © Ruggero Vanni/CORBIS: P. 67 (both) AA Photo Library: P. 68 JA006227 © James L. Amos/CORBIS: P. 69 (both) A.F. Kersting: P. 70 (both) A.F. Kersting: P. 71 (both) AA Photo Library: P. 72 AW002655 © Adam Woolfit/CORBIS: P. 73 (both) AA Photo Library: P. 74 (both) AA Photo Library: P. 75 CS005110 © Archivo Iconigrafico SA/CORBIS: P. 76 AA Photo Library: P. 77 AL004074 © Paul Almasy/CORBIS: P. 78 and 79 (both) AA Photo Library: P. 80 AL013111 © Paul Almasy/CORBIS: P. 81 AL004358 © Paul Almasy/CORBIS: P. 82 (both) Edifice/Norman: P. 83 © Werner Forman Archive: P. 84 (both) AA Photo Library: P. 85 CJ008459 © Charles & Josette Lenars/CORBIS: P. 86 AL003043 © Paul Almasy/CORBIS: P. 87 A.F. Kersting: P. 88 AA Photo Library: P. 89 (both) AA Photo Library: P. 90 and 91 (both) AA Photo Library: P. 92 AL012901 © Paul Almasy/CORBIS: P. 93 A.F. Kersting: P. 94 and 95 (both) AA Photo Library: P. 96 AA Photo Library: P. 97 (both) AA Photo Library: P. 98 AA Photo Library: P. 99 © TRIP/TH-FOTO WERBUNG: P. 100 AA Photo Library: P.101 (both) AA Photo Library: P. 102 (left) AA Photo Library: P. 102 (right) IH166872 © Richard T. Nowitz/CORBIS: P. 103 JB011287 © Jonathan Blair/CORBIS: P. 104 and 105 (all) AA Photo Library: P. 106 (both) AA Photo Library: P. 107 AW011771 © Adam Woolfit/CORBIS: P. 108 and 109 (both) AA Photo Library: P. 110 (both) AA Photo Library: P. 111 AA Photo Library: P. 112 and 113 (both) AA Photo Library: P. 114 and 115 (all) AA Photo Library: P. 116 and 117 (all) AA Photo Library: P. 118

(left) AA Photo Library: P. 118 (right) WS001869 © Patrick Ward/CORBIS: P. 119 (both) AA Photo Library: P. 120 and 121 (all) AA Photo Library: P. 122 AL003101 © Paul Almasy/CORBIS: P. 123 QU001782 © Chris Lisle: P. 126 AA Photo Library: P. 127 Edifice/Lewis: P. 128 VN002008 © Ruggero Vanni/CORBIS: P. 129 ME001076 G Macduff Everton/CORBIS: P. 130 and 131 (both) A.F. Kersting: P. 132 VU002776 © Sandro Vannini/CORBIS: P. 133 A.F. Kersting: P. 134 EG001331 © Carmen Redondo/CORBIS: P. 135 AA Photo Library: P. 136 MN001278 © Michael Nicholson/CORBIS: P. 137 FC001500 © Francesco Muntada/CORBIS: P. 138 and 139 (all) AA Photo Library: P. 140 and 141 (all) AA Photo Library: P. 142 and 143 (both) AA Photo Library: P. 144 (both) AA Photo Library: P. 145 DS002236 © Leonard de Selva/CORBIS: P. 146 and 147 (all) AA Photo Library: P. 148 A.F. Kersting: P. 149 VN002377 © Ruggero Vanni/CORBIS: P. 150 and 151 (both) AA Photo Library: P. 152 AA Photo Library: P. 153 EL005396 © Elio Ciol/CORBIS: P. 154 and 155 (all) AA Photo Library: P. 156 and 157 (both) AA Photo Library: P. 158–159 CS004571 © Archivo Iconigrafico SA/CORBIS: P. 160 and 161 (both) AA Photo Library: P. 162 DY001456 © Danny Lehman/CORBIS: P. 163 AA Photo Library: P. 164 and 165 (all) AA Photo Library: P. 166 (both) AA Photo Library: P. 167 Edifice/Darley: P. 168 and 169 (both) Edifice/Darley: P. 170 (both) AA Photo Library: P. 171 AA Photo Library; Photo by Tony Souter: P. 172 A.F. Kersting: P. 173 AA Photo Library: P. 174 and 175 (both) AA Photo Library: P. 176 A. F. Kersting: P. 177 A.F. Kersting: P. 178 and 179 (all) AA Photo Library: P. 183 A.F. Kersting: P. 184 and 185 (both) AA Photo Library: P. 186 and 187 (both) Edifice/Darley: P. 188 and 189 (both) A.F. Kersting: P. 190 and 191 (both) A.F. Kersting: P. 192 and 193 (both) AA Photo Library: P. 194 and 195 (all) Edifice/Darley: P. 196 and 197 (both) AA Photo Library: P. 198–199 HG002428 © Hans Georg Roth/CORBIS: P. 200 AA Photo Library: P. 201 AW025240 © Adam Woolfit/CORBIS: P. 202 and 203 (both) AA Photo Library: P. 204 and 205 (all) Edifice/Lewis: P. 206 and 207 (all) AA Photo Library: Page 208 (both) AA Photo Library: P. 209 A.F. Kersting: P. 210 and 211 (both) AA Photo Library: P. 212 Trip/M. O'Brien: P. 213 AA Photo Library: P. 214 TG004243 © Todd Gipstein/CORBIS: P. 215 (both) AA Photo Library: P. 216 and 217 (both) AA Photo Library: P. 218 CORBIS: P. 219 GM004027 © Carl Mooney/CORBIS: P. 220 and 221 (all) AA Photo Library: P. 222 and 223 (all) AA Photo Library: P. 224 and 225 (all) AA Photo Library: P. 226 (both) AA Photo Library: P. 227 (both) AA Photo Library: P. 228 (left) AA Photo Library: P. 228 (right) AA Photo Library; Photo by Tim Woodcock: P. 229 AA Photo Library: P. 230 and 231 (both) AA Photo Library: P. 232 and 233 (both) AA Photo Library: P. 234 HE001602 © Chris Hellier/CORBIS: P. 236 and 237 (all) Glasgow School of Art: P. 238 and 239 (both) AA Photo Library: P. 240 MT000459 © MIT Collection/CORBIS: P. 241 AA Photo Library: P. 245 AA Photo Library © Gordon D.R. Clements/Axiom: P. 246 AA Photo Library: P. 247 AA Photo Library © Gordon D.R. Clements/Axiom: P. 248 and 249 (both) Ffotograff © Patricia

Aithie: P. 250 UB003007 © Patrick Field/CORBIS: P. 251 DC007252 © Dean Conger/CORBIS: P. 252 and 253 (both) © Trip/P. Mitchell: P. 254 and 255 (both) AA Photo Library © Gordon D.R. Clements/Axiom: P. 260 AA Photo Library © 1995 Jim Holmes: P. 264 © Michael Yamashito/CORBIS: P. 266 RH011734 © Robert Holmes/CORBIS: P. 267 UB007000 © Frank Leather/CORBIS: P. 268 RH009883 © Robert Holmes/CORBIS: P. 269 (both) Trewin Copplestone: P. 270 and 271 (all) AA Photo Library © Gordon D.R. Clements/Axiom: P. 272 and 273 (both) © Trewin Copplestone: P. 276 A.F. Kersting: P. 277 A.F. Kersting: P. 278 A.F. Kersting: P. 279 Edifice/Mayer: P. 280 and 281 (both) Edifice/Mayer: P. 282 and 283 (both) A.F. Kersting: P. 284 and 285 (both) A.F. Kersting: P. 286 and 287 (both) A.F. Kersting: P. 288 IH030624 © Sheldon Collins/CORBIS: P. 289 IH033604 © Sheldon Collins/CORBIS: P. 290–291 AA Photo Library: P. 292 AA Photo Library: P. 293 (both) Edifice/Mayer: P. 294 and 295 (both) A.F. Kersting: P. 296 and 297 (both) A.F. Kersting: P. 298 and 299 (both) AA Photo Library: P. 300 © Trip/Trip: P. 301 A.F. Kersting: P. 302 HR003048 © Jeremy Horner/CORBIS: P. 303 A.F. Kersting: P. 304 © Trip, D./Saunders: P. 305 © Werner Forman Archive: P. 306 and 307 (all) AA Photo Library: P. 310 AA Photo Library: P. 311 (right) HG001174 © Hans Georg Roth/CORBIS: P. 311 (left) TRIP/TRIP: P. 312 AA Photo Library: P. 313 AA Photo Library: Photo by Julian Loader: P. 314 AA Photo Library: P. 315 AA Photo Library; Photo by Michelle Chaplow: P. 316 LJ001213 © Abilio Lope/CORBIS: P. 317 (both) AA Photo Library: P. 318–19 © Trip/J. Sweeney: P. 320 (both) AA Photo Library: P. 321 VN004723 © Gian Berto Vanni/CORBIS: P. 321–322 A.F. Kersting: P. 322–323 A.F. Kersting: P. 324 and 325 (both) AA Photo Library: P. 326 and 327 (both) A.F. Kersting: P. 328 HE002175 © Chris Hellier/CORBIS: P. 329 © Werner Forman Archive: P. 330 and 331 AA Photo Library: P. 332 (both) AA Photo Library: P. 333 AA Photo Library; Photo by Paul Kenward: P. 334 and 335 (all) © Werner Forman Archive: P. 336 RW002460 © Roger Wood/CORBIS: P. 336–337 A.F. Kersting: P. 338 and 339 (both) © Trip/C. Rennie: P. 340 and 341 (both) © TRIP/Tibor Bognar: P. 345 Edifice/Darley: P. 346 and 347 (both) © Thomas A. Heinz: P. 348 and 349 (both) © Thomas A. Heinz: P. 350 TE001916 © Ed Eckstein/CORBIS: P. 351 MK001092 © Michael John Kielty/CORBIS: P. 352 and 353 (all) © Thomas A. Heinz: P. 355 Bildarchiv Foto Marburg: P. 356 and 357 (both) AA Photo Library: P. 358 NB001499 © Neil Beer/CORBIS: P. 359 DH004717 © Dave G. Houser/CORBIS: P. 360 and 361 (both) Edifice/Darley: P. 362 © TRIP/Z. Harasym: P. 363 AA Photo Library: P. 364 and 365 (both) Edifice/Darley: P. 366–367 VN003750 © Ruggero Vanni/CORBIS: P. 368–369 AA Photo Library: P. 370–371 AX001770 © CRDPHOTO/CORBIS: P. 372 and 373 (both) AA Photo Library: P. 374 and 375 (both) Edifice © Gillian Darley: P. 376 and 377 (both) © Thomas A. Heinz: P. 378 and 379 (both) © Thomas A. Heinz: P. 380 IH166624 © Richard T. Nowitz/CORBIS: P. 381 YM013046 © Michael S. Yamashita/CORBIS: P. 382 and 383 (all) AA Photo Library: P. 384 and 385 (all) AA Photo

Library: P. 386 Edifice/Darley: P. 387 AH002177 © Angelo Hornak/CORBIS: P. 388 and 389 (both) © Thomas A. Heinz: P. 390 © Thomas A Heinz: P. 391 (both) © Trewin Copplestone: P. 392 Edifice © Heini Schneebeli: P. 393 © Sonia Halliday Photographs: P. 394 and 395 (both) Edifice © Heini Schneebeli: P. 396 MA11305A © Francis G. Mayen/CORBIS: P. 397 TG001931 © Todd Gipstein/CORBIS: P. 398 and 399 (both) A.F. Kersting: P. 400 and 401 (both) © Thomas A. Heinz: P. 402–403 VC004260 © Vince Streano/CORBIS: P. 404 KM 003284 © Kelly-Mooney Photography/CORBIS: P. 405 JS1000001 © Joseph Sohm, Visions of America/CORBIS: P. 406 IH027411 © Jeremy Horner/CORBIS: P. 407 AH001754 © Angelo Hornak/CORBIS: P. 408 and 409 (both) Edifice/Darley: P. 410 UB009877 © John Dakars; Eye Ubiquitous/CORBIS: P. 411 UB 004826 © Julia Waterlow; Eye Ubiquitous/CORBIS: P. 412 and 413 (both) © Thomas A. Heinz: P. 414 and 415 (both) © Thomas A. Heinz: P. 416–417 © Thomas A. Heinz: P. 418–419 Edifice/Darley: P. 420–421 AA Photo Library: P. 422 and 423 (both) Edifice/Darley: P. 424 and 425 (both) AA Photo Library: P. 426 DV002351 © WildCountry/CORBIS: P. 427 DV002332 © WildCountry/CORBIS: P. 428 RI002212 © Bob Krist/CORBIS: P. 429 KF001086 © Kevin Fleming/CORBIS: P. 430 Foster & Partners; Photographer Nigel Young: P. 431 Foster and Partners; Photographer Ian Lambot: P. 432 © Edifice/Darley: P. 434 UB010092 ©John Dakars; Eye Ubiquitous/CORBIS: P. 436 © Trewin Copplestone: P. 437 Edifice/Darley.